Building God's Kingdom

Building God's Kingdom

Inside the World of Christian Reconstruction

———◦◉◦———

JULIE J. INGERSOLL

OXFORD
UNIVERSITY PRESS

OXFORD

UNIVERSITY PRESS

Oxford University Press is a department of the University of Oxford.
It furthers the University's objective of excellence in research, scholarship,
and education by publishing worldwide. Oxford is a registered trade mark
of Oxford University Press in the UK and in certain other countries

Published in the United States of America by
Oxford University Press
198 Madison Avenue, New York, NY 10016,
United States of America

© Oxford University Press 2015

Library of Congress Cataloging-in-Publication Data
Ingersoll, Julie.
Building God's kingdom : inside the world of Christian reconstruction / Julie J. Ingersoll.
p. cm.
Includes bibliographical references and index.
ISBN 978-0-19-991378-7 (cloth : alk. paper) 1. Dominion theology. I. Title.
BT82.25.I54 2015
230'.046—dc23
2014038632

Justin L. Ingersoll, Jr.

*Dad and I would set out just before sunrise
in a rented rowboat. As the morning fog lifted
it would reveal the mirrored surface of the silent lake;
the only sound, the oars rhythmically slapping the still water.
We'd fish in silence, barely a word said between us.
Thanks, Dad.*

Contents

Preface

THIS PROJECT BRINGS together ethnographic fieldwork with historically informed close reading of the original work of several Christian Reconstructionists. I have worked to present religion as it plays out in the world (rather than presenting only the beliefs of elites) and to present it in ways that show clearly the complexity, variety, and divisions within fundamentalism and evangelicalism. I am committed to the academic study of religion; I believe we need scholars who strive to describe and explain religion apart from engaging in polemics.[1] To that end I see myself standing outside the groups I study, as a translator explaining how they see the world. I am under no illusion that I do so in a purely objective manner, but I do strive for neutral, accurate descriptions and explanations in terms of the variety of theories in my discipline. In showing how the Reconstructionists' world makes sense, to them, in terms of their own framework, it should be clear I am not advocating their views or their framework. I try to show the internal coherence as it appears to them. Ironically, while some will read this work as a defense of the people I am studying, Reconstructionists would say that my presuppositions are humanist, naturalist, and materialist (and they would call me liberal). They would deny that one can study religion without "doing" theology, and while this is a criticism I understand, it is not one I embrace.

Religious studies scholars often explain our discipline as an attempt to make *the strange familiar and the familiar strange,* and this is exactly what I seek to do. In fact, I think that this is the most important skill that religious studies scholars bring to scholarly discourse—and maybe to public discourse: the ability to comprehend someone else's perspective as it makes sense to them, to then see our own taken-for-granted-assumptions as they look to people who do not share them, and finally to reframe that effort in ways that help us better understand how "religion" functions in our world.

This book is the culmination of nearly thirty years of research, much of it informal, and I have published earlier versions of some sections along the way.[2] My interest in this topic began when I was an undergraduate political science major at Rutgers College in the early 1980s, when I first encountered Christian Reconstruction. During those years, and those immediately following, I worked in political campaigns and in a number of Washington-based groups as a volunteer, an intern, a writer, and a researcher. Those groups included the National Conservative Political Action Committee, the Free Congress Foundation, and the American Life Lobby. I attended the campaign schools conducted by the National Conservative Foundation, the Committee for the Survival of a Free Congress, and the College Republican National Committee Fieldman School. In 1983 I married a member of one of the Reconstructionist families about whom I write and met many of the others whose work I explore here. We were divorced in the early 1990s, but since those days I have carried with me a collection of books that have been invaluable to this project. One brother-in-law owned Thoburn Press and Fairfax Christian Bookstore; another worked for the Moral Majority. My father-in-law was a Westminster Seminary graduate who pastored an Orthodox Presbyterian Church congregation and with my mother-in-law founded and owned one of the original Reconstructionist Christian schools. I also cofounded a privately owned Christian school.

My place in that world was always uneasy. My politics were more libertarian than conservative, though those two perspectives seemed closer together to me then than they do now. My libertarianism was formed in the context of a small, generationally connected city in southern Maine, shaped by a puritan ethos in which we are all obligated to care for one another (the "city on a hill" as invoked by John Winthrop rather than the one invoked by Ronald Reagan); individualism tempered by communitarianism if you will. I now see serious problems with how contemporary libertarianism fails to recognize the degree to which we are interdependent.[3]

Moreover, I think I was born a feminist.[4] This was always a source of tension during my years in the Reconstructionist world. I remained an advocate for the Equal Rights Amendment and embraced what we called biblical feminism, arguing for women's equality in the home and in the church. I kept my name when I was married (something my husband supported but no one else did) and constantly chafed under the gender-based limitations placed on me. I was also a pro-life activist. I worked with a number of right-to-life groups, including Operation Rescue, with which I was arrested a handful of times, and Feminists for Life, where I served for a time as the California chapter president. I was aware of the antifeminist agenda of many right-to-lifers, but I was convinced that my feminist convictions and my opposition to abortion were not mutually exclusive, and there were many more like me. In the years since that time, the pro-life movement has shifted toward the larger agenda that I now see as irreconcilably opposed to women's rights. In the 1980s only a part of the pro-life movement, for example, had any misgivings about the use of contraception. Most understood that widely available contraception prevents unwanted pregnancies and abortion. Even more clear to me now, if pro-lifers really believe life begins at conception, preventing conception also prevents untold numbers of deaths by spontaneous abortion. Certainly Catholics opposed contraception in those days, but very few Protestant pro-lifers did. While conservative Christian families often had many children, there were no churches where this was the norm and the expectation. Quiverfull was not yet a movement, though in hindsight I can see that the seeds of it were there. In fact, in the 1980s, biblical feminism, or evangelical feminism, was in the ascendency. Now, some thirty years later, while much of the culture has embraced women's equality and even LGBT rights, these corners of the conservative Christian subculture seem more patriarchal than ever. And while the pro-life movement has changed, I've changed a lot since then too. It was the certainty about truth this world promised that once appealed to me; but everything seemed more black and white then, in a way that nothing does anymore.

It has taken me so long to write this book because I needed the distance from that time. I am now trained as a scholar of religion. I completed my master's degree in history and religious studies at George Washington University, where I wrote my thesis on Christian schools, homeschooling, and conservative Christian efforts to change public schools.[5] I received my PhD in religious studies at the University of California, Santa Barbara, where I wrote a dissertation on conflict over women's roles in conservative Protestantism, later published as *Evangelical Christian Women: War Stories in the Gender Battles*. My interest is understanding the social-cultural dimensions of religion in general, and in the contours and details of the religious right in American politics in particular. But this book is not a memoir, nor is it an exposé; I share these autobiographical details here only because they inform my work. When I say that Rushdoony influenced Jerry Falwell, for example, that observation begins with (though, of course, does not rest on) the fact that I knew Re-constructionists on his staff and saw Rushdoony's books in his office all those years ago. I leave it to readers to decide whether my former ties strengthen or weaken my work.

I can envision a number of criticisms that will be made of this book. Reconstructionists will think that, on the basis of my presuppositions, I cannot comprehend their view of the world. While I no longer share their presuppositions or their view of the world, I think they underestimate the possibility of "trying on" someone's presuppositions to see how the world might make sense from a different worldview. There will be evangelicals who are also unhappy, some, because I have treated Reconstructionists as "Christians," since they will think they miss the "real" message of Jesus. To them I take refuge in the academic study of religion in which we are (thankfully) not charged with, and are methodologically incapable of, dis-cerning who is the "real" Christian (or Jew or Muslim or Buddhist) or whether there even is such a thing. Those normative debates belong among members of religious groups, not between religious groups and religious studies scholars. Other evangelicals will argue that no one really follows these folks and that they are such a fringe group that most people haven't even heard of them. I'm not convinced by this argument, because I think we are rarely aware of our intellectual ancestors. How many of those same Christians are aware of Plato's influence on their belief system? How about Avicenna's? Lack of awareness of an influence does not prove that it is not there. Still other evangelicals will have an interest in arguing for the irrel-evance of Rushdoony and the Reconstructionists because they want to dis-tance themselves from them.

Some progressives and activists will likely think that I have been too easy on Reconstructionists. As I remind readers throughout the book, it is not my goal to argue for or against Reconstructionism. I invite readers to use the knowledge they gain from this book to do their own normative work. Other readers will be dissatisfied with the lack of quantitative data on Reconstructionists' influence in terms of book sales or website hits. Unfortunately, quantitative data seem, by design, impossible to obtain; these folks are notoriously secretive. In some cases the groups I have stud-ied are registered as nonprofits, making some data available through IRS records. I include that where I am able, but similar data on privately owned companies are rare. Reconstructionists publish their own books, sell them through "bookstores" that are run by people in their sympathetic networks, and maintain their own websites. They do not share such data and, indeed, kicked me out of a conference just for being there. Even if they did share book sales the value of self-reported data is suspect. I engaged several colleagues who specialize in either quantitative research or investigative journalism, to no avail, in an effort to develop strategies for more quantification. That leaves the strategy of trying to trace the influence in more subtle, nuanced, and admittedly interpretive ways. I propose that in the absence of substantial hard data, softer ethnographic evidence is even more valuable than it would otherwise be.

Finally, others will say that—as commenters have on my essays at *Religion Dispatches*—Reconstructionists are just "crazies," and it's a waste of time to try to understand them. To these folks (and others) I say that to see the influence, you have to know the Reconstructionists well enough to hear the echoes of their work. If all you know is that Rushdoony advocated the death penalty for gays and incorrigible teens (he did, and we'll get to that) you won't recognize the influence when you hear it. Please keep reading and give me a chance to change your mind.

Terminology

Studies of conservative Protestantism, evangelicalism, fundamentalism, and the religious right are plagued with difficulties related to language and terminology. One key problem stems from a tendency to try to define a movement based on some central characteristics without recognizing that boundaries and identifications shift over time. Is fundamentalism, essentially, as some have argued, separatist? It was at one time, but these days that is less clear. Are there central beliefs that can help identify fundamentalism, like premillennialism, or, more recently, opposition to women's ordination? Perhaps, but conservative Christians have disagreed over these issues too. What about biblical literalism? As we shall see, the claim to read the Bible literally is much more a rhetorical device used by conservative Protestants to legitimate their interpretation than it is an adequate description of how they use the Bible.

I use the terms "religious right" and "New Christian Right" interchangeably to refer to the politically conservative bloc of evangelical and fundamentalist Christians whose influence ebbs and flows in American culture and politics, around issues tied to what they see as family values, since at least the middle of the twentieth century. This movement replaced an older one that historian Leo Ribuffo called the Old Christian Right.[6] Randall Balmer has critiqued the Old Christian Right label, "Try as I might as a historian, I've never been able to determine what that [the Old Christian Right] was—unless it was the crusty anti-Communism of people like Carl McIntire and Billy James Hargis in the 1940s and 1950s or the stubborn segregationism of the Jim Crow era. Either attribution, I think, demeans the faith."[7] But Balmer speaks here more as a member of the faithful looking for authenticity than as an historian. It may or may not "demean the faith," but that is not an argument against its use. The Old Christian Right, indeed, refers to exactly those leaders and their followers' concerns over those issues. There is also technical theological language that must be used to explain the subtle similarities and differences among the groups of people I discuss. Throughout I strive to write in a manner that is clear and accessible, and I define technical terms when I use them. But the fact remains that when I explain how Reconstructionists' technically framed, theological views were popularized, I will need to use technical language.

Finally, there are issues relevant to my effort to portray Reconstructionists in a manner that is an honest representation of their views. The first has to do with gender-inclusive language. I find Reconstructionists' reliance on masculine pronouns jarring and even offensive. But I have not taken it upon myself to "correct" it when summarizing or quoting them. You should discern two voices on this point. In describing and analyzing I use my own language, which is gender inclusive. When I am presenting what they say, I use the terms "he," "man," and "men" as they do. Reconstructionists would often (not always) insist that those terms include women. When citing the creedal formulation "Who for us men and our salvation" the masculine is assumed to be generic. The difficulty is that, in Reconstructionist readings of the Bible, the masculine form often does *not* include women: "Elders in the church should be men of character, the husband of one wife" is understood to explicitly preclude women from leadership. More complex, for example, is "man's call to dominion." In some cases men and women are understood as called by God to exercise dominion. But in others dominion is primarily the calling of men, and the exercise of dominion by women is understood as limited to assisting men in their dominion. Ultimately readers must decide when to interpret them as intending masculine forms to be inclusive and when to not do so. There are other language-usage issues as well. I use the term "Hebrew Bible" to refer to the scriptures that Reconstructionists and other Christians call the Old Testament. Nonetheless, in describing their work and especially in quoting them I use the terminology they use. Rushdoony continued to use the archaic "Negro" as a term for African Americans throughout his life. As with gender-inclusive language, I replicate his language in quoted material, despite my discomfort with it. A final point is the manner in which I present quoted material from their work, both in terms of editing and emphasis. Because the topic of Christian Reconstructionism is fraught with division and disagreement (from scholars who disagree over their relevance, to activists who disagree over what they teach, to Reconstructionists themselves who disagree amongst themselves and insist that no one "gets them right"), I make use, in the chapters that follow, of material directly quoted from their work. I have occasionally edited the quoted material for length but have been careful to preserve the original meaning. Such edits are indicated by ellipses. Finally, Reconstructionists often use bold and italics for emphasis, and I have faithfully reproduced that here. Unless otherwise indicated, italics and boldface in quoted material were in the original texts. Many of the sources from which these quotes come are now available online for free, and I encourage readers to check for themselves to decide if I have accurately reproduced them.[8]

Acknowledgments

I WELCOME THE opportunity to say thank you to all the people who have helped bring this project to publication and am, at the same time, intimidated by the knowledge that I will never be able to do so adequately. While I could not have completed this book without the help of many, and it is much stronger thanks to the generosity of those noted below, the shortcomings, of course, remain mine.

To the people who talked with me and shared the details of their lives and their understanding of the issues about which I write, I am grateful. I encountered many such people at conferences and events and even more contacted me when they learned of my work on Rushdoony and the Christian Reconstructionists. There are too many to name but most importantly Mark and his family come to mind. Other people inside this world and outside of it have shared books and ideas over many years. Together they represent the core of this project and without them there would be no book.

My work on this project has been generously supported by the University of North Florida in the form of numerous summer research grants and a 2009 sabbatical grant. The Florida Blue Center for Ethics at the University of North Florida funded the research and writing of chapter 6 with a summer grant in 2009. Parts of chapter 7 were written in the context of a National Endowment for the Humanities Summer Seminar "Religious Diversity and the Common Good" directed by Alan Wolfe, also in 2009. Alan and the other seminar participants helped me hone the argument and connect the project to larger conversations about the role of religion in society. I have presented on this work in a variety of other academic venues, including a conference sponsored by the Russell Sage Foundation as well as the North American Association for the Study of Religion (NAASR), and the Society for the Scientific Study of Religion (SSSR). Those sessions facilitated conversations with colleagues that have been extraordinarily fun and have helped me sharpen my arguments and be clearer about their limits.

I have been the beneficiary of invaluable support and mentoring throughout my academic career but most especially from my teachers and colleagues in the Religious Studies department at the University of California, Santa Barbara. I enjoyed many late-night conversations on the topics in this book with Walter Capps when he and Lois allowed me the use of their guest room during the year I commuted from Santa Monica to Santa Barbara. Of course Wade Clark Roof remains a most important friend and mentor. But no one at UCSB took more interest in this project than Mark Juergensmeyer. We first began discussing Christian Reconstruction when he was working on *Terror in the Mind of God* and I was finishing my dissertation. He told me then, and every time I saw him after graduating, that I needed to write this book, and he supported and encouraged me all along the way. My long-time friend from those Santa Barbara days, Diana Butler Bass (thanks, Clark, for introducing us), has also been relentless in insisting that I bring this project to fruition.

Some of the framing and some of the content of the chapters that follow have previously appeared in print in "Religiously Motivated Violence in the Abortion Debate" in the *Oxford Handbook of Religion and Violence*, edited by Mark Juergensmeyer, Margot S. Kitts and Michael Jerryson (Oxford University Press, 2013); "Rank-and-File Evangelicals and the Activist Elite: Views of Pluralist Democracy," in *The Conservative Christian Movement and American Democracy*, edited by Steven Brint and Jean Reith Schroedel (Russell Sage Foundation, 2009); and "Religion and Politics: The Impact of the Religious Right," in *Faith in America*, edited by Charles Lippy (Praeger Press, 2006). In each case the anonymous reviewers and the editors of the respective volumes made valuable suggestions prompting revision and rethinking. In recent years I have greatly enjoyed being part of a public conversation about religion, American politics, and the culture wars. Many of the opportunities to do this have roots in my work at *Religion Dispatches*, where I have also published earlier versions of some of what follows. I am grateful to Sarah Posner, Evan Derkacz, Lisa Webster, and Gary Laderman for their work on the magazine and for the terrific work they have done as editors and as teachers as I have endeavored to learn to write for a non-academic audience.

Speaking of the value of skilled (and even merciless) editors, I am also grateful to Theo Calderera at Oxford University Press and the anonymous reviewers he solicited for comments on my manuscript. The reviewers helped me address important challenges and Theo's no-holds-barred critiques made me make changes that greatly improved the finished product. His expertise and professionalism made it easy to trust him; the book is better for it.

Over the years I have had the great fortune of challenging conversations with colleagues whom I am lucky to also be able to call friends. These include Diana Butler Bass, Randy Balmer, Anthea Butler, Shawn Landres, Russell McCutcheon, Colleen McDannell, Kathryn Joyce, Sarah Posner, and Winni Sullivan. Other generous colleagues whom I know not as well have, nonetheless, read all or parts of this manuscript and offered very helpful criticisms and suggestions. These include Cythina Burack and Michael McVicar.

Finally, I thank my dad (to whom this book is dedicated) and my mom, for always giving me room to explore, most recently literal "room" as I have worked on this book, in my writing space in their home in Maine.

Building God's Kingdom

Introduction

THE LATE HOWARD Phillips, one of the political operatives credited with building the religious right, called Rousas John Rushdoony the "most influential man of the 21st century," and someone who caused "historic changes in the thinking of countless leaders."[1] Yet that influence was largely hidden. When Rushdoony passed away in February of 2001, his son-in-law, Gary North, reflected on this:

> Rushdoony's writings are the source of many of the core ideas of the New Christian Right, a voting bloc whose unforeseen arrival in American politics in 1980 caught the media by surprise . . . *Newsweek* (Feb. 2, 1981) accurately but very briefly identified Rushdoony's Chalcedon Foundation as the think tank of the Religious Right. But the mainstream media did not take the hint. They never did figure out where these ideas were coming from . . . Rushdoony in 1981 was almost unknown outside of the leadership of New Right/ New Christian Right circles. So he remained at his death.[2]

The religious right was one of the defining forces of late-twentieth-century American politics, and Rushdoony was one of its intellectual godfathers—but he is often treated like a crazy uncle. He started a movement—Reconstructionism, which sought to remake the whole of society to conform to his reading of the Bible—that didn't attract much support, but the movement's ideas became a driving force in American politics. Reconstructionists found a home in Washington-based political organizations, such as the Moral Majority and the Christian Voice, that were prominent in the early 1980s. Reconstructionist books could be found in the offices of religious right organizations and Reconstructionists who worked on Capitol Hill.[3]

But while the movement's key theological positions echo throughout the fundamentalist worldview, the religious right never followed through on the implications of those ideas. Reconstructionists argue that American Christianity (including the religious right) is in thrall to individualism, the notion of freedom of conscience (Reconstructionists reject the autonomy of human reason), and a heretical discontinuity between the New Testament and the Old. In Reconstructionist terms, the religious right is philosophically schizophrenic, so its efforts to return America to its Christian moorings are doomed. The piecemeal character of the adoption of Christian Reconstruction is the reason, according to the Reconstructionists who refer to it as a lack of "epistemological self-consciousness," that the religious right has not, as yet, been able to transform society.[4] Reconstructionism hasn't failed; it's never been tried.

When I spoke with Howard Phillips during the summer of 2007, as part of my research for this book, he stood by the earlier statement, "the whole Christian conservative political movement had its genesis in Rush."[5] (Rush is the name many of Rushdoony's followers called him.) He then elaborated his point, telling the story of how the two met and illustrating Rushdoony's appeal to those who sought to put the Bible at the center of their politics:

> I first met him in the mid-1970s when I was handed a tract he'd written on socialized medicine; the best argument I'd ever seen against it, and it was all based in the Bible. Rush became a close friend and personal mentor; I devoured his books. Together we testified in cases of the "IRS assault" on Christian schools. Rush was "early and often" on all the big issues, and he was a pioneer in the homeschool movement.

Phillips described how he had played tapes of Rushdoony's lectures in his car all the time—his son Doug, he said, was practically raised on Rushdoony's Christian Reconstruction. Doug Phillips went on to build a homeschool ministry called Vision Forum, grounded in the principles of Christian Reconstruction. Until its collapse in 2014 it aimed to facilitate the development of a Christian worldview in families, in what is now known as the biblical patriarchy movement.[6] No doubt the elder Phillips overestimated the influence of Rushdoony. But another of the early religious right leaders, Robert Billings, the Moral Majority's first executive director, also credits Rushdoony with an important role in the movement's creation.[7]

In fact, the contemporary religious right is a complex movement, weaving together a variety of smaller movements that date as far back in

American history as one cares to look. Nonetheless, it is possible to trace the intellectual, theological, and strategic lineage of attempts to build a thoroughly Reconstructed culture rooted in biblical law through three generations—or four, if you count the children being shaped by the Christian homeschool movement and biblical patriarchy movement.

As we shall see, well into the twenty-first century, the arguments made by conservative Christians about biblical government that focus on the character and structure of families, free-market economics, the legal status of religion, the critique of public education, care for the poor, the right to own guns, the funding of health care, and more have their roots in the work of R. J. Rushdoony.

By the 1950s the steady decline of conservative Protestantism seemed well established; observers had written the obituary for American fundamentalism and ignored any counter-evidence as insignificant vestiges of the past—or as it was often put, "the last gasps of a dying movement." Following the 1980 elections, scholars scrambled to make sense of the seemingly meteoric rise of the religious right. A flurry of studies appeared, examining its organizational structure and worldview, evaluating its real impact and size, and exploring its similarities and dissimilarities with other fundamentalist movements around the world.[8]

A dominant narrative formed, which went something like this: with the public ridicule in the wake of the Scopes Monkey Trial, fundamentalists withdrew from public life and built their own parallel subculture including Bible colleges, publishing houses, and radio networks. They focused internally on maintaining fundamentalism and interacted with the larger culture only to evangelize and bring others into the fold. Fundamentalists became increasingly concerned about social and political changes in the 1960s and 1970s when, according to historian Randall Balmer, "a Southern Baptist Sunday school teacher, Jimmy Carter, began to lure Evangelicals out of their apolitical torpor."[9] But the engagement with Jimmy Carter and the Democrats was something of a false start. Conservative Christians came to see Carter as a poor representative of their interests, and then, in Balmer's words, "rapturous leaders of the religious right crawled into bed with the Republican Party in 1980 and heralded Reagan's election as a harbinger of the Second Coming."[10] Scholars gradually came to the conclusion that what was generically called "the moral majority" (referring to the movement rather than the specific organization) was first and foremost not as large as it had seemed. Clearly, creating the perception of big numbers was of benefit to the religious

right leaders. And since sensationalism sells newspapers, the media accepted and perpetuated the perception that a major political realignment was taking place. Those same scholars observed that, instead of a
populist groundswell, the religious right in the 1980s was primarily a
coalition of Washington-based political action committees (PACs) and
lobbying groups that had built a paper giant with sophisticated direct-
mail techniques.

With few exceptions these early studies focused on one of three primary questions: What do these Washington-based groups look like, and
how did they come into existence? How does the movement play into the
"culture wars"? And what impact does the vitality of the religious right
have on the widely held notion that the world was growing more secular
by the day? These studies typically assume that the movement originated
with those Washington-based political groups and begin their narratives
with the months leading up to the 1980 elections. In this version of history, the religious right is described as "bursting" onto the American political scene, with little or no warning, in 1980.

In fact, early scholarly versions of the beginnings of the religious right
are nearly identical to the one put forth by the movement itself. Richard
Viguerie is a conservative political operative and one of the pioneers of
direct-mail outreach to voters and donors. His self-published book *The
New Right: We're Ready to Lead* (1980) spells out how he and several other
conservative leaders (including Paul Weyrich and Howard Phillips) created several special interest groups to raise money and mobilize religious
conservatives. According to Viguerie, widespread dissatisfaction in America's heartland created an opportunity on which he and others capitalized.
Religious conservatives around the country were unhappy over the decline of religious influence in the public sphere as a result of broadening
interpretations of the First Amendment's establishment clause. They
were enraged over the increasing availability of legal abortion, disturbed
by the gender and sexual revolutions and the rise of communism, and
fearful of what they saw as the increasing willingness of the government
to intrude in their churches and private Christian schools. Some scholars
cite Viguerie's interpretation of the origins of the Christian Right and
others merely repeat it as the conventional wisdom.

More recently scholars have sought to document earlier roots of politically engaged conservative Protestantism, including several pushing the
origins back to the 1950s.[11] Darren Dochuk traces the Depression-era mi-
gration of Southern "plainfolk" to California, where their Southern religion

was transformed, giving rise to a religious-political culture in California that shaped Nixon's infamous "Southern strategy" and elected Ronald Reagan before becoming the crucible in which the religious right developed. Donald Critchlow connects the Old Christian Right's anticommunism with the New Christian Right's emphasis on family and morality by tracing the rise of Phyllis Schlafly as an anticommunist activist and then later as the architect of the Stop ERA campaign. Daniel K. Williams pushes the origins of politically engaged conservative Protestantism back even further to the early twentieth century. He argues that conservative Christians did not retreat from political life in the mid-twentieth century to return in 1980. According to Williams, their involvement remained consistent since the early part of the century; what changed in 1980 was not their political involvement, but their consistent commitment to the Republican Party.[12]

Debates about the origins of politically mobilized conservative Protestantism notwithstanding, each time the modern religious right has seemed to be in decline, it has reemerged in a new form. While subsequent cycles seem to come at increasingly rapid intervals, this movement continues to be a force in American culture and politics—most recently, as we shall see, as one component of the Tea Party movement.[13]

In this book I address one aspect of the story shaping contemporary conservative Christian subculture and the rise of the religious right: the impact of a small group of fundamentalists known as Christian Reconstructionists. While Reconstructionists have influenced the rise of politically mobilized conservative Protestantism, that is but one aspect of their broader effort to transform the larger culture to bring it in line with what they see as the requirements of biblical law. As early as the 1960s, Rushdoony and other Reconstructionists framed what they termed a "biblical worldview." They sought to spread that worldview through what they call the exercise of dominion, after the mandate given to Adam and Eve in the Garden of Eden. In the book of Genesis, God told Adam and Eve that they should go forth from the garden and have dominion over all of creation. Dominion theology has become the most recognizable and widely controversial component of Christian Reconstruction. The chapters that follow seek to explore the Reconstructionists' understanding of this biblical concept and trace its dissemination throughout the larger conservative Christian world.

Well before the establishment of the Washington-based political organizations designed to harness the growing dissatisfaction among conservative Christians, Reconstructionists were laying an intellectual foundation that would shape the twenty-first-century conservative Christian subculture, developing what would become the religious right's critique of the American social order, and plotting strategies to bring about change. They wrote on these topics extensively and made their writings widely available, actively promoting what they called "epistemological self-consciousness" and a blueprint for transforming society to align with their biblical worldview. Reconstructionist ideas made their way into evangelical and fundamentalist churches through study guides and Christian school (and later homeschool) curricula, giving rise to an integrated worldview and a distinct subculture. In fact, their early work was foundational to the philosophical and theological critiques of public education and the argument for a distinctly Christian education that they believe flows from biblical requirements. Reconstructionist work influenced the mid- to late-twentieth-century leaders of the religious right who found, in that distinct subculture, fertile ground for their organizing efforts in the 1970s and 1980s. That influence continues, although often until recently unacknowledged and sometimes denied.[14]

There is now a growing body of work on the religious right that acknowledges the importance of Christian Reconstruction, though often in passing.[15] These works often lack a thorough focus on the movement or its significance, or are alarmist in tone, warning of an impending theocratic takeover.[16] The alarmists are dismissed by scholars who point to the very small numbers of people who claim the label Reconstructionist, the absence of significant self-described Reconstructionist groups, and the assertion that most conservative Christians have never heard of them. I contend that both the alarmists and their critics misunderstand the influence of the Reconstructionists. While it is true that many of the early thinkers have passed away or moved on, and that there are few clearly identifiable leaders who embrace organizations explicitly identifying with Christian Reconstruction, they *are* influential. But their influence is subtle, implicit, and hidden. It is neither consistent across, nor acknowledged by, the movement we know as conservative Protestantism, which is itself complex and composed of many smaller movements.[17] But the popular translation of Reconstructionist ideas to the broader conservative Protestant subculture is so consistent, often even including the obscure terminology and phrasing used by the Reconstructionists, and the evidence of ties between the Reconstructionists and the early leaders of the religious right are common enough, that the influence is undeniable and that a more thorough treatment of Christian Reconstruction is warranted.[18] I am not saying that Reconstructionists birthed the religious right, nor am I denying that there were other influences—such as Francis Schaeffer or the anticommunist movement—that were equally if not more important.[19] Finally, to argue that Rushdoony and his followers have had a role in shaping contemporary conservative Protestantism is not to claim that contemporary Protestants will ultimately embrace the theocratic extremes of Christian Reconstruction. I make a more modest claim: that Reconstructionists have been an important influence that has been inadequately studied.

Religion and Politics in America

Many people believe that the religious right is violating a longstanding tradition of separation between church and state when, in fact, there are few things more "American" than political activism rooted in religious conviction. The notion that religion and politics have ever been separate in America is something of an illusion put forth by liberal Protestants who saw their brand of Protestantism as neutral. This is evident in the fact that Protestant prayer and Bible reading were not successfully challenged in the public schools, despite Catholic claims that they inculcated Protestantism, until the 1960s. When the Puritans came to the Americas it was not to establish freedom of religion but rather to embark on a holy experiment: to build a model of the Kingdom of God on earth. The American Revolution followed on the heels of what has been called the First Great Awakening, and the case can be made that the evangelists, traveling the disparate colonies and giving rise to a national consciousness, made the Revolution possible. Likewise, the Second Great Awakening immediately preceded the Civil War, with both sides drawing on revivalist religion and contributing to regional divisions that caused major religious bodies to split over slavery.

By the end of the nineteenth century, American domestic politics was dominated by a series of social reform movements that all had their roots in revivalist evangelicalism: women's suffrage, Prohibition, and the labor movement. Internationally, at this same time, a desire to "share the Gospel" took missionaries around the world. They brought American democracy and capitalism with them, legitimizing expansionism and giving rise to both a peace movement and, ultimately, anticommunism. In the early twentieth century, revivalist religion split into two camps we now call fundamentalist and modernist and provoked a political fight over evolution. By the middle of the twentieth century, religious groups

were on both sides of the debate over the Vietnam War, with some advocating peace and others concerned that communism threatened faith and
freedom. The civil rights movement, the fight against nuclear power and
nuclear weapons, the environmentalist movement, and even the feminist
movement all had roots in religion. Religiously motivated political activism is not limited to one side of the political spectrum.

In fact, in some cases, religiously motivated people defy our contemporary model dividing the Left from the Right: the movements for women's
suffrage and Prohibition, for example, were intimately tied together to the
point of sharing leaders. There is a core group of antiabortion activists
who are also peace activists and center their notion of the Gospel and their
political goals on meeting the needs of the poor.

Yet, for nearly fifty years American politics has been dominated by the
religious right and its concerns that center, overwhelmingly, on issues of
gender and family: specifically the roles of women (including abortion),
gay and lesbian rights, and the education of children. The Christian Reconstructionists were one important force in the development of the character of that political movement, but Reconstructionists insist that their
movement is not primarily political. Indeed, to suggest that they have had
political influence is not to say that political influence is their primary
goal. As we shall see, they define "politics" as having to do with the regulation of power within civil government, and, in that sense, political goals
are but one small part of their vision for a Reconstructed society. Since
the 1960s conservative Christians have slowly and steadily built an insti-
tutionally integrated, mutually reinforcing, and self-sustaining subculture that exists alongside the world in which most of us live. The religious
right may be one of the most visible manifestations of that subculture,
but it is not the full expression, nor the most influential aspect, of it. This
subculture is often invisible, but it is so pervasive that there are now adult
Americans who were raised in Christian homeschooling families, who
believe that America is a Christian nation; that there is no separation of
church and state implied in the Constitution; that authoritarian patriarchy is the God-ordained structure for families; that the functions of
civil government are limited to providing for national defense and punishing crimes outlined in the Bible; that the Bible speaks to every aspect
of life; and that we are all obligated to live under the law contained therein,
law that is anchored in the literal six-day creation described in Genesis.
Furthermore, this integrated worldview includes an ideological structure

for identifying, explaining, and then dismissing any alternative ways of seeing things.

There are two key aspects of Christian Reconstruction expressed theologically as presuppositionalism and postmillennialism, culturally as theonomy and dominion, and cast in accessible popular terms as the critique of secular humanism and the effort to restore America as a Christian nation. These ideas will be explored in the chapters that follow, but, briefly, presuppositionalists hold that all knowledge is derived from presuppositions; reasoning always begins with premises that cannot be proven. One cannot, for example, prove that God exists. But you cannot prove that God does not exist either. Christianity and atheism each requires a "leap of faith," as it were. Reconstructionists operate from the presupposition that God exists and that the Bible is true; everything must be seen through that lens. They acknowledge this presupposition, but they contend that the alternative view is equally presuppositionally dependent. The corollary to presuppositionalism is "theonomy" (meaning God's law), which asserts that there can be no neutral, objective way to determine ethics and law, and that God's law, as revealed in the Bible, is inescapable. Humans must either choose to live under God's law or reject it and substitute some humanistic value system; the only alternatives are an objective, absolute standard (the Bible) or abject moral relativism resulting in chaos. For Rushdoony the fundamental issue is one of authority, thus the title of his early work: *By What Standard?*[20]

The second key point in Christian Reconstructionism is postmillennial eschatology. Briefly, Reconstructionists hold that Satan was defeated by Christ's resurrection and that we are currently living in the millennial reign of the Kingdom of God. They have a trifold understanding of individual salvation. Christians are saved instantaneously at the point of conversion, they increasingly experience the fruits of that salvation as they work through it in their daily lives, and they are finally and completely sanctified at the culmination of history, when Christ returns. Postmillennialist Reconstructionists see a similar process at work in creation, which was redeemed with the resurrection. The Kingdom of God, they believe, becomes increasingly apparent as history progresses (and as Christians acknowledge God's authority and labor to build it) and will be perfectly established at Christ's second coming (thus, his coming is postmillennial). The task of furthering the Kingdom falls to the epistemologically self-conscious Christians as they exercise dominion and seek to bring all aspects of life under the authority of biblical law.

For Christian Reconstructionists, the issue of authority binds together what otherwise appear to be disparate conflicts across the American religious landscape. The first decade of the twenty-first century, for
example, saw a growing division within the Episcopal Church. On the
surface, the division seems rooted in the question of whether gay people
can be bishops and whether same-sex unions should be recognized and
blessed by the church. Those who have broken from the American
church, who call themselves Anglican, believe that they remain in communion with the worldwide Anglican Church and that it is the Episcopal
Church that has "left."[21] Furthermore, they are quite insistent that the
issue is not really homosexuality. So what is it? In 2007, the Christian
ministry Answers in Genesis opened a 70,000-square-foot museum, a
short drive from the airport in Cincinnati, devoted to presenting the origins of life as described in the book of Genesis. In its first three years of
operation, it saw over a million visitors. All the while conservative Christians continue to fight at the local and state levels over how, and whether,
evolution should be taught in public schools. From the outside some
wonder why they care about this particular issue as much as they do.
After all, there are many aspects of contemporary Christian culture that
fall short of what these Christians believe to be right. And yet, aside from
the issues of abortion and homosexuality, no other issue generates the
intensity that evolution does.

Underneath these controversies and so many others is the issue of
authority. Traditionally Episcopalians believe in the church's authority to
interpret the Bible (which led them to install gay bishops and the bless
same-sex unions) but dissenters believe that the meaning of the Bible is
plain on its face, that there is no interpretation required, and they therefore deny the authority of the church to interpret the text. The factions
have divided over who is to have the authority to shape the future of the
church. Creationists fight against evolution because they believe their
reading of Genesis to be the necessary reading if their assumptions about
how to read the text in general and about the authority of the text are sus-
tainable; their whole worldview falls if they give up their understanding
of Genesis. This book will trace one thread in the systematic development, promotion, and defense of this conservative Christian worldview,
which is self-consciously rooted in a thoroughly detailed perspective on
authority. I will draw centrally on the work of Rushdoony, who spent most
of his life as an independent scholar and author, working from his Chalcedon Foundation in Vallecito, California. I will also expand that focus to

some key figures who have built upon his work, many of whom worked for Chalcedon at one point or another. First and foremost among those figures is Gary North, Rushdoony's son-in-law, and the central figure in a branch of Christian Reconstruction that developed in Tyler, Texas, around North's Institute for Christian Economics (ICE) and Institute for Biblical Economics. Other important early figures include Greg Bahnsen and David Chilton. Bahnsen built on Rushdoony's work in presuppositionalist apologetics, which serves as the basis for Christian Reconstruction. Chilton developed the postmillennialist framework upon which dominion theology relies. Among these early architects of Christian Reconstruction only North is still living. Doug Phillips of Vision Forum in San Antonio, Texas, and Gary DeMar, now at American Vision outside Atlanta, have also played important roles in the dissemination of various aspects of Christian Reconstruction, most especially the understanding of America and American history that has become known as Christian American history and providential history.

Theory and Method in the Study of Religion

This project has two scholarly goals. The first is to explore some of the key dimensions of the Reconstructionists' worldview, goals, and strategies. I look at how they develop this worldview in their written work and then explore, ethnographically, a number of sites where that worldview currently finds expression. The second is to place the study of this movement in the context of larger questions about the way in which religion functions in society. The second part of the project is rooted in the work of religious studies scholars, such as Bruce Lincoln and Russell McCutcheon, who explore how religion serves to authorize and reproduce certain social structures.[22] Indeed, these two endeavors are complementary in that the Christian Reconstructionists are clear that this is what they are doing. They believe, or at least they claim to believe (like all religious groups), that they do this because their view of things is true.[23] But Reconstructionists assert that the question of authority is at the root of every issue, every conflict, and every institution. They see clearly that, outside their theonomic system, the social order is arbitrary, though they argue that biblical law resolves the arbitrariness and replaces it with order by rooting ethics in God's divine plan. They seek to subject the arbitrary social order to biblical law, in fact, to inculcate a worldview that will perpetuate a biblical social order. As Reconstructionist Gary North

and others say, Reconstructionism is not "primarily" political—in the
sense of expecting the changes they seek to come explicitly through a
political process. Their real goal is much broader; it is a complete transformation of every aspect of culture (including, but not limited to, politics). Every aspect of culture is to be brought into conformity with biblical
law. Their strategy for bringing about that transformation has resulted in
significantly more influence than they could have achieved through narrowly political efforts. It is the broad-based systematic worldview that has
made Reconstructionists influential in the conservative Christian subculture and in the religious right. While Reconstructionists define the
"political" in such a way as to declare that their efforts are not political,
in a broader sense, of course they are intensely political. Their worldview
requires a wholesale overturning of authority and political order. And it
secures for them continued influence on the broader conservative Christian subculture.

Chapter Outline

The broad influence of Christian Reconstruction is derived from its systematic character, its long-term strategy, and its ability to make meaningful the mundane details of day-to-day life by situating them in a sweeping
historical narrative framed as the fundamental purpose of God and his
creation. Reconstructionists assert that the Bible speaks to every area of
life, and they have articulated the ways in which they believe it does so.
The result has been a self-reinforcing web of meaning that has now
shaped multiple generations of believers for whom this vision of reality
seems indisputable as well as essentially, inevitably, and irreconcilably at
odds with the vision of reality of modern secular culture. The book is divided into two parts: the first outlines the theological system and resulting worldview, and the second explores the application of Reconstructionist
influence in a variety of contexts.

The first part lays out the basic argument that the New Christian Right
is not new and that it can be traced to the Old Christian Right and the rise
of fundamentalism at the turn of the twentieth century, and that the Christian Reconstructionists played an important role in laying out a framework
that helped the movement take root in the conservative Protestant subculture. It outlines the theology of the Christian Reconstructionists, explores
contemporary dominion theology and the fight against secular humanism, and shows how theological ideas were popularized in forms embraced

by evangelicals and fundamentalists who did not explicitly identify with the Reconstructionists. The final chapter in the first part outlines the Reconstructionist vision for culture as presented in Gary North's *Biblical Blueprint Series*.

The second part of the book takes seriously the Reconstructionists' assertion that their movement is not primarily political but that it seeks to transform culture more broadly. Here I add fieldwork to explore contemporary sites of influence: Christian schools and Christian homeschools, the creationist movement, and two organizations that identify explicitly with Christian Reconstruction: Vision Forum and American Vision. I explore David Barton's "Christian American history" that is rooted in Rushdoony's philosophy of history, which has gained a wider audience with the Tea Party. Finally, I look at the relationship between Christian Reconstructionism and violence, highlighting anti-Semitism, racism, and abortion-related violence.

I

Christian Reconstructionist Theology

R. J. RUSHDOONY DEVELOPED AND then helped popularize what he called a "biblical worldview," which was rooted in historic Calvinism. In this view the Bible speaks to every aspect of life and provides a blueprint for living according to the will of God. This chapter traces Rushdoony's intellectual heritage, contextualizing his work within the larger Christian tradition.[1]

The influences on Reconstructionist theology date back at least as far as St. Augustine and can be traced through the Reformation theologian John Calvin to nineteenth-century Calvinist Abraham Kuyper, and twentieth-century Calvinists Herman Dooyeweerd and Cornelius Van Til.[2] The broad name for this theological perspective is "Reformed," and it can be found, to some degree, in several American Protestant denominations. Presbyterian and Christian Reformed churches are primarily in this tradition, but many Episcopalians and Baptists are as well. In fact, most Baptists were "Reformed" until the period known as the Second Great Awakening in which they traded the predestination of Calvinism for a more "preachable" Arminian theology, which did not understand salvation as limited to a predetermined elect. Calvinism, however, has made a comeback among some Baptists. Specifically, the Baptists who led the late-twentieth-century conservative takeover of the Southern Baptist Convention (SBC) and the subsequent purge of the SBC seminaries were Baptists who had returned to Calvinism. *Time* magazine called New Calvinism one of the ten ideas "changing the world."[3] *Christianity Today* editor Collin Hansen has tracked the development of this movement in his book *Young, Restless, Reformed.*[4] And by the annual meeting of the SBC in June of 2013, divisions between the Arminian faction and the Calvinist faction (sill a minority but a vocal one) had become so strong that it led to a plea for getting along in the form of a report entitled "Truth, Trust, and Testimony in a Time of Tension," by a nineteen-member Calvinism Advisory Committee.[5] Reconstructionists are all Reformed in their theology—that is, they are Calvinist. Perhaps it goes without saying, but not all Calvinists or Reformed Protestants are Reconstructionist. These New Calvinists, in particular, though generally very conservative on issues like the roles of women, often seek to distance themselves from theonomy, the Reconstructionists' understanding of the implications of the absolute sovereignty of God's law.

The shorthand version of Calvinism emphasizes five key points; some Calvinists will identify themselves as "five-point Calvinists," indicating their adherence to the entirety of the teaching, as opposed to those who have modernized their Calvinism by dropping out one or more points. Briefly, the first point, *Total Depravity*, refers to the character of the human condition at least since the Fall. The human soul is corrupted, and we are inherently sinful. Because of the condition of the human heart, free will is not possible. The second point, *Unconditional Election*, refers to the belief that God "elects" some to salvation in a manner that is not conditioned on anything they do or can do. It rests on the first point in that the totally depraved human is incapable of doing anything worthy of salvation, so the only way salvation can occur is if God initiates it. The third point, *Limited Atonement*, asserts that the effectiveness of the atoning death of Christ on the cross is limited to those whom God has elected. Other forms of Christian theology teach, for example, that atonement is effective for everyone, returning humans to a state in which they are capable of accepting salvation. Calvinists reject this idea, in part because human autonomy comes at the expense of the sovereignty of God. In the fourth point, *Irresistible Grace*, Calvinists believe that when God elects one to be the recipient of saving grace, a beneficiary of the atonement, that election is irresistible. Again, the first point, depravity, makes this necessary. If God grants grace and if grace is to be effective, the sinful heart must be incapable of resisting it. Finally, the fifth point is *Perseverance of the Saints*. Once one is saved there is nothing that can make him or her unsaved. Calvinism has no notion of backsliding. This does not mean that the elect can behave badly. Since it is expected that salvation will bear fruit in the life of the believer, unrepentant sin is seen as evidence that one is not actually saved. So while salvation is in no way dependent upon the actions of humans, one's behavior is not irrelevant. Calvinists believe that the life of one who is truly regenerated will exemplify that fact. In effect, since unbelievers can also exhibit such evidence, one can know if one is *not* saved (the absence of evidence), but one can not know for sure that one *is* saved. From these five points follows the

Calvinist teaching on predestination and, together, they all rest on the assertion of the absolute sovereignty of God.[6]

While Calvinism has seemed, to many, to be a dour theological system, its appeal for those who hold it lies in both its elegant internal logic and the way in which it consistently, emphatically preserves the notion of a majestic, all-powerful, all-knowing, eternal, uncreated deity; literally an awesome God. The Calvinist God is beyond human comprehension and yet has reached across the gulf between Creator and fallen creation to restore humans to the purpose for which they were created: dominion. For Reconstructionists, dominion is a creative act reflecting the way in which humans were made in the image of God the Creator.

From the sovereignty of God follows, for Reconstructionists, the authority of biblical law and the obligation to submit to it. This is where Reconstructionists and other Reformed Christians sometimes part company. The biblical worldview put forth by Rushdoony can be understood in terms of these interlocking notions: Presuppositionalism (leading to theonomy) and postmillennialism, to which we will return.

Southern Presbyterianism Survives

We began this chapter discussing some of the influence of widely regarded Christian theologians on Rushdoony's views: Augustine, Calvin, Kuyper, Dooyeweerd, and Van Til. There remains one more important thinker in Rushdoony's conceptualization of a biblical society: Southern Presbyterian theologian R. L. Dabney. Dabney was the premier theologian of Southern Presbyterianism; an apologist for slavery; and a defender of the agrarian, patriarchal ways of life that characterized the Old South. By most accounts, Dabney's influence had waned when C. Peter Singer and Rushdoony resurrected his work in the middle of the twentieth century.[7] Yet Dabney has been called prophetic by Reconstructionists from Rushdoony to Doug Phillips.[8] While much of Dabney's work was republished by Lloyd Sprinkle, Rushdoony's Ross House Books also republished some of it.[9] Rushdoony publicized those books through Chalcedon Foundation newsletters, public lectures, and his very early "podcasts" sent to subscribers on audiotape. According to Edward Sebesta and Euan Hague:

> Rushdoony's promotion of Sprinkle's reprints brought them to the attention of the wider Christian Reconstructionist movement in the United States [leading] to their discussion and review in

magazine articles, books, audio cassettes, videotape sets, and other pro-Confederate theological and political venues. By the end of the 1970s, therefore, Sprinkle, Rushdoony and others had republished and reinterpreted the historical record and, based on the evidence of a few atypical nineteenth century texts, claimed the 1861–1865 Confederate army to be populated by theologically driven Christian Reconstructionists fighting to preserve their orthodox Christian nation against heretical Union troops.[10]

For Rushdoony, the Civil War was not fought over slavery. It was a religious war. The North had abandoned Christianity in favor of humanism, and the South was fighting to defend a Christian civilization. In the South, civil authority was decentralized and severely limited. Instead, family authority was exercised by patriarchs to whom submission was due.[11] Following Dabney, Rushdoony idealized the pre–Civil War Southern civilization as exemplifying biblical values in contrast to the Unitarian-transcendentalism of the North. These biblical values included God-ordained social hierarchy and patriarchy, by which he meant a social order governed by family authority in the context of a very weak civil government.

Rushdoony does not see the US Constitution as a document rooted in democratic, egalitarian, or secularist values. His view is that, at the beginning of the constitutional era, the various states had established Christianity; they were Christian republics. To "read the Constitution as a charter for a secular state is to misread history," he wrote; it was "designed, rather, to *perpetuate* a Christian order."[12] He maintained that the federal Constitution omits references to religion because it was intended to be a matter left to the states. "The freedom of the first amendment from federal interference is not *from* religion but *for* religion . . . In many areas, laws against unbelief were on the books. A man could be imprisoned for atheism."[13] Yet, unlike in contemporary conservatism, "states' rights" is not Rushdoony's ideal alternative to federal rights; county rights are the "basic unit of the American system" of government. In addition to power over religion, he claimed that counties had "full jurisdiction . . . in the areas [that] constitute the essence of civil government," including taxes, criminal law, and civil law.[14]

Rushdoony saw the Enlightenment promotion of equality as anathema and democracy as nothing more than an attempt to govern civil society according to humanism rather than God's word. Dabney's critiques of public education (and widely available education generally, including education for women and African Americans) and his denunciations of early efforts for women's equality, including speaking in public and voting, were carried over by Rushdoony and fit neatly within his notion of a biblical worldview.

> The law cannot favor equality without ceasing to be law: at all times, the law defines, in any and every society, those who constitute the legitimate and illegitimate members of society . . . the fact of law introduces a fundamental and basic inequality in society. The abolition of law will not eliminate inequality, because then the very fact of sheer survival will create an elite and establish fundamental inequality.[15]

In Rushdoony's 1965 critique of democracy as "the obedience of man to man," we find his articulation of what, today, has become a commonplace inversion of the notion of religious freedom where the term refers not to the freedom of individuals to practice or not practice religion according to the dictates of their consciences, but to the freedom of members of the dominant religion to exercise privileges afforded by its dominant status. In 1965 Rushdoony wrote: "There are two major stages in the attack on religious liberty. First the state is secularized in the name of freedom and, second, every prerogative of the church is attacked in an indirect manner so that . . . its right to exist is denied." Present-day demagoguery about "tyranny" echoes Rushdoony's early work:

> The word *tyrant* from the Greek . . . means a secular ruler, one who rules without the sanction of religious law . . . its new principle of law was *democracy* . . . Instead of a higher law, the tyrant sees his mandate in the will of the people . . . Tyranny is thus inevitably in conflict with religion because it cannot tolerate a law which denies that the people are the source of law . . . By affirming as his principle "The People, Yes," the tyrant must sooner or later logically affirm its corollary by saying to God an empathetic *no*.[16]

Many observers have noted that the dividing line in America's culture wars is roughly the same as the Mason–Dixon line. Red state–blue state divisions follow slave state–free state or Confederacy–Union divisions. While certainly the Nixon-era "Southern strategy" is rightly marshaled to account for that, it's also the case that the Southern strategy was success-ful because it tapped into existing values and tensions. Rushdoony and other Reconstructionists have had a role in reinvigorating this distinctly Southern form of Christianity found in the work of Robert L. Dabney and others. Edward H. Sebesta and Euan Hague have traced the development of the idea of the Civil War as a religious war from its origins among Southern Presbyterians, most especially Dabney, through its period of obscurity and its repopularization among neoconfederates via the work of Rushdoony.[17] According to Sebesta and Hague, Dabney remained outside the mainstream of Protestant theology but, after World War II, became central to a developing neoconfederate revisionist history of the Civil War and the more widespread claim that the "real America" is Southern and rural, which has an appeal much broader than far-right neoconfederacy. To take but one example of the genre:

> orthodox Christianity, honor, hierarchy, loyalty to place and kin, patriarchy, and respect for the rule of law—represents an obsta-cle to the left-liberals' lust for power . . . The treason of the Left involves such unconstitutional and immoral enormities as glo-balism—the selling-out of American national sovereignty to in-ternational agencies and interests; radical egalitarianism; feminism; sodomite rights; abortion; Third-World immigration; gun control; hate crime legislation; . . . judicial tyranny; burden-some taxation; multiculturalism and diversity (code words for anti-white, anti-Christian bigotry); the universal rights of man; and other manifestations of a new brand of politically-correct totalitarianism.[18]

This could easily have come from Rushdoony or a Tea Party rally, but it actually comes from the president of the League of the South, a neocon-federate organization.

Presuppositionalism: Secular Humanism and the Myth of Neutrality

A key point of Christian Reconstructionism is presuppositional epistemol-ogy, which was translated into a popular form in the critique of secular humanism. Rushdoony adapted this particular typology from Calvinists Abraham Kuyper and Herman Dooyeweerd, who argued that faith in

Christ should impact all of life. Rushdoony read Kuyper and Dooyeweerd through the lens provided by Cornelius Van Til's assertion that all knowledge is based on inescapably religious presuppositions. Kuyper developed a doctrine known as "sphere sovereignty," in which biblically derived authority is understood as existing in three distinct spheres: the state, society (which included the family), and the church.

Rushdoony's unique contributions to sphere sovereignty are the specific framing commonly invoked by contemporary conservative Protestants (family, church, and civil government) and the application of biblical law as the method through which faith should shape all of life. The limits on the role of each institution are much more sharply drawn in Rushdoony's writing (and contemporary usage) than in Kuyper's. This view was developed by both Rushdoony and Francis Schaeffer, who is often considered the most influential evangelical theologian of the twentieth century. Both Rushdoony and Schaeffer argued for the philosophical impossibility of epistemological neutrality (Schaeffer had studied with Van Til). Schaeffer's critique of humanistic presuppositions reached a much broader—and more decidedly evangelical—audience than did Rushdoony's.[19] They were aware of each other's work, and there is evidence of the exchange of ideas between the two in what was likely an example of two thinkers working on similar issues and drawing on similar sources, rather than the direct influence of one on the other. Yet, given Schaeffer's stature in the evangelical world, it is worth examining them in relationship to each other.[20]

When I visited Schaeffer's L'Abri Fellowship in Switzerland in the late 1980s, the staff and other guests readily discussed Reconstructionism. William Edgar of the Christian magazine *First Things* attests to the much earlier presence of Rushdoony's work at L'Abri:

> I first encountered Rushdoony's work at L'Abri, a Christian Community high in the Swiss Alps. The year was 1963. Francis Schaeffer, the founder and director of L'Abri, had recently come across a little book by Rushdoony called *This Independent Republic: Studies in the Nature and Meaning of American History*, and he made it the basis for a seminar with the students at L'Abri . . . Those were heady days at L'Abri, which in the sixties was a seedbed for ideas that captivated our imaginations and sought to link every area of our lives to a Christian worldview.[21]

The point is not that Rushdoony rather than Schaeffer promoted this view but, instead, that Rushdoony was an important figure in addition to Schaeffer, most significantly because while they popularized a similar critique of culture based in Reformed theology, and both argued for a thoroughgoing biblical worldview, it was Rushdoony who spent his life developing that systematic worldview. Rushdoony's work (and that of those who followed him) focused much more specifically on developing a biblical alternative to humanism. Indeed, Francis Schaeffer's son Frank has written extensively on the influence of his father as well as the broad-based cultural influence of Rushdoony on American evangelicalism and fundamentalism. The elder Schaeffer acknowledged the ties between his work and Rushdoony's in a warm, highly personal 1978 letter to Rushdoony, which included kind words about their mutual work and well wishes to Gary North.[22]

Underlying Rushdoony's disdain for secularism was his contention that no legal, economic, or political system could be religiously neutral; all claims to knowledge not based in biblical authority are illegitimate because they rest on the claim of the autonomy of human reason, elevating it above the authority of God. According to Van Til's presuppositionalism, on which he built, there can be no knowledge without presuppositions, which are inherently religious; therefore, there can be no religious neutrality. There can be no religiously neutral legal systems or economic systems (all law is someone's view of what is right imposed on others; the originator of law can be God or "man" but it can never be neutral). In Rushdoony's language this is "inescapable." Similarly—and crucial to Rushdoony's critique of public schools—no educational system or curriculum could be religiously neutral. Believers and nonbelievers have no common ground on which to engage. All presuppositions not derived from God (i.e., from the Bible) are derived from human beings' desire to be gods unto themselves, determining for themselves what is good and what is evil.

For Reconstructionists, this is the essence of humanism. Presuppositionalism, sometimes explicitly acknowledged but often not, is the intellectual and theological foundation for the popular critique of secular humanism offered by important religious right leaders like Tim LaHaye and later David Barton. The critique is often rooted in Reconstructionist writings.

Strategically, the effort to bring the entirety of culture "under the Lordship of Christ" has been two-pronged. There is the short-term effort to engage in electoral politics and then bring pressure on elected officials.

The more long-term strategy is to "raise up generations of leaders" with the skills and the worldview to "usher in the Kingdom of God." This second strategy is deemed "not political" by Reconstructionists because it is not explicitly directed toward the transformation of civil government but rather the transformation of all aspects of culture and society.

The influence of Rushdoony's presuppositionalism is evident in the writings of numerous leaders important to the early religious right. For example, Rus Walton, longtime director of the Plymouth Rock Foundation and one of the earliest promoters of "Christian American history," lays out a critique of secular humanism in his *Fundamentals for American Christians* (1979) and later *One Nation Under God* (1986), putting forth a "biblical" political philosophy and citing Rushdoony and North throughout. Walton also relied on books that were important in the dissemination of these ideas in churches and in Christian schools: Rosalie Slater and Verna Hall's three-book series (affectionately called "the big red books" by Christian schoolers), Slater's 1965 *Teaching and Learning America's Christian History,* and Hall's 1966 *The Christian History of the Constitution of the United States.* Though Slater and Hall were not Reconstructionists, they were figures in 1950–1960s patriotic anticommunism, where the Reconstructionists encountered their work and incorporated it into their own efforts to promote the vision of America as a Christian nation. John Whitehead, on the other hand, identified early with Rushdoony. In *The Separation Illusion* he "documents" the shift from America as a "nation founded on God's law" to one founded on "secular humanism."[23] The book contains a foreword by Rushdoony, it references the work of Rushdoony throughout, and Whitehead thanks Rushdoony, in his acknowledgments, for the use of his library.

Before Tim LaHaye was a bestselling apocalyptic Christian novelist (the *Left Behind* series), he was a critic of secular humanism. His books *The Battle for the Mind* (1980), *The Battle for the Family* (1982), and *The Battle for the Public Schools* (1983) cite Francis Schaeffer and Rushdoony, as well as John Whitehead (specifically the parts of Whitehead's work that draw on Rushdoony). LaHaye's work demonstrates how Reconstructionist thought has been translated for and incorporated into fundamentalist popular culture.

LaHaye uses presuppositionalism and theonomy to argue that there are only two sources of knowledge: God and human. All that is not based on God is humanism. This is all drawn directly from Rushdoony, and the sources cited bear that out. The framing of the LaHaye series borrows from Rushdoony's version of the typology in which biblical authority resides in three distinct—and limited—spheres: family, church, and civil government. This is even truer of LaHaye's later book *Faith of our Founding Fathers*, in which he argues for the view that America was founded as a Christian nation; it was published, incidentally, by a small (short-lived) press with Reconstructionist ties: Wolgemuth and Hyatt.[24]

Theonomy and Submission to Biblical Law

The other pillar of the Christian Reconstructionist framework is theonomy. Literally meaning "God's Law," theonomy refers to the view that the God of the Bible is the ultimate source of authority. Claims of human autonomy are not merely false, but sinful. Most contemporary Christians see the New Testament as replacing the Old. Mainstream Christians tend to read the Old Testament through what they understand as the life of Jesus. They draw on the parts of the Old Testament that are reaffirmed in the New, like the Ten Commandments and the parts that seem to them to be in keeping with New Testament teachings about self-sacrifice, equality, concern for the poor, and so on. But even most fundamentalists who invoke the Old Testament do so less literally than they claim and in a manner that Christian Reconstructionists see as selective and inconsistent. They will, for example, draw on Genesis to support creationism or Leviticus to support their hostility to LGBT concerns, but they avoid the sections of the Old Testament that describe a wrathful, angry, and violent God.

Christian Reconstructionists see the Bible as a coherent whole, a doctrine they refer to as the "unity of Scripture." While Rushdoony held this view, it found its fullest expression in the work of Reconstructionist theologian and professor of apologetics Greg Bahnsen. He writes:

> Within the Scriptures we should presume continuity between Old and New Testament moral principles and regulations until God's revelation tells us otherwise . . . Therefore . . . the Old Testament law continues to offer us an inspired and reliable model for civil justice or socio-political morality (a guide for public reform in our own day, even in the area of crime and punishment).[25]

There are parts of the Old Testament that Reconstructionists see as no longer applicable (by virtue of being "ceremonial" law that is fulfilled in Christ), but by and large the Old and New Testaments are integrated and remain authoritative. This is a view developed by John Calvin during the Reformation and is, in some ways, influential in all of Protestantism, but like Calvin's predestination, it is, today, self-consciously embraced in its full form in only the most extreme branches of Protestantism like Christian Reconstruction. The God who commanded Moses to commit genocide, telling him, "You must utterly destroy the Hittites, Amorites, Canaanites, Perizzites, Hivites, and Jebusites, just as the LORD your God has commanded you" (Deuteronomy 20:1), is that same God worshipped in the New Testament as Father, Son, and Holy Spirit. The way these Christians understand the Trinity makes Jesus present at creation and throughout the Old Testament period—indeed, it's the reason they insist that Muslims and Christian do not worship the same God, and one of the reasons the Genesis account of creation is so important to them.

This God, whose greatest act of love is the violent execution of his Son (Himself?) as the only adequate resolution to sin, is a wrathful, vengeful God who sits in judgment of disobedient nations. For these Christians, most of the explicit condemnations in the Old Testament are still applicable. Reconstructionists don't see them as being outside the "character of God," as many other Christians might. Moreover, according to Reconstructionists, Christians who find it hard to countenance the God of the Old Testament are guilty of presuming that their own reason is adequate to question the sovereign God who is Lord and Creator of all. To embrace those aspects of God's character that strike us as angry, harsh, and violent is the very test of obedience. By accepting what God tells us in scripture rather than what seems to our own minds to be right, we humbly acknowledge the limits and contingent character of human reason.[26] To presume to judge God is hubris. Bahnsen points to the Puritans as an example of believers who refused to subject the demands of God's law to the standards of human reason:

> The Puritans were zealous to live in the moral purity which reflects God's own. Consequently they upheld the honor and binding quality of every command from God . . . Thus the Puritans did not, like many modern believers, tamper with or annul any part of God's law . . . Unlike modern theologians who evaluate God's requirements according to their cultural traditions and who follow the Satanic temptation to define holiness according to their own estimate of moral purity, the Puritans did not seek schemes by which to shrink the entire duty of man in God's law to their preconceived notions.[27]

Reconstructionists' insistence on continuity between the Old and New Testaments shapes their understanding of every aspect of the character of God and his relationship to us as individuals and as nations. Yet beyond the theoretical subordination of one's reason to God's authority, what constitutes obedience in terms of day-to-day behavior? How is one to know what God requires? The Reconstructionist answer to this question can be found in Rushdoony's first book, *By What Standard?*, published in 1958. But it was Greg Bahnsen, in *By This Standard* and *Theonomy and Christian Ethics,* who developed the theonomic philosophical framework for applying biblical law to contemporary society.[28] Bahnsen explains that the proper approach to the Old Testament is to presume continuity except in cases where the New Testament, in some way, indicates we should not do so. In Bahnsen's view, the revealed word of God must be used to interpret itself rather than making the text subject to interpretation based on human reason. Addressing the responsibilities of government to enforce biblical law he writes:

> Consequently, instead of taking a basically antagonistic view of the Old Testament commandments for society and the state, and instead of taking a smorgasbord approach of picking and choosing among those laws on the basis of personal taste and convenience, we must recognize the continuing obligation of civil magistrates to obey and enforce the relevant laws of the Old Testament, including the penal sanctions specified by the just Judge of all the earth. As with the rest of God's law, we must presume continuity of binding authority regarding the socio-political commandments revealed as standing law in the Old Testament.[29]

Bahnsen traces the departure from what he sees as the proper grounding of Christian ethics in biblical law, beginning with the medieval church, which proposed a division between revealed religious knowledge and other knowledge that is accessible by human reason or the laws of nature. It was the Reformers who challenged this epistemology with their claims of *sola scriptura* (scripture alone). And, again, according to Bahnsen, it is the Puritans who provide the model of an effort to build a society rooted in biblical law.

> That is why the Puritans strove to let God's word form their lifestyle and regulate their behavior in every sphere of human endeavor . . .

The Puritans even took God's law as their yardstick for civil laws in the new land to which they eventually came, and we have enjoyed the fruits of their godly venture in this country for three centuries now.[30]

With the "alleged enlightenment," Bahnsen argues, the West increasingly shifted toward the mistaken emphasis on the autonomy of human reason and the abandonment of biblical law as the standard for ethics and morality.

More recently, Reconstructionists have built upon the gendered implications of their understanding of the unity of scripture and the character of God. Christianity has traditionally held that God is neither male nor female; that despite the gendered pronoun "He," God is beyond gender. But Reconstructionists and other fundamentalists ground their conception of human nature of the gendered nature of God. We see this in the development of biblical patriarchy (see chapter 7) and we see it here, in the argument that a distinction between Old and New Testaments that replaces God's wrath with God's love is a fatally feminized or even neutered Christianity.[31]

Postmillennialism, Dominion Theology, and the Faithful Remnant

The notion that there is some perfect place and time, whether literal or metaphorical, whether earthly or heavenly, runs through all of Christianity. We have come to categorize the various versions of this teaching in terms of the relationship between the timing of the perfect place and time and the return of Jesus Christ: as premillennial (Jesus will return before the millennium), postmillennial (Jesus will return at the culmination of the millennium), or amillennial (the millennium is a heavenly, rather than earthly, reality). Dimensions of each of these views have been present throughout the history of Christianity, but the distinct categories as they exist today have not. So, for example, while St. Augustine is typically considered an amillennialist, as is John Calvin, postmillennialists claim them both on the basis that their work included both amillennial and postmillennial themes.[32] Though it too has earlier roots, the premillennial dispensationalism present in Hal Lindsay's *Late Great Planet Earth* and the *Left Behind* series by Tim LaHaye and Jerry Jenkins developed in the nineteenth century. It added to the earlier form of premillennialism a framework dividing historical periods into distinct ages called dispensations.

The majority of contemporary fundamentalist Christians are premillennialist; so much so that those who try to define fundamentalism in terms of a list of specific beliefs usually include this. In fact, contemporary fundamentalists subscribe to a very particular version of premillennialism that dates to the mid-nineteenth century and the work of John Nelson Darby. Premillennial dispensationalism teaches that God "dispenses" grace in different ways during different periods of history and sees the biblical books of Daniel and Revelation as prophecies about the future. According to dispensationalism, we are now living in the end of the second to the final age—the "church age." In this period, the world will tumble in decline until things are so bad that Jesus must return to establish the Kingdom of God (thus his return is premillennial). The details of this decline are debated, but they include the Great Tribulation (described in the Gospels and Revelation as a period of turmoil and violence immediately preceding the second coming of Christ), the battle of Armageddon, and the Rapture (in which it is thought that Christians will be rescued from the chaos of the Tribulation). Briefly, there are three versions that divide over when the Rapture will take place in relationship to the Great Tribulation. That is, there is a pretribulation version that holds that Christians will be taken away by Jesus before the Tribulation; a midtribulation version that holds that Christians will have to live through part of the Tribulation; and a posttribulation version. Both the midtribulation and posttribulation versions hold that through the Tribulation, Christians do not escape and must persevere in obedience to God's will as the "faithful remnant." This notion is present in the biblical text, for example in Romans 11:5 and Revelation 12:17. But historian Michael McVicar credits Albert J. Nock with bringing the concept of "the remnant" into the broader milieu of American conservatism. Rushdoony adopted it from Nock and incorporated his own version of it into his theological worldview.[33]

Reconstructionists, on the other hand, are postmillennial. They hold that the Kingdom of God is a present, earthly reality and that the second coming of Jesus will mark the culmination of the Kingdom (thus it is postmillennial). For postmillennialists, Jesus defeated death (and Satan) at the cross, thereby establishing the Kingdom of God. Postmillennialists teach that it is the work of Christians to restore the damage done by the Fall; to bring the blessings of the Gospel to the whole earth. They believe that salvation is both spiritual and historical, as well as individual and cultural. Gary North claims that postmillennialism goes back to at least the early fourth century, that it was "pioneered in part by Augustine and John Calvin, and developed more fully by the Puritans of the seventeenth century."[34] Reconstructionist postmillennialism has roots in the work of Roderick Campbell and Marcellus Kik who shaped Rushdoony's views, which were in turn developed by David Chilton, among others.

While postmillennialism was common among nineteenth-century evangelicals—and, in fact, the many social reform movements of the period can be understood as a result of evangelical efforts to build the Kingdom of God—Reconstructionist postmillennialism is distinct from most earlier forms by virtue of its emphases on theonomy and dominion (bringing all areas of life under the lordship of Jesus through the application of biblical law). Also called covenantalism, it is one of the features that unites Reconstructionists with New England Puritans, who understood their "errand into the wilderness" as an effort to expand the Kingdom, such that North calls the Reconstruction movement "social neo-puritanism."[35]

For Reconstructionist postmillennialists creation is redeemed in ways directly parallel to the ways in which individual humans are saved. One is saved when he or she becomes a Christian, salvation is worked out in the imperfect life of the believer, and it is perfected for eternity at Judgment. Similarly, they believe, all of creation was restored to its original purpose with Jesus' resurrection, restoration and/or redemption is worked out in history as Christians fulfill the Great Commission and take dominion over the world, and it will be perfected when Jesus returns. The Great Commission in Matthew, "go therefore and make disciples of all the nations, baptizing them in the name of the Father and the Son and the Holy Spirit, teaching them to observe all that I have commanded you" is seen as a postredemption restatement of the "dominion mandate" given in Genesis: "And God blessed them; and God said to them, 'Be fruitful and multiply, and fill the earth and subdue it; and rule over the fish of the sea and over the birds of the sky, and over every living thing that moves on the earth.'"[36]

Just as Greg Bahnsen established himself as the Reconstructionist specialist on presuppositionalism by building on the work of Rushdoony, David Chilton did so in the area of postmillennialism. In the introduction to *Paradise Restored*, Chilton tells us what he believes is at stake in the debate between premillennialists and postmillennialists: "The fact is that *you will not work for the transformation of society if you do not believe society can be transformed.*"[37] In other words, because premillennialists believe the world will spiral ever downward until Christ returns, they won't work to build his Kingdom on earth. Chilton takes on premillennial dispensationalism and fundamentalist rhetoric about "literal readings" of scripture and offers instead a "prophetic pattern" laid out in the book of Genesis and repeated throughout as "the Biblical Story."[38] Chilton argues that "we must allow the Bible's own structure to arise from the text itself, to impose itself upon our own understanding. We must become accustomed to the Biblical vocabulary and modes of expression, seeking to shape our own thinking in terms of Scriptural categories."[39] He begins by making the case that the "eschatology of defeat" is not in keeping with the historic teachings of the Christian church. He argues:

> Until fairly recently *most Christians held an eschatology of dominion.* Most Christians throughout the history of the Church regarded the eschatology of defeat as a doctrine of crackpots. The Hope of world-wide conquest for Christianity has been the traditional faith of the Church through the ages.[40]

He claims that "the eschatology of dominion radically shaped Western civilization," from architecture and art to the exploration of Christopher Columbus.[41] Chilton points to the unparalleled success of the Gospel as the source of all that is good in the West.

> The whole rise of Western Civilization—science and technology, medicine, the arts, constitutionalism, the jury system, free enterprise, literacy, increasing productivity, the high status of women— is attributable to one major fact: *the West has been transformed by Christianity.*[42]

Chilton's postmillennialism is "preterist" (technically, partial preterist). That is, he believes that the biblical "prophecies" are indeed prophecies foretelling the future, but he believes that many of them foretold a future that has now already occurred.[43] He dates the fall of the Temple in Jerusalem to 70 AD and argues that the events foretold in the Bible refer to this period. He rejects fundamentalist claims for reading the Bible "literally," arguing that all interpretations include both literalism and symbolism.[44] Chilton recognizes the Bible as literature, albeit "divinely inspired and inerrant literature"; he says that unless we learn its literary styles, we will not be able to understand what it means.[45] Chilton's point is that the division between literalists and nonliteralists is artificial, that the real division is between biblical interpretation and speculative interpretation; those who go to the text itself to understand how to interpret the text, and those who go to outside sources—what he labels speculation."[46] And indeed, there are points on which Chilton is much more literal than the premillennial dispensationalists who call themselves literalists. An interesting example is the biblical text addressing the period known as the Great Tribulation. Jesus tells his disciples, "Truly I say unto you, this generation will not pass away until all these things take place."[47] Chilton writes:

> It has become fashionable over the last 100 years or so to teach that He was speaking about the end of the "Church Age" and the time of His Second Coming. But is this what He meant? We should note carefully that Jesus Himself gave the (approximate) date of the coming Tribulation, leaving no room for doubt after any careful examination of the text . . . This means that *everything* Jesus spoke of in this passage . . . *took place before the generation then living passed away.*[48]

And again:

> As is pointed out in Matthew, the Great Tribulation was to take place, not at the *end* of history but in the *middle*, for nothing similar had occurred "from the beginning of the world until now, *nor ever shall.*"[49]

It would seem unnecessary to replicate each point of Chilton's exegesis here. My intention is to illustrate the style in which he engages his fundamentalist opponents. He is, clearly, one of them: engaging them in their own terms and within their own framework. And he goes on to do this with each of the key points of their system. Chilton's discussion of the symbolism of the Bible is sophisticated; it's not a "this means that" symbolism that serves no purpose other than to create a mysterious code. On the contrary, Chilton holds that the symbolism serves the purpose of integrating the whole; of making each reference call attention to all the other similar references. He uses the example of the symbolism of water to illustrate the point, citing just twelve of the many Old Testament references.

He writes: "In principle, the whole Story of redemption is taught in the early chapters of the Bible: the rest is simply built upon the foundation laid there."[50]

If Rushdoony is the architect of the theological and philosophical system, and Chilton is the general contractor in charge of developing and popularizing postmillennialism, Gary North is the site foreman with the on-the-ground plans for taking dominion. While Chilton focused on biblical exegesis to develop and defend his postmillennialism, North has engaged more directly in debate with premillennial dispensationalists and sought to work through the implications of postmillennialism for the church and society as a whole. While this is generally true of North's work, it is especially so in his 1990 work *Millennialism and Social Theory* and his *Biblical Blueprint Series*. Much of North's work is conspiratorial and survivalist. Titles include *None Dare Call it Witchcraft* (1976), *The Last Train Out: The Essential Survival Manual for the 80s and Beyond* (1983), *Government by Emergency* (1983), *Fighting Chance: Ten Feet to Survival* (1986), *Conspiracy: A Biblical View* (1986), and *The Pirate Economy* (1987).[51] One of the paradoxes noted by those who study the rise of the religious right is that premillennialists, who believe that the end of the world and the return of their savior are imminent (and who enthusiastically look forward to those developments), were mobilized to change the future: to (re) build a Christian nation. By reframing postmillennialism as "dominion theology," Reconstructionists helped fundamentalists square this circle, even while they continued, to the unending frustration of Reconstructionists, to embrace premillennialism.

Journalist Jeff Sharlet tied the Reconstructionists to the religious right by way of Tim LaHaye.[52] In response, *Christianity Today* ran a critical review by Alan Jacobs and then an exchange between Sharlet and Jacobs. In it Jacobs argues:

> Sharlet surely must know that Dominionists like Rushdoony believe that Christ will not return until his Church has established its rule, its Dominion, over the world; and he must also know that dispensationalists like Tim LaHaye believe that the Church will *never* establish such dominion, that the world will just become more and more of a mess until Christ returns to rescue, to judge, and to bring an end to history. It could not escape him that these vast differences in eschatology yield vastly different political programs—and if they don't, then that indicates a

certain incoherence, a lack of fit between theology and practice, which renders doubtful the notion that theologians can be Svengalis to their "students" and "disciples."[53]

Indeed, it's not a lack of "fit between theology and practice" but rather an example of how fluid theology is in the lives of everyday people. Those of us who study religion too often demand a coherence of ideas that most people don't. What we have here is an ethos in which the contradictory edges of the theological systems are smoothed over in practice; a powerful example of the inadequacy of reducing a "religion" to its theological system or, for that matter, its sacred texts. In this particular instance, it's the theology of dominion and the concept of the faithful remnant that serve as a bridge between the two systems.

For Reconstructionists, dominion theology is the practical outworking of postmillennialism. In simple terms, God created Adam and Eve to have fellowship with him and have dominion over the Garden of Eden. With the Fall, both their fellowship with God and their place in the Garden were lost. Postmillennialists believe that all of creation was restored with the resurrection and that the "garden" is now the whole earth, so Christians should exercise dominion over it in the name of Christ. The concept of "dominion" in Reconstructionist writing is closely tied to the Reformed notion of stewardship, which lends "dominion" a slightly different cast than it might have outside this context.[54] It really does not mean "to dominate," exactly, though certainly it does not mean only "to care for" either.[55] It is, rather, a paternalistic "caring for" that includes both ideas. Gary North writes: "The will to dominion is . . . not the quest for power apart from ethical law, but the quest for authority by means of ethical action."[56] In fact, North sees power and dominion as oppositional, representing, respectively, humanistic and godly religion: "power" is the usurpation of authority under the presumed autonomy of human reason, while "dominion" is the legitimate exercise of delegated authority under biblical law. In North's work, especially, the "dominion mandate" and postmillennialism are explicitly tied to the Reformed notion of "common grace," as it is outlined by Cornelius Van Til. North's book *Dominion and Common Grace* is a response to Van Til's earlier work *Common Grace and the Gospel*.[57] Without becoming bogged down in the details of this debate, it concerns the question of the degree to which the benefits of the grace of God fall to the unsaved as well as the saved.

According to Reconstructionists, order and rationality upon which we (believers and unbelievers alike) depend comes from God; apart from God there can be no order and therefore no rationality. Apart from God, what seems like knowledge is actually irrational because it denies its own foundation. Unbelievers (and most Christians who deny presuppositionalism and theonomy) depend on God's order and rationality but at the same time deny it because acknowledging it would require submission to biblical law—in this sense they are said to be schizophrenic and lack epistemological self-consciousness. According to North, God restrains unbelievers from rejecting him entirely (and allows them their schizophrenia) temporarily. This, in turn, allows unbelievers to continue to prosper despite their disobedience but, as Christians bring God's law to bear on all aspects of life, God will increasingly withdraw his "common grace" and unbelievers will be subject to the implications of their defective worldview.

Fundamentalists adopted Reconstructionist postmillennialism in a piecemeal way. While most did not explicitly jettison their premillennial dispensationalism, they adopted, instead, dominion theology. They chose to stop focusing on what would happen eschatologically and, instead, focused on Christ's command that, until he returned, Christians were to "disciple the nations" and "occupy" the land. Fundamentalist Christians began to organize over concern that America was drifting from its holy calling as a Christian nation and specifically over concern that the changing values of America were impinging on their own family and church lives. As Matt Moen has argued, it was often issues about taxation (IRS "tyranny") and regulation of Christian schools that propelled fundamentalists into local politics.[58]

In its popularized form, dominion theology was separated from postmillennialism. This move was, perhaps, best facilitated by the version of postmillennialism and dominion theology put forth by North (though unintentionally so, as Reconstructionists consistently find this troubling).[59] In many ways North's postmillennialism is typical of other Reconstructionists' (and nineteenth-century postmillennialists'). In *Conspiracy: A Biblical View,* for example, North argues that society will be saved by the "covenantal faithfulness" of the people.

> Our job is not to "throw the rascals out" in one glorious national election. Our job is to replace them steadily by our own competence. God did not promise Moses that the Hebrews would conquer

the Canaanites overnight . . . God promised them victory and he promises us victory, too.[60]

And later:

> A counter-offensive is called for. Not a defensive holding action [that is, premillennial dispensationalism]. Not a retreat into the historical shadows. A counter-offensive. It must be a *bottom-up* decentralized offensive campaign. The top-down centralized strategy is the strategy of our opponents [he is referring to communists who are but one kind of humanist]. What we need is a long-term grass roots campaign at every level of politics, economics, and institutional influence, in every region of the country—indeed every region of the world.[61]

But in his other writings we find a sense of urgency and impending catastrophe more like that which we find in premillennialism, combined with a long-term postmillennialist vision. The impending catastrophe may be brought about by the forces of communism, Eastern religions, New Age religion, witchcraft, a global shutdown as a result of computer failure, or an economic crisis, but, in any case, faithful Christians (the remnant) will survive to pick up the pieces and build the Kingdom of God. The churches, having embraced premillennialism or amillennialism, do not have the framework to "reap the harvest." That is, people are converting and the churches are not prepared to disciple them, by which Reconstructionists mean mentoring them in the application of their faith to every aspect of their lives. Christians have not prepared for a transformation of culture because they believed that it could not happen. In this scenario, the "faithful remnant" that North envisions will be prepared to lead and other Christians will have no choice but to follow. It is after this event that Christians will be able to build the Kingdom of God in earnest. Unlike the theology of nineteenth-century optimistic postmillennialists, North's postmillennialism develops in the context of his larger vision of history shaped by the anticommunist movement of the 1950s in general and the John Birch Society in particular.[62] For decades North produced a subscription-based newsletter that offered economic advice, called the *Remnant Review*, and he is perhaps most widely known for leading the chorus of dire predictions associated with Y2K. He also says that before he met Rushdoony and went to work for him he was an ardent premillennialist.

In his 1990 *Millennialism and Social Theory*, North lays out the reasons for his sense of urgency, why he expects catastrophic destruction and how that fits into his larger postmillennialist views. While he believes that it may be a very long time before Christians have fulfilled the Great Commission, the short-term scenario he envisions blends easily with the expectations of premillennialists. North believes that two facts necessitate a cataclysmic crisis that will occur relatively soon: the rise in global population and the fact that people are more open to conversion when facing difficulty than when enjoying prosperity. He argues that, by virtue of obedience to God's command in Genesis to multiply and fill the earth, we have a population bomb, though his worry is not an environmental one: "If nothing changes, the mere birthrate differential between the saved and the lost will guarantee the triumph of Satan's kingdom in history."[63]

> I prefer to believe that in the coming millennium . . . God is going to send [revival]. I cannot be sure, but it seems to me that this is the way God works. I think this will happen fairly soon. If it doesn't, then Satan will be able to boast: "they obeyed your rule (Gen. 1:28) and therefore I will spend eternity with vastly more souls." . . . This is not prophecy; this is simply applied covenant theology. You do not need a degree in theology to figure this out; a hand held calculator is sufficient.[64]

Oddly enough, this view is reminiscent of the arguments made by premillennial dispensationalists in the nineteenth century about why Jesus would return soon. According to historian George Marsden, William E. Blackstone helped popularize premillennial dispensationalism with charts depicting the number of people of the world and their respective religions to argue that the rapidly growing numbers of "heathens" as compared to "True Christians" disproved postmillennialism.[65]

Drawing historical comparisons, North argues that periods of peace and prosperity do not typically lend themselves to people seeking deeper spiritual meaning.

> A meaningful, culture transforming spread of the gospel is unlikely to happen without the crises . . . I am not talking about a short term emergency. I am talking about a new way of life for at least a generation. The bubonic plague forced this in 1347–48, and it returned, generation after generation, for over three centuries,

until the last major outbreak in London in 1665. The next year London burned to the ground. It will be a time of despair for billions of people. This is the softening up process that has always been necessary in advance for widespread repentance.[66]

North's work is focused on concrete ways in which the faithful remnant can survive the catastrophe and do so with the skills necessary for rebuilding. This is not inconsistent with certain versions of premillennialism. Whether they anticipate the gradual "replacing evil with good" or the faithful remnant picking up the pieces after an apocalyptic cataclysm, Reconstructionist postmillennialism, in the form of dominion theology and popularized as the "(re)establishment of America as a Christian nation," is a rallying cry for the religious right.[67]

The work of religious right leader and best-selling author Tim LaHaye is a good example of the hidden influence of the Reconstructionists on early religious right leaders, as well as the way in which Gary North's style of postmillennialism can be reconciled with premillennialism, if not in theological detail, at least in ethos. As noted above, LaHaye's early work is rooted in Rushdoony's critique of secular humanism.[68] The books cite Rushdoony and illustrate the incorporation of Reconstructionist work. LaHaye's more recent books, the very popular *Left Behind* novels, are rooted in the familiar "end times prophecy" of premillennial dispensationalist. The Rapture has taken place and those "left behind" must hold back the forces of Satan to remain a faithful remnant until Jesus returns. But "the believers" are not hiding out and awaiting that return. They form the Tribulation Force that infiltrates the Global Community located in New Babylon. While God metes out punishment to "the enemies" by causing the sun to burn hotter and hotter or causing total darkness for a time, the remnant is kept safe. In one example at the end of the tenth book in the series, actually entitled *The Remnant*, God first "turned out the lights" and then later caused the whole world to exist in darkness. Except that the believers, and only the believers, can still see.

> Chang [one of the believers] wanted to laugh. He wanted to howl from his gut. He wished he could tell everyone everywhere that once again God had meted out a curse, a judgment upon the earth that affected only those who bore the mark of the beast. Chang could see. It was different. He didn't see lights either. He simply saw everything in Sepia tone, as if someone had turned down the wattage on a chandelier.[69]

The book ends:

> What better advantage could the Trib Force have than that they
> could see? They would have the drop on everyone and everybody.
> With but a year to go until the Glorious Appearing, Chang
> thought, the good guys finally had a better deal than they had
> when the daylight hours belonged solely to them. Now, for as long
> as God tarried . . . everything was in the believers' favor.[70]

This may not be a postmillennial building of the Kingdom of God on earth,
but neither is it the older helpless resignation of premillennialists "letting
the world go to hell in a hand basket." North's postmillennialism has the
Kingdom of God established at the resurrection but the world currently in
a state of decline, awaiting a major revival to be brought on by a great disaster of some sort. With the revival, the only people who understand what is
happening will be the faithful remnant whose members have been schooled
by the Reconstructionists. The church will turn to them to lead and will get
on with the business of reconstructing all of society and bringing it under
the dominion of Christ. Dispensationalists will disagree about the theological details of North's scenario, but they expect a rapture to remove
Christians from earth before a period of great disaster. The removal of the
faithful will cause revival in which some will "come around" to become a
faithful remnant who will be saved. They will be the only ones who understand what is going on and will fight through the period of disasters, exercising dominion, until Jesus returns to establish the Kingdom.

In both systems we find ourselves currently in the period immediately
before the disaster. Postmillennialists believe that the disaster is, to some
degree, the fault of the church for not adequately understanding and
teaching obedience to biblical law. But from the point of view of the premillennialists, the instructions about what to do in response to the disaster
are virtually the same. Millennialist systems make the present moment
the culmination of all of history and the lives of those of us living in this
time of cosmic importance. The human desire to be special and important can be so powerful it can make global cataclysm appealing.

Conclusion

This is not the first time in American history that a populist conservative
Protestantism has blended theological traditions to construct a "biblical" ra-
tionale for bringing the culture in line with their views. In the midst of the

fundamentalist–modernist controversy at the turn of the twentieth century, pietistic fundamentalism, more concerned with personal holiness than with the state of American culture, was drawn into engagement when believers felt their way of life was challenged by cultural shifts. Those conservative Protestants (the original fundamentalists) drew on the intellectual and theological foundation established by the "Old Princeton" theologians J. Gresham Machen, Benjamin Warfield, and Charles and A. A. Hodge, creating such an odd coalition of populist pietism and highly intellectual Reformed theology that historian George Marsden has called them "preachers of paradox."[71] It is a mistake to think of religious systems as clearly bounded, consistent structures that must be embraced in their entirety or rejected completely. Meaning making is a much more ad hoc process than that. Not coincidentally, the Reconstructionists see themselves as the true heirs to this Reformed tradition—holding Old Princeton (and especially Machen) in high esteem. Yet they critique Old Princetonians, too, for their failure to work out the implications of their otherwise sound epistemology. As North writes: "It was only with the publications written by R. J. Rushdoony, beginning in the early 1960's, that any theologian began to make a serious, systematic, exegetical attempt to link the Bible to the principles of limited civil government and free-market economics."[72]

The Christian Reconstructionists can be seen as a link between the early-twentieth-century Old Christian Right and the early-twenty-first century resurgence of Southern religious conservatism and the Tea Party.[73] At the turn of the twentieth century, fundamentalism was given intellectual foundation by the theologians at Old Princeton and given political expression from the 1930s to the 1950s in the Old Christian Right. In the 1960s and early 1970s, the Reconstructionist movement laid a parallel intellectual foundation that was given political expression by the New Christian Right. Phillip Hammond and James Davison Hunter have argued that the rise of the religious right of the 1980s can best be seen as the "second installment" of the conflict between fundamentalists and modernists that began at the turn of the twentieth century.[74] The fundamentalists lost the theological conflict early on, but the cultural war was yet to be fought. The second half of the war would be fought by a similar coalition of conservative religious leaders.

2

Jurisdictional Authority and Sphere Sovereignty

WHILE CONTEMPORARY RELIGIOUS right leaders and activists are hardly committed Reconstructionists, they have inherited a postmillennialist ethos, some organizing philosophical commitments, and a significant portion of the Reconstructionist political program. Call it soft Reconstructionism. From the early work of Tim LaHaye and John Whitehead to the Tea Party "historian" David Barton, Rushdoony's version of a traditional Reformed framework—called sphere sovereignty or jurisdictional authority—remains at the heart of the "biblical worldview." As early as the 1960s, and well into the 1980s, Christian Reconstructionists advocated that Christians should go about transforming the world by bringing it "under the Lordship of Christ." This transformation was to be partly political but is much broader than that: Christians are to transform every aspect of culture to bring it in line with Bible, their biblical worldview. The political transformation will follow from this broader, comprehensive transformation.

In the more than fifty years since R. J. Rushdoony published *By What Standard?*, there have been significant changes, developments, variations, and even divisions within the Reconstructionist movement. Rushdoony's earliest works lay the epistemological foundation to argue that theonomy (that is, God's law as it is revealed in the Old and New Testaments) is the necessary foundation of all knowledge. In addition to *By What Standard?* (1958), these works include *Intellectual Schizophrenia* (1961), *The Messianic Character of American Education* (1963), *The Mythology of Science* (1967), and *Law and Liberty* (1971). Rushdoony then moved on to explicate the biblical worldview in his *The Institutes of Biblical Law* (1973). In other words, the earliest works seek to explain what's wrong with the world and then *The Institutes of Biblical Law* lays out a vision for a better world, one based on biblical principles.

For Rushdoony, the fundamental question all humans must face, the inescapable question, concerns authority: what is its source and how do we live appropriately according to it. His answer is that there are only two possible sources for authority (and therefore law): God (leading to life) and Man (leading to death). *The Institutes of Biblical Law* lays out Rushdoony's vision of a world grounded in biblical law by way of a lengthy (890 pages in the first of two volumes alone) commentary on the Ten Commandments and the relevant "case law" from other parts of the Bible.[1] It has often been called Rushdoony's most important work and was named the most important book of 1973 by *Christianity Today*. Written over a three-year period, it represented something of a culmination of his previous work.

In the introduction, Rushdoony rejects the dominant Christian approach to biblical law. Most contemporary Christians see the Old Testament as a book of law that has been replaced by grace in the New Testament, making biblical law no longer applicable to God's people. For Rushdoony, this is heresy.

> It is modern heresy that holds that the law of God holds no meaning nor any binding force for man today. It is an aspect of the influence of humanistic and evolutionary thought on the church, and it posits an evolving, developing god. This "dispensational" god expressed himself in law in an earlier age, then later expressed himself by grace alone, and is now perhaps to express himself in some other way. But this is not the God of Scripture, whose grace and law remain the same in every age.[2]

He explains that the Ten Commandments lay out general principles of law but that a true understanding of biblical law requires the detailed examination of the application of the principles in specific cases found throughout the Bible. "The law, then, *first* asserts principles, *second*, it cites cases to develop the implications of those principles, and, *third*, the law has as its purpose the direction and *the restitution of God's order*."[3] Later, he writes:

> We must conclude therefore that *authority is not only a religious concept but also a total one*. It involves the recognition at every point of our lives of God's absolute law-order. The starting point of this recognition is the family: "Honor thy father and thy mother." Out of

this commandment, with its requirement that children submit to and obey the authority of their parents under God, comes the basic and fundamental training in religious authority. If the authority of the home is denied, it means that man is in revolution against the fabric and structure of life, and against life itself. Obedience thus carries the promise of life.[4]

According to Rushdoony, biblical authority is God's authority delegated to humans, who exercise dominion under God's law in three distinct God-ordained institutions: the family, the church, and the civil government. Each of those institutions has carefully delineated and limited responsibilities. When humans decide that those institutions should serve any functions beyond the ones ordained by God, they presume the autonomy and supremacy of human reason and thus violate biblical law.

Biblical Authority and Family

There is no more important key to understanding Christian Reconstruction than Rushdoony's concept of the family, which undergirds everything else. While Rushdoony argues that God has ordained authority to function in three distinctly separate spheres—familial, ecclesiastical, and civil—familial authority is the most fundamental and, in many ways, the model for the others.[5] He writes, *"The meaning of the family is thus not to be sought in procreation but in a God-centered authority and responsibility in terms of man's calling to subdue the earth and exercise dominion over it."*[6]

Cognitive linguist George Lakoff suggests that we can understand the competing worldviews that divide our contemporary culture through the metaphor of the family.[7] He uses the notion of "folk theories" to articulate the distinction between what we think is going on in our everyday reality from what current work in cognitive linguistics suggests is really going on. Much of our thinking, Lakoff says, is not conscious. Moral thinking, on issues like freedom and justice, is imaginative and depends fundamentally on metaphorical understanding. Lakoff argues that family-model metaphors provide the basis for contemporary political worldviews, and he specifies two versions. Conservatives, he argues, see government as a strict father, while liberals believe it should be a nurturant parent.[8] Exemplifying a worldview rooted in the strict father metaphor, Rushdoony argues that freedom is found most fully in "obedience" as decreed in the commandment to honor one's parents. He says:

> It is commonly held, by the humanistic mind, that the unquestioning and faithful obedience required by law of children is destructive of the mind . . . But the best functioning mind is the obedient and disciplined mind. The child who is disciplined into obedience is not the servile youth but the free man.[9]

Rushdoony is emphatic that freedom is not autonomy for individuals. Freedom, as Christian Reconstructionists understand it, is for each of the biblically ordained institutions (family, church, and civil government) to function autonomously from each other under the sole authority of God. For Rushdoony, freedom is rooted in the family insofar as the family is seen as the most central of these institutions. Families are free when they are protected from the usurpation of their authority by the other two, especially the civil government. It is this particular family model that grounds Rushdoony's worldview and finds expression in the contemporary conservative understanding of freedom as the removal of government restraints.

We can see Lakoff's strict father metaphor at play. The family, with the father as authority, mirrors the cosmos, with God as authority. Rushdoony makes this explicit as he explores the implications, for family and by extension for all of society, of the recognition that all legitimate authority comes from God:

> Four laws deal with the family, three of them directly: "Honor thy father and mother," "Thou shalt not commit adultery," "Thou shalt not steal." . . . The fact that property (and hence theft) were family-oriented appears not only in all the law, but in the tenth commandment: to covet, whether property, wife, or servants of another was a sin against the neighbor's family.[10]

The centrality of the family's authority is evident, for Rushdoony, even in the creation account. Before there were gatherings of God's faithful or civil societies, there was the family and its primary function: to exercise dominion over the earth and subdue it. The whole purpose of humans is seen in the calling given Adam (and by implication, though secondarily, Eve) in Genesis, and that calling rests on the authority given by God to the family.

Although originally only Adam was created (Gen 2:7), the creation mandate is plainly spoken to Adam in the married estate, and with the creation of woman in mind. Thus, essential to the function of the family under God, and to the role of the man as the head of the household, *is the call to subdue the earth and exercise dominion over it* . . . Man must bring to all creation God's law-order, exercising power over creation in the name of God. The earth was created "very good" but it was as yet undeveloped in terms of subjugation and possession by man, God's appointed governor. This *government* is particularly the calling of the man as husband and father, and of the family as an institution.[11]

It might seem obvious that from these views of family flow certain notions about the relationships between men and women and the relationships between parents and their children, both of which would be characterized by submission and obedience. Rushdoony is very explicit about this, and he finds in the fifth commandment—"honor thy father and mother that thy days may be long upon the land,"—much more than one might expect. Rushdoony points to Isaiah 3:16–26 as an illustration of what happens when men fail to exercise their God-given prerogative of dominion in the family: "Women rule over men; children then gain undue freedom and power and become oppressors of their parents; the emasculated rulers in such a social order lead the people astray and destroy the fabric of society."[12] Rushdoony anticipates a future collapse of society like that depicted in Isaiah in which "the once independent and feministic women are humbled in their pride and seek the protection and safety of a man."[13] His analysis is grounded in essentialized views of gender in which males, by nature, fight for territory and status while females' instincts are "personal and anarchistic." He writes, "the woman becomes absorbed with problems of law and order in a personal way, i.e. when her family and her family's safety are endangered by its decay. The man will be concerned with the problems of society apart from the condition of crisis."[14] In what could be lifted from a Promise Keepers tract more than thirty years later, Rushdoony writes:

Today, men, having abdicated extensively their masculinity, are less concerned with order and more with gratification. As a result, women, because their security, and that of their children is at stake, become involved with the problem of social decay and law and order. Social and political action thus becomes a pressing feminine concern. Their concern underscores the decay of society and the failure of men.[15]

But, because this commandment is addressed to children, most of Rushdoony's focus in the chapter is on discussing the implications of the place of children in the family and the mutual relationship and responsibilities between them and parents. Rushdoony argues that not only is the family the most influential school but also that God has given the family—not the church and not the state—the authority to train children. Public schools, according to Rushdoony, usurp the authority of the family and in the process destroy it. Children's most important responsibility is to be obedient, and chief among parents' responsibilities is to provide an education "in the broadest sense of the word," by which Rushdoony means both discipline and schooling.[16] Lakoff's strict father model could have no clearer expression. In a hearty endorsement of corporal punishment Rushdoony writes: "parents then [in biblical times] were as inclined to be tenderhearted as now, but the necessity for chastening cannot be set aside by a foolish pity. Chastisement can be a lifesaver to the child."[17] But it's in his discussion of schooling that Rushdoony lays out what has, for many in the religious right, become the basic framework for understanding education:

> It needs more than ever to be stressed that the best and truest educators are parents under God. The greatest school is the family . . . The moral training of the child, the discipline of good habits, is an inheritance from the parents to the child which surpasses all other. The family is the first and most basic school of man.[18]

Furthermore, public schools, which Rushdoony calls "government schools," contribute to the destruction of society: "The statist school . . . basically trains women to be men; it is not surprising that so many are unhappy to be women. Nor are men any the happier, in that dominion in modern education is transferred from man to the state, and man is progressively emasculated."[19] In another example, Rushdoony writes: "The major casualty in modern education is the male student, since any education which diminishes man's calling to exercise dominion also diminishes man to the same degree." Conservative commentator and author Christina Hoff Sommers made the same point twenty years later.[20] More recently, former Florida congressman and Tea Party leader Alan West made the same argument.

Education, for Reconstructionists, is to be Bible centered. Efforts at critical thinking and concerns over freedom of inquiry are humanistic— rooted in a false religion. And students are to learn in obedience; teaching the value of questioning, let alone the value of challenging authority, is not part of the curriculum. For Rushdoony, even student government violates this principle. "The child has no right to govern his parents, the student their school, nor the employees their employer," he says.[21] This early rejection of the notion of children's rights plays out today in the fight over the United Nations Declaration of the Rights of the Child, as well as legal controversies over homeschooling and regulation, in which the Home School Legal Defense Association specifically opposes the notion of children's rights.

Lakoff sees clearly that conservative views of economic freedom are individualistic and private, that they are fundamental to other freedoms, and that they are believed to be based in nature. What Lakoff misses (though it is stronger evidence for his larger theory) is that, for conservatives, these economic views are also grounded in very specific notions of family. The commission given to Adam and Eve in the Garden is, in essence, an economic mission: be fruitful and multiply, fill up the earth, and subdue it. Rushdoony finds this in the fifth commandment.

> The first general principle inherent in this law . . . is . . . the basic law of inheritance. What we inherit from our parents is life itself, and also the wisdom of their faith and experience that they transmit to us . . . the continuity of history rests in this honor and inheritance . . . [W]e do not enter an empty world. The houses, orchards, fields, and flocks are all the handiwork of the past, and we are richer for this past and must honor it . . . The basic and central inheritance of culture and all that it includes, faith, training, wisdom, wealth, love, common ties and traditions are severed and denied where parents and elders are not honored.[22]

In a section entitled "The Economics of the Family," Rushdoony explores the relationship between family, property, and liberty, with family members having "property rights" in each other. "It can be said that a man holds his wife as his property and his children also. But because his wife and children have certain, individual, particular, special, and continuing claims on him, they have a property right in him."[23] For Rushdoony, Western metaphors of progress (and even postmillennialism itself) are "the second general principle" derived from the fifth commandment.[24]

> In Biblical faith, the family inherits from the past in order to grow firmly into the future . . . Scripture declares, "Therefore shall a man leave his father and mother and cleave unto his wife: and they shall be one flesh" (Gen. 2:24). Marriage calls for a move forward by the man and his wife; they break with the old families to create a new one. They remain tied to the old families in that both represent a cultural inheritance from two specific families. They remain tied further by their religious duty to honor their parents. The growth is real, and the dependence is real: the new clearly and plainly grows out of and realizes the potentiality of the old.[25]

Opposition to abortion also is rooted in the family as understood by Rushdoony, and he ties his views to biblical law. In one of the most frequently cited aspects of his work, Rushdoony examines the law in Deuteronomy 23:17 pertaining to incorrigible youth. The rebellious youth is to be chastened and if he will not reform, he is to be brought before the elders of the city who are to put him to death. Rushdoony carefully explains this in detail—though the explanation is not likely to make the solution seem more reasonable to modern ears; we must follow it closely to understand its relationship to abortion. The passage, Rushdoony says, actually limits parental authority (only the representatives of the community as a whole had the authority to execute the death penalty) at a time when, under Roman law, fathers had absolute authority over the life and death of their children.[26] In the years before *Roe v. Wade*, Rushdoony argued that the legalization of abortion would cause a return to Roman pagan law in which fathers were the life givers and had, therefore, the right to take life. Rushdoony grounds his conservative notions of "limited government" in this aspect of the law.

> Life is created by God, governed by His law, and to be lived only in terms of His law-word. All transgression faces ultimate judgment; capital offenses require the death penalty here and now, by civil authorities. *Neither the parents nor the state are the creators of life, and therefore cannot fix the terms of life.* In this fact is man's greatest safeguard for freedom; the godly state does indeed deal severely with

offenders, but it strictly limits the power of the state . . . the power of the parents is similarly limited.[27]

Rushdoony supports the death penalty but only for those crimes for which he understands the Bible explicitly calling for it.

Biblical Authority and the Church

Under sphere sovereignty, it is the responsibility of the church to preach the Gospel. This is much more than the contemporary evangelical formula "Jesus died for your sins." Reconstructionists mean the "entirety of the good news": that the resurrection has restored the original purpose of creation, calling "men" to salvation and to dominion, in obedience to biblical law. The Reconstructionists envision a process they call covenantal displacement: they anticipate that, over time, there will be increasing numbers of people who embrace the covenant and through their influence culture will become more biblical. Calling people to embrace the covenant is the work of the church. North writes: "Christians are to destroy the enemy's city (civilization), though normally through voluntary conversions and progressive, long term, cultural displacement."[28] He outlines what he calls "the biblical program for cultural transformation":

> *First*, the Church is to bring continuous positive sanctions into a covenant-breaking culture: preaching, the sacraments, charity, and the disciplining of its members . . . *Second*, the Holy Spirit must also bring positive discontinuities into individual lives: conversion. That is at His discretion, not ours. *Third*, a sovereign God in heaven must bring His discontinuous, corporate, negative sanctions against covenant breakers in history. Notice, above all, that it is God who brings negative corporate sanctions in society, not the Church. *The Church is an exclusively positive agent in society.*[29]

The question arises, however, how the faithful are to come to understand what is required of them. How can Reconstructionists claim that the Bible gives standards for all of life when they don't even agree on those standards among themselves? Or better yet, even if the Bible does give standards, if they can't agree on what they are, how are we to obey them? The answer to this is found in another dimension of Reconstructionism that is rarely explored. Unlike most fundamentalists,

Reconstructionists embrace the idea of theological development over time. North uses the examples of the developing precision of the Christian creeds to demonstrate how the church's understanding of "truth" has changed over time. For him, this is how truth is revealed in history—and how Christians participate in the process of bringing forth that revelation. North finds a "five point covenantal model" embedded in the Bible and uses this to develop an argument for how the church is supposed to, over time, refine its understanding of the application of God's law and to school believers in how to be obedient to it.[30] He describes it as a trial-and-error process that is built upon "positive and negative sanctions" for covenant-keeping and/or covenant-breaking. For North, there are rewards that result from obedience to God's law. Those rewards are personal and cultural, they are historical and eternal, and they are part of how fallen humans come to know the requirements of God's law. Historically speaking, at least in the short run, the rewards benefit all those in an obedient society—not just the believers. Human beings cannot earn salvation, but they can earn earthly rewards both for themselves and for those around them; furthermore, they can receive rewards they do not earn.

Biblical Authority and the Civil Government

The question of whether the religious right seeks to build a theocracy is a central focus for journalists and most of the scholars who have written about Christian Reconstruction. Reconstructionists do not deny that theirs is a strategy for complete transformation of all aspects of culture; they merely reject the use of the term "political" to describe that strategy. That said, the question of whether Reconstructionist thinkers advocate the implementation of theocracy is more complicated. First, they don't all agree. Second, the notion of theocracy they do embrace must be understood within a larger context.

As I've said, Reconstructionists insist that their movement is not primarily political. Rushdoony writes:

It is *not* the purpose of the state and its law to change or reform men: this is a spiritual matter and a task for religion. Man can be changed only by the grace of God through the ministry of his word. Man cannot be changed by statist legislation; he cannot be legislated into a new character.[31]

Gary North and Gary DeMar have, together, written extensively asserting that Reconstruction is only "peripherally" related to politics.[32]

> Christian Reconstructionists are falsely accused of saying that men are saved in some way through political activism. This is utter non-sense. Men are saved by grace through faith, and nothing else . . . Critics who accuse Christian Reconstructionists of teaching a doc-trine of political salvation are spreading a grotesque falsehood. If they had read our materials—and very few of the published critics have—they would know better.[33]

These examples are representative of the perspective of Reconstruction-ists generally. Reconstructionists, being strong five-point Calvinists, be-lieve that, by virtue of original sin, all humans deserve eternal damnation, but that God unconditionally chooses to confer unearned and irresistible grace on some. In Calvinism, there is nothing one can do to earn salva-tion. Not only is it impossible for fallen humans to do anything worthy of grace, it is also predestined from the beginning of time who will be among "the elect." How can teaching and exhortation change the political system when it cannot even convert a sinner to a believer? Furthermore, Recon-structionists are political conservatives in the way we use that term in contemporary American politics: they advocate what contemporary con-servatives consider "limited government." North and DeMar write:

> Reconstructionists believe in a "minimal state." The purpose of getting involved in politics, as Reconstructionists see it, is to *reduce* the power of the State. Reconstructionists are not calling on the State to mandate prayer and Bible reading in public (government) schools, as most fundamentalists advocate. Neither do we advocate teaching "Creation Science" [in those public schools].[34]

Yet how do we make sense of this? On one hand it might seem that North and DeMar are being deceptive. But to understand how they can ad-vocate broad involvement of religion in every aspect of life and, at the same time, claim they aren't advocating theocracy, we need to both clarify their use of the term "politics" and place these views in the larger context of Christian Reconstruction. In his 1990 *Millennialism and Social Theory*, Gary North connects postmillennialism with theonomy to develop what he calls a biblical social theory. The book offers a relatively concise exposition of the dimensions of a Reconstructionist theocracy, developing themes that are often lost in discussions of Reconstructionism. For example, North begins by explaining that the book is actually about evangelism. He is critical, however, of what he calls pietism—by which he means Christianity that focuses on the spiritual condition of individuals; privatized religion, or what religion scholar Bruce Lincoln calls minimalism.[35] So Reconstructionist evangelism is different from the witnessing and altar calls of most conservative Protestants. Those who would evangelize should preach the Gospel but then disciple new converts so that they reshape every dimension of their lives in terms of the requirements of the Bible. This, in turn, impacts the culture. According to North, this is the theme that underlies the Bible, making it a coherent whole:

> The New Testament's emphasis is *personal* deliverance from *eternal* wrath to eternal blessing. The Old Testament's emphasis is *corporate* deliverance from *temporal* wrath to temporal blessing. These dual emphases do not cancel out each other. The theme of eternal personal deliverance is not entirely absent from the Old Testament, and the theme of corporate historical deliverance is not entirely absent from the New Testament. But each Testament has a particular emphasis. *Neither emphasis denies the other.*[36]

After listing a series of academic fields, North says:

> The experts in each of these fields, as well as all the others, are required by God to go to the Bible in search of their field's operational first principles, as well as for some of the actual content (facts) of their fields . . . This means that the Bible is relevant for social theory . . . there is only one self-conscious body of literature that relies solely on the Bible in order to establish its first principles of social theory: theonomy or Christian Reconstruction.[37]

So not only are individuals "saved," but they also begin to live in such a way that the societies in which they live become increasingly sanctified. North writes, "a day is coming when men's *cultural deliverance* will be so widespread, because of men's *widespread repentance*, that God will bring unprecedented blessings in history . . . The Bible teaches that *this fundamental historical transition from wrath to grace is* [in addition to being personal] *also social and cultural.*"[38] This view is rooted in the

"Great Commission" given to Christians in the Gospel of Matthew. Christians are told to go into all the world and preach the Gospel, baptizing converts and teaching them. For Reconstructionists, "evangelism is comprehensive."[39] Reconstructionists understand "politics" to be the process by which individuals seek to influence the policies of the institutions of civil government, but they consider it to be humanist heresy to think of government solely in terms of civil government. They write, "Christians today think just as humanists do regarding social change. When they hear the phrase 'social change,' they automatically think to themselves 'politically directed change.' This is humanism's view of social change, not the Bible's."[40]

Reconstructionists argue that "politics" pertains only to the sphere of civil government. They advocate a theocracy in that they believe that each of the spheres is ordained by and under the authority of God—but they are decidedly separate and each is limited. The role of civil government is

> the public suppression of evil. The State imposes negative sanctions against evil public acts. The civil magistrate is in fact a minister of God . . . But the State is not an agency of salvation. It does not save man by making him positively good . . . Christianity teaches that the reform of society must begin with the individual. To sustain a positive reform of society, God must initiate His transforming grace among many people. He is the agent of positive transformation, not the State.[41]

Reconstructionists disagree over whether the family or the church is the most central institution to a biblical social order, but they agree that both are more important than the state.[42] Elevating the state is humanistic, in their view, because it makes the state the source of salvation; it is a "messianic view of the state." So for Reconstructionists, their system is not centrally "political." But the civil magistrate is still governed by God's law. Their detractors, on the other hand, use the term "political" in a way that is much more broadly construed, referring to the various processes by which institutions in society determine what is, and what is not, a legitimate use of coercive force. A fight within a Christian denomination over whether women may be church leaders is "political" in this larger sense of the word but not in the way the Reconstructionists use it.

Reconstructionists are insistent that they are not advocating an imposition of biblical law from the top down, by the power of a civil government overseen, in some way, by ecclesiastical authority. North argues that, in his model, a separation of church and state is emphatically biblical.

> [The biblical program for cultural transformation] *militates against ecclesiocracy:* the fusion of church and state. If the Church is to bring exclusively positive sanctions in society rather than negative, and if the State is to bring primarily negative sanctions, then *Church and State are inherently separate institutions.* They have two separate functions covenantally.[43]

But of course what he means by the phrase "separation of church and state" is decidedly different from the way that phrase is used in the broader American political discourse.

North anticipates a war over "cultural and judicial standards."[44] It is clear from his work that that is not always a literal war, though at times it is, indeed, literal.

> The enemies of God seldom surrender peacefully. They correctly perceive that they're fighting to the death covenantally, both personally and institutionally. This is what the Bible teaches: either the old Adam dies spiritually through the new birth in history or else God will publicly execute him eternally on Judgment day. Covenant breakers clearly perceive the life and death nature of the struggle for civilization.[45]

In his view, though, it is the covenant breakers who initiate war. North is focused not on what Christians ought to do but what he anticipates will happen in history as a result of what covenant breakers do and what God does in response. Despite a biblical separation of the institutions of church and state, theonomy does not separate religion and state (or religion and any other institution).

> The goal of biblical covenantalism is to bring all the institutions of life under the rule of God's covenant law. The State imposes negative sanctions against specified *public* acts of evil. The churches preach the gospel and proclaim God's law. The family acts as the agent of dominion. Voluntary corporations of all kinds are established to achieve both profitable and charitable goals.[46]

Much of North's work is marked by repeated criticisms that theological opponents of Christian Reconstruction do not read Reconstructionists' work and then disingenuously repeat inaccurate criticisms. He frequently cites theologian Richard John Neuhaus, who admitted in a critical article that he did not have time to read the Reconstructionists' works because they write so much. There is no issue more marked by this kind of dialogue than the disagreement over the degree to which Reconstructionists rely on politics to bring about the Kingdom of God. North insists that, since he so often argues that Reconstruction is not primarily political, his detractors violate the commandment against bearing false witness by lying about what Reconstructionists believe. In the end, the disagreement hangs on whether "politics" is defined narrowly (relevant to civil government alone) or broadly (relevant to all public affairs) and whether one considers a union of civil government and religion "political"; but, in either case, the Reconstructionists' strategic efforts to transform culture in all its dimensions have put them in a position to have continued influence, whether or not that influence shows in electoral politics at any given time. The questions of how much emphasis they put on politics and the degree to which they want to "impose" a "theocracy" will be explored further in the next chapter.

3

Building a Reconstructed Society:
Gary North's Biblical Blueprint Series

THE EFFORT TO articulate a biblical worldview to replace the dominant, but doomed, humanist worldview is at the heart of Christian Reconstructionism. While much of this worldview is articulated in philosophically and theologically dense volumes, Reconstructionists have also been adept at producing accessible versions, stripped of technical language and packaged such that churchgoers, conference goers, even high schoolers and college students can learn how to structure their lives according to this biblical model.

One of the most direct and systematic efforts at popularization is the *Biblical Blueprint Series*, edited by Gary North. Published in 1986 and 1987 (by North's Dominion Press), the ten volumes in the series are authored by six different people. Each explores a dimension of the reconstruction of society, taking seriously the Christian Reconstructionist assertion the "the Bible speaks to every area of life." Underlying each of the books is the coherent integration of presuppositionalism, postmillennialism, and theonomy. Each volume begins with an introduction by North placing the book in the larger context of the series, and each volume ends with the same essay by North outlining his vision for the *Blueprint Series*. According to North, the argument that the Bible is "not a textbook" and does not provide "blueprints for living" is made by Christians who are embarrassed by the Bible and draw a distinction between the God of the Old Testament and the God of the New. Modern Christians, he says, who believe the New Testament replaced the Old Testament, see God as a "God of love not wrath," rather than as a God of both love and wrath. Yet the very heart of Christianity—which claims that God sent his son, who is also God, to be crucified for human sin—becomes incomprehensible without the recognition of God's wrath.

We must never doubt that whatever God did in the Old Testament era, the Second Person of the Trinity also did. God's counsel and judgments are not divided. We must be careful not to regard Jesus Christ as a sort of "unindicted co-conspirator" when we read the Old Testament . . . If we as Christians can accept what is a very hard principle of the Bible, that Christ was a blood sacrifice for our individual sins, then we shouldn't flinch at accepting any of the rest of God's principles. As we joyfully accepted His salvation, so we must joyfully embrace all of His principles that affect any and every area of our lives.[1]

Once Christians come to see the New Testament as a commentary on the Old, rather than a replacement for it, North argues, they will have a fuller, more accurate picture of God, of the Bible, and of demands of God's law. Obedience to biblical law is the prerequisite for Christian Reconstruction and the exercise of godly dominion. In Reconstruction, such obedience is liberating; it brings freedom from enslavement to sin. North's essay outlines the Reconstructionist vision of dominion in terms of the spheres of God-ordained authority as laid out in Rushdoony's work.

Dominion Christianity teaches that there are four covenants under God, meaning four kinds of *vows* under God: personal (individual), and the three institutional covenants: ecclesiastical (the church), civil (governments), and family. All other human institutions (business, educational, charitable, etc.) are to one degree or other under the jurisdiction of these four covenants. No single covenant is absolute; therefore, no single institution is all-powerful. Thus, Christian liberty is *liberty under God and God's law*.[2]

The volumes also share a format in which each begins with an epigraph from Rushdoony, the introduction by North, and then an introduction by the volume's author. Part I of each volume lays out the Reconstructionists' vision of the relevant biblical perspective on the issue at hand. Part II of each volume addresses how to bring about reform and is usually divided into three chapters that outline a strategy for reconstruction in terms of the delineated spheres of authority: what the family can do, what the church can do, and what the civil government can do. Several of the volumes engage the question of the degree to which Christian Reconstruction is correctly understood as "political," as well as the question of whether Reconstructionists want to "impose" biblical law. Just as important is the often-ignored Christian Reconstructionist emphasis on economics.

Gary North's Biblical Economics

North wrote four of the volumes, three of which are centrally about what he calls biblical economics: *Liberating Planet Earth: An Introduction to Biblical Blueprints; Honest Money: Biblical Principles of Money and Banking;* and *Inherit the Earth: Biblical Principles for Economics.* The fourth deals with international relations: *Healer of Nations: Biblical Principles for International Relations.*[3]

North anticipated the economic downturns of the 1980s and 2000s, though he predicted not just recessions but catastrophic collapses. Of course, North has spent his life predicting one economic collapse after another, so the fact that he anticipated these is not necessarily evidence of his insight or acuity. For North, economic collapse is not merely an economic prediction but a theological necessity. It is in the context of this collapse that biblical Christians will come to exercise dominion. North's interest in history and economics, as well as his ties to the earlier anti-communist movement, are ever-present in his framing of these issues. The first volume in the *Blueprint Series* was initially written as a response to Latin American Marxist liberation theology. He frames Christian Reconstruction as the only true "liberation theology." In his view other theologies that promise liberation are ultimately philosophically inconsistent and fraudulent.[4]

Published two years before the fall of the Berlin wall in 1989, the focus on communism and socialism may seem rather dated. Yet in the context of the rise of the Tea Party and its accusations that President Obama is a socialist, it has renewed currency. Without a doubt, Reconstructionists have been advocates for, and activists within, the Tea Party. North is a long-time supporter of—and former staffer for—Ron Paul and is now helping Paul launch a homeschool curriculum. North writes a free daily "newsletter" he calls *The Tea Party Economist*, in which he refers to himself as "Ron Paul's original staff economist" and maintains a Facebook page by the same name. Both focus on economics and gun rights and while the newsletter is identified with North's name, the Facebook page gives no indication of its source. Both fit the religiously sanitized, tax-focused mold of much of the Tea Party material. North has written "open letters" to Sarah Palin as well as laudatory assessments of the strength of the Tea Party.[5]

Scholars of the religious right and new religious movements generally, and liberal and progressive political activists and commentators, have puzzled at the Tea Party accusations that President Obama is a socialist and dismissed the use of the term as empty inflammatory rhetoric. As with so many points of conflict between these two worlds, much depends on definitions. When scholars, or liberal activists and commentators, hear the label "socialist," they understand it to mean a political and economic system where the government centralizes ownership and control in the hands of the state, eliminating private property. When the Reconstructionists use the term, they mean a system in which salvation (in its earthly historical manifestation) is thought to be found in government and in politics; a system that by its very nature seeks to replace God. In this view the legitimate role of government in the economy is limited to ensuring that people deal honestly with one another. Tea Partiers and Reconstructionists see socialism in the "government takeover" of major functions of other institutions. But it is also much broader than this, as socialism is understood as a systematic world and life view (tied very closely to evolution). This view of the relationship between biblical Christianity and Marxist socialism is outlined by North in *Liberating Planet Earth*.[6]

> This is a book about liberation theology. In fact, it's a book about two radically different types of theology, each of which claims to be preaching liberation. One of these systems is Marxist, and the other is Christian . . . Marx . . . argued for humanism, the idea that mankind is the highest form of being—in other words, that man is god . . . There can be no compromise here. It is either faith in God or faith in man. It is either Christianity or Marxism. There is no honest and accurate way to put Marxism together with Christianity. These two deeply religious systems are at war with each other. Marx understood this completely.[7]

In this conceptualization, "socialism" is when the civil government usurps authority "legitimately granted" to the individual, the family, and the church. It is in this sense that these critics call liberal and progressive views on economics and social policy (especially health care and public education) socialist. North proposes the "true liberation" of the family and the church from the "false dominion" of the state.

Honest Money is a relatively straightforward primer in economics from the perspective of the Austrian School to which North subscribes, but which he understands as "biblical economics." The result is a broad-based critique of contemporary banking from the Federal Reserve to fractional reserve banking, all of which were relatively obscure for decades until former congressman and presidential candidate Ron Paul, and now his son, Kentucky senator and presidential candidate Rand Paul, gained a wider audience. North's book was written during the lead-up to the international debt crisis of the 1980s, but the arguments put forth are identical to those he continues to espouse in the context of what he believes to be a contemporary domestic debt crisis and the economic collapse that it will precipitate. While he doesn't use the labels "too big to fail" and "toxic debt," North explains that the banks were sitting on massive bad debt in the 1980s, owed by "third world countries that would never be paid back" and for which the American taxpayers were ultimately going to be made liable. He anticipated a collapse and argued that biblically based Christians needed to be ready with answers as to why it happened and what should be done. Those answers, he believes, are to be found in the Bible.

North considers most forms of debt to be unbiblical, with just two exceptions: charitable loans (for which interest may not be charged) and business loans (which effectively form business partnerships between people contributing capital and people contributing ideas and/or labor). Indebtedness is a form of slavery and even those loans that are permitted are to be tightly regulated. So North refers to biblical limitations on collateral for a charitable loan. Collateral can be required but the lender's possession of the collateral is limited. The poor person who gives his cloak as collateral must be able to retrieve it at night to keep warm. According to North the necessity of returning it during the day gives the borrower incentive to repay the debt and prohibits him from using it to fraudulently secure another loan, creating what North calls "multiple indebtedness." Inasmuch as the Bible requires a system of just weights and measures, and according to North manipulation of those weights and measures is theft, business loans require that both borrower and lender live up to their agreement. A borrower cannot repay a loan with devalued currency (say "silver" coins that have been altered to contain less actual silver). Beyond this, however, borrowers and lenders, as well as buyers and sellers and employers and employees, should be free to negotiate whatever terms they can agree upon. By analogy with the prohibition on multiple indebtedness, North argues that fractional reserve banking, the common practice in which a bank must keep only a portion of deposits on hand, loaning out the rest, is "legalized counterfeiting."

> If I loan you $100, I can't use that $100 while you're using it . . . Not so in a fractional reserve banking system. I have the right at any time to spend the money I deposited, even though 90% of it (or more) was loaned out already. Where does the banker get the money to honor my check? From some depositor who deposited his paycheck today. . . . Fractional reserve banking violates the Biblical principle against multiple indebtedness. When bankers violate this law (with the consent of the State), it leads to inflation and economic booms, followed by deflation and economic depressions.[8]

Furthermore, in buying and selling bonds and manipulating interest rates and reserve rates the Federal Reserve, according to North, fraudulently manipulates the value of money (weights and measures), effectively stealing from those who have it and giving it to those who owe it. More importantly, these practices, combined with a paper money system and a government monopoly on money, centralized power in the hands of an unaccountable and unrestrained institution.

In *Honest Money* he described the inevitable economic collapse:

> First, the bankers and the politicians will continue to try to make the present system work. This will make the present system worse. Second, there will be a collapse in stages: inflation, then mass inflation, then price controls, then tyranny, and finally a worldwide deflationary depression. At that point, there will be new demand from the voters for answers. Third—and this is my hope and my prayer— people will at last decide that they have had enough moral and legal compromise. They will at last decide to adopt a simple system of honest money, along with competitive free market principles throughout the economy. They will stop stealing from each other.[9]

Economic crises result from the ways in which the Federal Reserve System and fractional reserve banking devalue money by increasing the money supply, either by manipulating interest rates or by allowing banks to loan out money they don't actually have on hand. Both practices create inflation, encouraging debt over savings and making the wealth earned and saved worth less. In North's view both of these practices constitute theft. While gold and silver have historically served as guarantors of the value of paper money, North sees no biblical requirement for a gold or silver standard; the Bible requires only that paper money be secured by a valuable asset and that the value of it not be manipulated.

In *Inherit the Earth,* North returns to the topic of socialism as the effort to put the State in the place of God and to make humans the measure of all things.

> The primary welfare institution is the family. Parents are to protect, educate, and support young children. Older children are to protect their parents when the parents grow too old . . . Socialism is primarily a war against the family . . . State-financed "neutral" education, State-financed charities, State-financed retirement programs, and State-financed medicine. With each new welfare program, the politicians transfer responsibility to the bureaucrats, and with every increase of State responsibility comes an increase of State power. The State is . . . doing it for political and ultimately religious reasons. The central planners want to take over the role of God in people's thinking. The State, not God, will protect them. The State, not God, will educate them, employ them, exercise power over their employers, establish the terms of trade. The State becomes the final court of appeal. The State becomes the new God of world civilization.[10]

North outlines theologically inflected libertarian, free-market views of economics derived from his understanding of dominion as the central task of human beings and his understanding of the family as the central institution though which dominion can occur. For Reconstructionists, dominion is not individual but is, rather, a multigenerational achievement. Therefore, biblical economics depends on the authority of the family to raise children who will exercise godly dominion, with each generation building upon the work of the previous generations. Scarcity is rooted in the Fall, the very first example of theft (Adam and Eve ate of the tree that had not been given to them). Taxation, beyond the tithe and for uses beyond limited, biblically permissible purposes, is a form of theft from individuals, families, and generations, since inheritance is the mechanism for family accountability and for building dominion.

It is often assumed that the exercise of political power is at the heart of Reconstructionists' goals for dominion and this view is discussed at length in the media, by Reconstructionists' critics, and by the Reconstructionists themselves. The degree to which Christian Reconstructionists understand a biblical worldview to be rooted in economics, however, is vastly underexplored. The very sovereignty of God, for Reconstructionists, is expressed in terms of property rights: God "owns" everything and insofar as humans have ownership they do so only by virtue of God's grace and under God's authority and primarily in the context of families and for the purpose of dominion.

In every instance, North articulates the theological, social, and ethical aspects of economic decisions. Inflation is immoral because it is theft. Democratic elections in which a majority of people vote to "confiscate" the wealth of some to pay for the programs desired by others are, likewise, theft. Economic freedom (the right to buy and sell at whatever price one can—as long as one does so honestly) is a necessary corollary of the fact that humans are accountable to God for the use of the wealth that God has allowed them to have.

> Individuals are responsible before God for the administration of whatever assets they have been delegated, and therefore they have to make the initial decision about what should be done with these assets. They take their own knowledge, their own skills, their own abilities and their own perception of what the market requires and they must work to the best of their abilities to meet market demand.[11]

This accountability promotes efficiency and ultimately a division of labor, all of which produce an increase in productivity and the accumulation of wealth. The problem, as North sees it, is that the state has overstepped its legitimate authority and taken over functions that God assigned to the family (and which, in North's view, the family can do much better). It's the centralized planning of the modern "welfare state" that inhibits efficiency, productivity, growth, and ultimately dominion.

According to North, there is very little that the family can do, beyond taking responsibility for itself, to reverse the trend toward increasing consolidation of power within government. Only when the "inevitable" economic collapse arrives will the failure of government become obvious, resulting in decentralization. In the meantime, the steps he suggests for families are, in his view, not political. Families must take back the functions that they have abdicated: they should refuse to take advantage of public schools, welfare, and social security. They should teach their children at home or in Christian schools, they should take care of the poor in their families and in their communities, and they should prepare for retirement and raise their children to care for them in their old age. In short, Christians who seek reconstruction are to build a system of alternative, biblical, institutions. In his scenario, Christians who have "reconstructed" their families in these ways will be independent from the economic structures when they do collapse. The churches, too, have a role to play in the economic reconstruction of society. According to North, they need to retake the social welfare function, overseeing nonfamilial charity.

Finally, North says, Christians have a responsibility to participate in politics and the civil government as citizens with the goal of eliminating programs and policies that are extra-biblical:

> Christians need to begin a long-term strategy of capturing authority at every level of civil government. This will not be successful until they believe that God calls them to freedom from the State. Also, it will not be done until they have already begun to support private charities (beginning with family welfare obligations) with their own hard-earned money. It probably will not happen until the State bankrupts itself and millions of voters in a wave of financial crises that the State's own policies have created. The goal is to *roll back the State*. The goal is to get the State's hand out of our wallets, even if it's doing so "in the name of the People."[12]

We find here a framework widespread among conservatives where "the government" is not seen as the elected representative of its citizens in a social contract for their mutual benefit, but rather an alien intrusive institution at odds with "the people" and always on the verge of becoming tyrannical. The economic model is an ideological/theological system rather than a theoretical model developed from economic data. The basic building block of the economy, as it is understood here, is a simple exchange between two free individuals, calibrated to be of mutual benefit by virtue of supply and demand; the global economy is understood merely in terms of these small-scale simple free-market exchanges writ large. There is no recognition that unrestrained global corporate capitalism fosters something entirely different from a small-scale free market: the centralization of wealth and power in massive corporate institutions with every bit as much potential for tyranny as government. Indeed, "free

markets" are understood as the antidote to tyranny and the most fundamental protection of every kind of freedom. The degree to which North
claims that Christian Reconstruction is not primarily political is especially evident here. He repeats that the problems are primarily moral and
religious and that the most important solutions are also moral and religious. There are, nonetheless, important political implications.

A City on a Hill? Politics in a Reconstructed World

North wrote an additional volume in the series entitled *Healer of Nations:
Biblical Blueprints for International Relations,* in which he argues that the
various nations that made up Christendom during the Middle Ages
should serve as a model for the ways in which plurality and unity can co-
exist today.[13] This volume emphasizes presuppositionalism (the myth of
neutrality) and postmillennialism to argue that all nations exist in the
context of a covenant—either the biblical covenant with God or a covenant
with Satan—and that, inevitably, all nations will ultimately come under
the biblical covenant. North invokes the Puritan dream to build a "city on
a hill," from John Winthrop's sermon aboard the Arbella, *A Model of
Christian Charity,* in which Winthrop outlines the obligations of the covenant the Puritans had made with God.[14] They were to be faithful and
care for one another in exchange for God blessing them to the degree that
other nations would want to become like them.[15] The Reconstructionist
global vision is for an international theocracy.[16] This, in his view, is the
only avenue to international peace. As in each of the volumes in the series,
North argues that the realization of theocracy is only possible when the
overwhelming majority of citizens are biblical Christians. It must come
from "the bottom up," he likes to say.

   Healer of Nations is helpful in understanding the overall Reconstructionist vision, because North lays out explicitly just what a Christian
nation would look like. Here is one of the clearest articulations of this
vision.

1. *A Common View of God* All citizens would acknowledge the sovereignty
   of the Trinitarian God of the Bible . . . His Word, the Bible, would be
   acknowledged as the source of the nation's law-order.
2. *A Common System of Courts* . . . A Christian nation would follow the
   example of Exodus 18 and establish an appeals court system. Men
   would be free to do as they please unless they violated a specific piece

of Bible-based legislation or a specific Biblical injunction that the Bible says must be enforced by the civil government . . .

3. *Common Biblical Law* The Bible as the Word of God would be the final standard of justice . . . The national constitution (written or unwritten) would be officially subordinate to the Bible . . .

4. *Judgment by Citizens* The judges in Exodus 18 were to be men of good character . . . Covenanted citizens alone may serve as judges. All other civil rights (legal immunities) belong to every resident . . .

5. *Continuity* . . . Each succeeding generation would be trained by Biblical law by parents (Deuteronomy 6:6–7) and by the civil government through public instruction in God's law (Deuteronomy 31:10–13).[17]

A country with these characteristics would, in North's view, be a Christian nation. As we have seen, his goal is to transform (or "restore") the United States along these lines. The Bible, he insists, both demands and promises this transformation in all nations. "Statist," "humanist" efforts to bring change to other nations by force are the "methods of the covenant of Satan," the legacy of which is imperialism and colonialism and is doomed to failure.[18] The transformation of "other nations" can occur through the work of missionaries (as an extension of the church) and through the effects of international free trade (as an extension of the exercise of dominion by families), but the civil government has no role. In a move that will surely provide evidence to dismiss him as too fringe to be taken seriously, he advocates replacing the State Department with missionaries and businessmen. Yet despite these ideas, he remains a revered figure among his followers, and his views have gained traction in other sectors of the religious right.

Amidst the insistence that Christian Reconstruction is not primarily political, two volumes of the *Biblical Blueprint Series* deal directly with politics: Gary DeMar's *Ruler of Nations: Biblical Blueprints of Government* and George Grant's *The Changing of the Guard: Biblical Principles for Political Action.*[19] The tripartite description of legitimate authority, drawn from Rushdoony's work, serves as the underlying framework to the entire *Biblical Blueprint Series.* It is DeMar's volume *Ruler of Nations: Biblical Principles for Government,* however, that most explicitly lays out this division. DeMar is president of American Vision. This volume is a popularized version of the notions put forth by Rushdoony and essentially a rehashing of the material DeMar presented in the American Vision editions of his three-volume series *God and Government,* published between

1982 and 1986. He begins by raising the criticism that the term "government" has been conflated with the notion of civil government when civil government is only one of four forms of biblically sanctioned government (self-government and then the three institutions: family, church, and state). But it is the State with which this volume is concerned. DeMar is insistent that the idea that government is a "necessary evil" is unbiblical and that Christians are to submit to civil government and recognize its God-given authority over them. Moreover, in a system such as ours Christians are to serve in government insofar as they are equipped and called.

DeMar argues that our constitutional republic is a clearly biblical system: he says that the checks and balances in our system create a multi-level authority structure that replicates the jurisdictional separation in the biblical structure he is advocating, and is ultimately rooted in the Trinity.[20]

> Only God is ultimate; the one and the many are governed by God's Law in all things. Thus, the one and the many in society are balanced under the one authority of the Triune God . . . Corruption and tyranny are heightened when authority structures, from the individual to civil governments at the local, county, and state levels, break down, and all authority then rests in one institution, usually the State. Reclamation of multiple authorities comes about when the individual assumes his responsibilities under God and thoroughly transforms his family, and working with other like-minded individuals, transforms his school, church, vocation, local community, state, and national civil government.[21]

This system, he argues, protects freedom by limiting the ability of one institution to become tyrannical:

> God establishes multiple government jurisdictions, and therefore multiple hierarchies, in order to reflect His own plural nature, but also to restrain the sinfulness of man. He brought judgment in history against the builders of the Tower of Babel because they proposed to build a one-world messianic State. . . . This representative character of all civil and ecclesiastical offices is basic to every human government. God brings His people freedom. One means to this freedom is a system of potentially competing delegated sovereignties. When men sin, and overstep their limits (the

meaning of sin), they often try to extend their authority over others. Parallel governments help to reduce the extent of such lawless behavior. This is the meaning of federalism, of checks and balances.[22]

But this does not mean that DeMar believes in separation of church and state in the way that that term is employed in contemporary American politics. Like other Reconstructionists, he argues for a jurisdictional separation in which all institutional authority is derived from and subject to God and biblical law.[23] Echoing Rushdoony: there is no neutrality and there is no legitimate authority outside of God.[24]

The Changing of the Guard by George Grant—pastor, author, and founder of the King's Meadow Study Center—is also explicitly about the application of the Bible to politics and government. Grant begins by exploring whether, under what circumstances, and in what manner Christians should be involved in politics. The volume culminates in a discussion of specific actions to be taken by individuals, families, and churches with regard to civil government. In this volume we return directly to the issue of the degree to which Christian Reconstruction is focused on politics, as well as whether they intend to impose a theocracy. Reconstructionists insist, across the board, that the centrality of politics to the modern worldview is essentially humanistic. They emphasize that law is not, properly understood, a means of salvation, justification, or redemption. The notion that salvation can be brought about by law is rejected as heresy. "Christians are politically active *because* of salvation *not* to provoke salvation."[25] Invoking what he calls the "American Legacy," Grant argues that "the founders and early leaders of the American republic had no trouble whatsoever acknowledging the theocracy of heaven and earth. Their political actions were thoroughly rooted in the realization that God rules."[26] Even skeptics and deists such as Jefferson and Franklin are marshaled to support his position:

Thomas Jefferson, primary author of the Declaration of Independence and the third president, was also quite forthright in his acknowledgement of universal theocracy . . . [and] *Benjamin Franklin*, the patriarch of the fledgling American republic, said, "A nation of well informed men who have been taught to know the price of the rights which God has given them, cannot be enslaved."[27]

He acknowledges that many of the founders were not "self-conscious Trinitarian Christians" but insists that each "retained enough of a Christian memory to acknowledge the *rule of Christ*."[28] Theocracy, in Reconstructionists' view, *already exists*—we are already subject to God's rule. There is a distinction between a political order that acknowledges this and an ecclesiocracy in which religious authorities rule the civil government.

Critics of Christian Reconstruction often charge that Reconstructionists reject the democratic process as unbiblical. While Rushdoony took a stronger stand on this question than many of his followers have, it is also important to pay careful attention to their definitions. When Reconstructionist writers claim that democracy is unbiblical, they are using a precise (and technically accurate) meaning of "democracy" rather than the one Americans tend to use in public discourse. While it is certainly true that they see democracy as humanistic (deriving its authority from "the people" and making them the ultimate arbiters), Reconstructionists, and many conservatives, argue that the American constitutional system is more accurately understood as a "republic" (a representative democracy). When they oppose "democracy," they are opposing a system of direct democracy that is relatively rare in our current system. This stance leads them to support the Electoral College, and to believe that we should return to the election of US senators by the state legislatures. Moreover, many of them are Presbyterians of one sort or another whose church governance follows the model of a democratic republic, as opposed to the democratic style of congregationalism.

Grant draws this distinction and roots it in the founders.

> But then neither did they desire to establish a democracy, where the majority controls the state. Democracy too has been denounced and rejected by Bible-believing Christians ever since the medieval era. They did not desire either the tyranny of the cloth or the tyranny of the fifty-one percent. Instead, they sought to imitate the Hebrew *theocratic republic . . .*

He concludes this section with the claim that the form of government established in the Constitution, when read in the context of the invocation of the Creator in the Declaration of Independence, is explicitly drawn from the blueprints in the Bible.

> Consequently, nearly all the distinctive ideas of the American Constitution were derived from the Scriptures: the balance of powers

(Exodus 12:21, 28; Numbers 11:16-17, 24-26), the upper and lower legislatures (Numbers 10:2-4), the covenant of rights (Deuteronomy 28:1-68), the electoral college (Numbers 1:16; 16:2), the popular vote (Exodus 19:7-9), and the chief executive (Numbers 27:1-9).[29]

Despite their protestations to the contrary, to those of us with modern ears this seems profoundly "political." Reconstructionists insist that their views are misconstrued by people who have not read their work, yet as we shall see the situation is more complicated than this. In part, this disjuncture is rooted in the fact that they are using a very narrow definition of "politics." In his Editor's Introduction, North defines politics for us as "the means of establishing and controlling civil government."[30] So when the church, through its system of church courts, rules on a charge of adultery, or refuses to sanction marriages between same-sex couples, or excommunicates someone for having an abortion, none of these actions is understood as political. Leaving aside, for the moment, the definition of the term *theocracy*, Reconstructionists argue that biblical law cannot be imposed from the top down but must be embraced by willing "men" who have been converted to Christianity by the ministry of the Holy Spirit. Because we tend to identify conservative Protestantism with the urgency of the dispensationalists, who are forever anticipating the rapture in the immediate future, we often miss the fact that Reconstructionists, as postmillennialists, are thinking in terms of 200-year plans and multigenerational family dynasties. Their time horizon is hundreds or even thousands of years. Furthermore, Grant insists that the establishment of a political theocracy is not the goal of Reconstruction; that a theocracy is already a spiritual reality. Grant presents it this way: "The goal of Christian political action then is not to *usher in* a theocracy but to *acknowledge* the theocracy that *already exists* (Proverbs 3:6). Christian political action is not supposed to impose a messianic kingdom from the top down."[31]

But inasmuch as this implies placing Christians committed to biblical law in positions of civil authority in order to make "politics openly and publicly under God," it would be, to those of us who do not believe in their God, the imposition of a theocracy from the top down. It is worth noting that even the Reconstructionists, in denying that they would impose biblical law by force, insist that reconstruction can only occur when the vast majority are converted. They never claim that they anticipate unanimity, acknowledging at least some coercion implicitly. And it's in this context that we find some of the most inflammatory material that opponents have cited, such as this passage from Grant:

> Christians have an obligation, a mandate, a commission, a holy responsibility to reclaim the land for Jesus Christ – to have dominion in the civil structures, just as in every other aspect of life and godliness. But it is dominion that we are after. Not just a voice. It is dominion we are after. Not just influence. It is dominion we are after. Not just equal time. It is dominion we are after. World conquest. That's what Christ has commissioned us to accomplish. We must win the world with the power of the Gospel. And we must never settle for anything less.[32]

And some relatively obscure Christian Reconstructionist work has made its way into contemporary politics. Ray Sutton's first volume in this series, *Who Owns the Family: God or the State?*, was at the root of a controversy in the 2009 governor's race in Virginia. Republican Bob McDonnell, who was elected and then later convicted on corruption charges, was criticized for views he outlined in his master's thesis, written under Reconstructionist Herb Titus, Professor of Law at Pat Robertson's CBN University, now Regent University, in 1989 (for more on Titus see chapter 8).[33] While pundits reviewing the thesis did not see McDonnell's Reconstructionist ties; the family views he advocated were drawn from Sutton. Sutton's book, in which he advocates the use of deception to destroy public education, is cited in several places in the thesis.[34] Here we can see one of the sources of Tea Party rage against public employee unions. Furthermore, McDonnell grounded his thesis in Rushdoony's ideas about biblical spheres of authority.[35]

In the beginning of *Who Owns the Family: God or the State?* Sutton exemplifies the alarmist tone that characterized religious right rhetoric on the family in the 1980s and which, in many ways, remains unchanged today: "The family in America is under *siege*, I know it. You know it . . . But when I say the family is under siege, I mean an all-out war is being waged against it! It seems like everything and almost everyone in our society is against the family."[36] The litany of issues is predictable: "women's lib," "homosexuality and lesbianism," welfare, which undermines families and makes them dependent, promiscuity, and high divorce rates, all of which arise as a result of government overreach. But Sutton does not advocate political solutions to these social problems. He invokes this notion of the separation of legitimate authority to argue that efforts to use government to solve the problem are in fact the source of the problem. As an example, he argues that promiscuity "should be restricted by government, but not the *civil* government . . . The civil government doesn't have any independent authority in this regard; it simply supports the decision of legally sovereign parents [whether to force a marriage] (Deuteronomy 22: 28–29)."[37]

The rhetoric about the relationship between the government and the family is more than the inflammatory ranting that it first appears to be; it is rooted in a holistic system.

In keeping with the structure of the books in the series, Sutton argues that there are only two potential sources for authority: God and humans (or Theism and Humanism, as he labels them here). "Theism teaches that *God's Word* is the infallible rule of faith and life, the final authority . . . Humanism on the other hand places final authority in man. Man sits in judgment of God and all things."[38] Humanism, according to Sutton, allows the state to illegitimately claim authority over the family. The Bible, on the other hand, divides authority delegated by God among the family, the church, and the state. The family, in Sutton's argument, is weakened nearly to the point of destruction as the state usurps its legitimate authority. It does so in many ways—allowing abortion, limiting inheritance, and legitimating homosexuality—but the most important is education. This critique runs throughout the book. And, of course, it runs centrally throughout all the Reconstructionist literature. Sutton argues that the state has no authority over education. When the state establishes public schools (which Reconstructionists call government schools) it usurps the authority legitimately given to the family. Public education is inevitably indoctrination into a humanistic worldview. When families give over responsibility for the education of children, they abdicate their responsibilities and authority.

At the heart of Sutton's prescription for reconstruction of the family is the idea that families must retake authority for educating their children by either homeschooling them or putting them in Christian schools, and should only attend churches in which the leadership has also done this. The responsibility of the churches is to press families to remove their children from public schools and to develop biblical mechanisms to "support the family" through church discipline (see chapter 7 for an examination of this process). Finally, Christians can get involved in civil government to limit its intrusion in family authority and to subvert this public education system to facilitate its replacement (i.e., elimination) with more biblical forms of education. He writes:

> If you run for the public school board, do it with one intention only: to create an orderly transition to exclusively private education. If you can't be elected on this platform (as seems likely), then become the candidate who wants to reduce waste. (The Biblical definition of wasteful public schools: "public schools.") Your real agenda: no more pay increases for teachers, no more school building programs, and a reduction next year in property taxes. Forever. Until the last public school superintendent is strangled in the non-negotiable demands of the last National Education Association union president, the humanists' war against the family isn't over! ! !39

For Sutton, reconstruction of families is key to the reconstruction of society as a whole: "America was claimed long ago by the Church of Jesus Christ. Our presidents are sworn in with their hands on an open Bible. They take their *oath of office* with a commitment to the Christian faith."40

It bears repeating that this book served as part of the framework for a thesis written by someone who was later elected governor of Virginia and, until his involvement in a financial scandal, was often in the list of GOP leaders likely to be considered as a vice presidential or even presidential candidate.

Biblical Law and Divorce

Conservative Christians tend to think divorce is unbiblical except in some very limited circumstances, such as adultery and abuse, where guilt and innocence are central. Even in cases such as these, remarriage is not always considered permissible. This is not to say that divorce and remarriage is less common than outside the Christian world, only that the teachings would not seem to permit it as frequently as it occurs.

In Sutton's second volume in the *Biblical Blueprint Series, Second Chance,* he suggests that the covenantal model he advocates greatly increases the permissible instances of both divorce and remarriage of the "innocent party" or repentant "guilty party."

According to Sutton, divorce is permissible in a number of instances in which the marital covenant has been broken. As he points out, the Bible says more about the death penalty than it does about divorce, yet for him the two notions are related as marriage is a metaphor of the covenant between the believer and God. Any crime that called for the death penalty would by definition have included the notion of the ending of a marriage. Moreover, Sutton argues that commission of a capital crime implicitly ends the marriage covenant, potentially allowing the innocent party to obtain a biblical divorce. Sutton's development of this line of reasoning is especially interesting in that it gives insight into the frequently decried but rarely examined place of the death penalty in Christian Reconstruction. It is certainly true that Reconstructionists in general, and Rushdoony in particular, argue that the capital sanction provided for certain offenses in the Old Testament—ranging from adultery and homosexuality to incorrigibility—is applicable today under biblical law.

It is also true, however, that there is debate among the Reconstructionists as to exactly what this means. Sutton and some others argue that those sanctions are not the mandatory sanctions but are limits placed on permissible punishments. That is, only certain crimes can be punished by death and the sanctions for those crimes described in the Bible are maximums, not requirements. Invoking the notion of the covenant, Sutton argues that one can be metaphorically dead as a result of covenant-breaking, making literal execution only one way to apply the "death penalty."

Sutton employs a variety of biblical texts to make his case, but discussion of two of them here will suffice. In the Garden of Eden, Adam and Eve were told that the penalty for eating of the forbidden tree was death. And yet they were not killed. What actually happened, at least in an immediate sense, is that they were sent out from the Garden. In Sutton's view this is evidence that excommunication (covenantal death) is one version of the "death penalty." In the New Testament, Sutton cites the story in which Mary's husband Joseph had the option of invoking the death penalty for what would have seemed, at the time, to be her rather obvious adultery. And yet, the text tells us that, instead of seeking her execution, and because he was "just," he thought to "put her away quietly."[41] And Sutton argues, "if God can create a new covenant between man and Himself, then there can be such a thing as remarriage."[42]

Second Chance lays out a theology in which divorce is legitimate in certain cases—adultery, for example—and the innocent party is free to remarry. By repenting and offering restitution, which Sutton construes as a form of metaphorical death, even the guilty party may remarry under some circumstances. The second part of Sutton's book is a marriage manual for divorced biblical Christians seeking to remarry. Sutton draws on examples from his work as a pastoral counselor (the characters seem loosely based on real stories but also seem somewhat contrived) to write in a way that is common in self-help books, presenting problems confronting people and then working through those problems by reasoning from biblical texts and requirements. An Old Testament statute of limitations becomes an argument for allowing time to pass after a "covenantal death" before remarrying. A New Testament admonition to avoid being "unequally yoked" (pertaining to regulations about agreements between churches) becomes a requirement that one marry only other Christians who understand their Christianity in rather specific ways. Much of Sutton's advice is the same as you would find in any self-help book addressed to divorced people considering remarriage. What is unique is the underlying framework, which builds extensively on the Christian Reconstructionist reading of the Bible, and especially the Old Testament (and the notion of the covenant drawn from it), for the purpose of assessing the legitimacy of divorce and for resolving the issues that arise in second marriages:

> The arguments of this book stand on the idea that marriage is a *covenant*, as expressly stated in the Bible (Malachi 2:14). If it is a covenant, and I believe it is because I believe the Bible, then it will have all of the marks of a Biblical covenant. Not only will it have those marks in its formation, but it will have those marks in its dissolution. Accordingly, divorce and remarriage, as painful as they may be, can at least be understood with this simple, yet profound, covenantal model. As covenant is the key to everything in the Bible and life, so it is the key to divorce and remarriage![43]

Biblical Law, Charity, and Poverty

In *In the Shadow of Plenty*, George Grant explores the implications of Christian Reconstruction for the poor. In a reconstructed society, authority for all social welfare is removed from civil government. For the most part the book is addressed to Christians whom Grant believes have failed to live up to their responsibility to care for the poor through charity. Grant details the ways in which the Bible requires that people make provision for the poor: to take care of widows, orphans, and strangers.

Gleaning, for example, is the practice of going through harvested fields to collect the remainder of the crops. In the Old Testament, God's people were required to leave parts of their fields unharvested to allow for this practice. The story of the Good Samaritan is an important touchstone. Grant emphasizes "dominion through service" and explains how charity functions as evangelism. Not only may the poor be brought to church by the promise of assistance, but more importantly Christians can demonstrate the authenticity of their faith through their self-sacrifice. Grant details how, throughout history, the flourishing of Christianity has been accompanied by efforts to care for the poor. From Augustine to Moody, converts have fed, clothed, and housed the poor, and built orphanages and hospitals. "Charity was, and is, central to the gospel's task. And as a result, souls were saved, nations converted, and cultures restored."[44] In many ways Grant's vision seems much like that of any number of other Christian thinkers. It is useful to remember that Reconstructionists are Calvinists. Three aspects of Calvinism are relevant here. The first is the notion of calling: one's life's work, that which one is created to do. There's a very real sense in which Calvinists understand the purpose of life to be work. Adam and Eve were created and given the task of keeping the garden. All work is to be done to the glory of God; there is a worshipful component to it. Whether one is a successful business person, a minister, an artist, or a ditch digger, striving to be the best at that to which we are called is an act of worship and one of the most important ways in which humans are to be obedient to God's will for their lives. Second is that Calvinism is individualistic and covenantal. Christians are individually accountable to God for their actions. The community is important, but it is essentially a collection of individuals. It is this combination of work as calling and the emphasis on individualism that Max Weber saw as the explanation for the ease with which Protestant countries took to capitalism, over against the struggles of Catholic countries to do the same.[45] Third is the Calvinist notion of the total depravity of all human beings. Human nature is sinful. Original sin is not the same as particular sin, something one might do or fail to do. Original sin is not something we do; it taints who we are, every one of us. When Grant argues that there is a connection between sin and poverty he is invoking this traditional Christian perspective: poverty exists as a part of the human condition and is a result of our innate depravity, apart from individual behavior and actions. Yet as we shall see, Grant also roots the causes of poverty in the sinful individual and makes assistance to the poor dependent upon their submission.

For Grant the only path out of poverty, individually and covenantally, is obedience to biblical law. Grant cites the story of the way God dealt with Adam and Eve as a model for how to address poverty: God called them on their sin and then showed them mercy.

> Adam and Eve impoverished themselves amidst the riches of Eden by sinning against God and transgressing His Law. Suddenly, there in the shadow of plenty, they knew real lack. . . . When God came to them in the cool of the day, they were huddled together in their misery and their shame (Genesis 3:7-8). He looked upon their broken estate and saw their pitiful poverty. So how did He respond to them? First, He pronounced a Word of judgment on them . . . (Genesis 3:14-19). Next, He pronounced a Word of hope for them. He opened the prophetic books and revealed the promise of a Deliverer, a Savior (Genesis 3:15). And finally, He confirmed His Word with deeds . . . He covered them. He showed them mercy. He matched judgment and grace with charity (Genesis 3:21).[46]

Grant sees this as the model for charity. Poverty is directly connected to the human condition of original sin. Grant develops this point, rooting a traditionally conservative view of poverty and welfare in the requirements of biblical law. He sees two types of poor people in the Bible: those who are *"denied* the opportunity to work and those who *refuse* the opportunity to work."[47] As one would expect, he draws a distinction between the two groups in terms of who is deserving of help. Grant is very clear that, according to the Bible, those who will not work should not eat. They should receive a "Word of judgment" calling them to account for their behavior. And if they are repentant, as Adam and Eve are, they should receive hope and help. If they are not they should receive nothing; the poor people in his latter category receive no charity. They should not receive housing benefits or job training programs. In Grant's vision, the Bible requires that they not even be given food—but as we shall see willingness to work is not the first criterion.

While Grant sometime uses the term "the oppressed" to refer to those deserving of charity he does not recognize any systemic sources of poverty, racism, sexism, other forms of discrimination, or shifting economic conditions. He focuses, instead, solely on the ways in which assistance can foster a lack of productivity or how a welfare system controlled by the government is subject to manipulation for political purposes.

More importantly, he does not say much about how to discern who fits in which category, which is, of course, the heart of the matter. Charity, in his view, should be first the function of the family and then the function of the church. So it is these institutions that would decide whether someone was "lazy" or "slothful." Moreover, he gives almost no criteria by which one might make such an evaluation. No criteria, save one:

> Even more than these [hard work and diligence], though, *obedience* is required. *Submission* to the standards of the Kingdom is required. In order to take advantage of the covenant privileges, a man must be *in* the covenant or dependent *on* the covenant. Even when the church reaches out into the streets, and lanes, and hedgerows, drawing in the cast-offs and dregs of the land, responsibility must be enforced.[48]

He points to Rahab the Harlot, who made herself "dependent on the covenant" by lying to protect Israel's spies and was thereby eligible for the blessings and protection of the covenant (he does not note that she also worked): "only those who are either *in* God's covenant or are dependent *on* God's covenant may receive charity . . . [which] extends to . . . all who will submit to God's Word."[49]

Grant's prescription for poverty takes a predictable conservative/libertarian form. Families and churches must do way more than they have to address the needs of the poor; civil government must be made to do nothing. Specifically, government should stop "paying people not to work." Grant construes welfare as racist. It fosters dependency, creating a "separate class of people who are not like all others."[50] Government should eliminate minimum wage laws because they "cause high unemployment among low skilled workers . . . exclud[ing] them from the economy altogether." And in an argument about racism and minimum wage laws, Grant makes the following point, which is that racism is the solution to racism.

> Besides the questions of skill or experience, minimum wage laws also raise, the question of *race*, to the detriment of minorities. If a racist employer is forced by the government to pay the same minimum wage to blacks, whites, and hispanics, his hiring criterion ceases to be economic and becomes instead preferential. Whom will he hire, an unskilled, inexperienced black, or an unskilled,

inexperienced white? By leveling the market interests, racists are *encouraged* to discriminate. Blacks and other minorities suffer.[51]

Grant seems to be arguing that racists who would rather not hire minorities will do so out of their own economic self-interest, if they are permitted to discriminate against them by paying them less than equally qualified whites.

Grant also argues against "occupational licensing" because it professionalizes fields that have been traditionally open to the poor unskilled labor force as a means to "work their way out of poverty."[52] Subsidies to industry weaken American business by lessening its need to compete effectively, ultimately hurting the poor.[53] The harshness for which Reconstructionists are criticized is evident throughout: the causes of poverty are attributed entirely to the poor and only those who submit to the covenant are eligible for help. North's introduction exemplifies this:

> The Bible also has a more earth-bound answer to the question of why people are hungry. This answer doesn't make humanists happy, either, but there is one. The Biblical answer is: "People who don't produce anything of value are going to starve, whether we legislate any tax-financed welfare programs or not" . . . There is a tight relationship between wickedness and poverty. There is also a tight connection between righteousness and having enough to eat. God places the unrighteous under covenanted judgment: *cursing*. Their descendants are cut off. He places the righteous under covenantal judgment, too: *blessing*. They are never found begging, and their descendants inherit the earth.[54]

Conclusion

The *Biblical Blueprint Series* shows the ways in which Reconstructionists understand the Bible to speak to every aspect of life. The books take the technical and dense work of Rushdoony and bring it to bear on aspects of life that, for the most part, Reconstructionists see as outside the realm of politics. The focus is overwhelmingly on the family, with economics seen as in the family's domain. The authors argue both that the family is the central unit of a biblically ordered society, and that private property rights are central to the family and the entire message of the Bible.

The accessible paperback books originally sold for $6.95 each and are now available for free on the Internet. Dominion Press does not make sales or distribution figures available. North's volume *Honest Money* was reprinted in 2005 by the Ludwig von Mises Institute and that version is also available for free online. The series makes complex theological, philosophical ideas (including discussions of economic theory) accessible and relevant to a popular audience, demonstrating how important Gary North has been to the dissemination of these ideas. Moreover, the series offers a powerful glimpse into what Christian Reconstructionists envision when they say they expect every knee to bow to the Lordship of Christ and every aspect of culture to be brought under God's authority.

4

Raising a Godly Generation: Christian Schooling

EVEN AS THEIR critics focus relentlessly on politics, Reconstructionists channel their energies elsewhere. Their most important strategy for taking dominion over every aspect of culture is to produce generations of Christians who have been protected from the influences of humanism and who are thoroughly imbued with a biblical worldview. Far more important than their political work, this is a long-term, multigenerational strategy designed to build a thoroughly Reconstructed society. It remains at the heart of their continuing influence even as the political fortunes of the religious right ebb and flow.

From the beginning of his writing career, Rushdoony laid a philosophical and theological basis for dismantling public education in favor of Christian education. His work as an expert witness helped lay the legal foundation for the right of "parental choice" in education as a matter of religious freedom, and he aided Christians across the country in the establishment of Christian schools and homeschooling. In 1981 Rushdoony published a collection of lectures he had given before various Christian school audiences entitled *The Philosophy of the Christian Curriculum*. Reconstructionists produced much of the early material to help start Christian schools and to help parents homeschool their children. Materials developed by Reconstructionists included why-to and how-to guides for starting a school, as well as ready-made curricula. Reconstructionists were also active in the courts, seeking to carve out legal space for parental autonomy from government in their children's education, which became the legal foundation for both Christian schools and Christian homeschooling.

The use of the courts to further policy goals, and to do so by carving out broad religious exemptions from seemingly secular laws, is a well-worn strategy at this point. One of the first organizations founded by the religious right for this purpose was John Whitehead's Rutherford Institute, founded in 1982. Whitehead rejects the Reconstructionist label, but it's not clear why. He articulates a worldview very much like Rushdoony's and cites him as an influence. There are no clear points of disagreement, and Whitehead doesn't accompany his denials with an explanation of his differences. In any case, the purpose of the Rutherford Institute is to defend Christian homeschoolers and church-run Christian schools against truancy and certification laws. Rushdoony's involvement with the Christian Schools of Ohio included serving as an expert legal witness on their behalf in court cases such as the one detailed in Alan Grover's 1977 *Ohio's Trojan Horse: A Warning to Christian Schools Everywhere*. Grover was executive director of Christian Schools of Ohio, and his book detailed a lengthy court battle over the rights of Christian schools to function autonomously from any and all government regulation as a matter of religious freedom. Rushdoony's books, tapes, lectures, and an unpublished work are cited throughout.[1]

There was a time when public schools were celebrated by Protestants as quintessentially American institutions: the training grounds for godly patriotism. Roman Catholics who perceived the schools as anything but "neutral," and put their children in parochial schools, were viewed with suspicion by many Protestants, who considered their actions unpatriotic. After all, the antecedents to today's public schools were supported by the Puritans. American civil society had a strong religious (Protestant) quality to it, such that Protestants of all denominations were comfortable with public education and religious instruction well into the middle of the twentieth century.[2]

But by the 1960s and 1970s, after Supreme Court decisions removing daily prayer and devotional Bible reading from public school classrooms, the veneer of Protestantism was slowly being replaced by modern secularism and pluralism.[3] As they lost their favored status, some Protestants began to reexamine the foundations of public education. While many were critical of public schools for teaching sex education or evolution or for forcing racial integration, others came to the conclusion that public education is, by definition, unbiblical. This more radical conclusion was articulated and extensively disseminated by Reconstructionists.

Rushdoony develops his critique of public schools from the basic framework we have already explored: presuppositionalism (all knowledge derives from God), theonomy (biblical law is our only legitimate source for authority, and biblical law makes the family responsible for education, precluding any role for the state), and postmillennialism (the purpose of human life is dominion).

For Reconstructionists, public education is unbiblical on two grounds. First, all education is essentially religious in character so secular education is humanistic education. Second, education is the responsibility of parents rather than the state. No amount of reform can fix either of these fundamental flaws. Rushdoony had an undergraduate degree in education from the University of California at Berkeley, and he began publishing critiques of public education as early as 1953. When Rushdoony went to work at the Volker Fund in the early 1960s, the fund supported his writing, which included one of his earliest and most important books, *The Messianic Character of American Education.*[4]

Throughout the 1970s and 1980s, Rushdoony served as an expert witness supporting Christian parents facing legal challenges to their right to make educational choices for their children apart from state regulation. Returning to his basic philosophical commitment to presuppositionalism, Rushdoony argued that biblical schools must be more than public schools with the addition of religious observance. Education itself is inescapably religious and biblical schools will be thoroughly infused with religion in every aspect:

> The function of education is thus to school persons in the ultimate values of a culture. This is an inescapably *religious* task. Education has always been a religious function of society and closely linked to its religion. When the state takes over the responsibility for education from the Church or from Christian parents, the state has not thereby disowned all religions but simply disestablished Christianity in favor of its own statist religion, usually a form of humanism.[5]

As we have seen, for Rushdoony, the conflict between humanist education and biblical education is a conflict over the meaning of freedom. The "liberal arts" curriculum defines freedom as "autonomy," such that the basis of the curriculum presupposes human autonomy and derives from it; Rushdoony traces this influence to Enlightenment philosophy. The commitment to human autonomy elevates the "pupil as judge before he has any learning or wisdom."[6]

[By comparison, Christian education has as its first presupposition]
the sovereignty of God and the authority of his infallible word. Both
sovereignty and infallibility are necessary and inescapable con-
cepts. If they are denied to God, they accrue to man, or to some
aspect of the universe or of history . . . there can be no compromise
between the two positions.[7]

Additionally, the explicit goal of Christian education is dominion.
Rushdoony writes, "The purpose of Christian education is not academic:
it is religious and practical . . . the creation mandate, the call to man to
know, subdue, and use the earth under God."[8] In *The Philosophy of the
Christian Curriculum* Rushdoony shows in detail how a biblical approach
to various aspects of a school curriculum differs, fundamentally, from a
humanistic approach. This, and its significance for Christian schools and
conflicts between conservative Christians and public schools, is nicely illustrated in his chapter "History vs. Social Science."

Rushdoony sees history as distinct from social science and more
closely aligned with theology. In social science, he writes, "history and
society must be studied scientifically, that is, in terms of purely naturalistic considerations, without reference to God or eternal law. This
methodology of necessity requires ultimately a materialistic philosophy of history."[9] For Rushdoony, history, taught from a Christian perspective, is the story of God's sovereign interaction with his people
over time. History taught from a humanist perspective is the history of
human action over time; it is "anti-Christian." This is what is at stake
for the Christians in the fight over Christian American history. This is
the perspective with which Tea Party "historian" David Barton ap-
proaches the study of history at the Christian school founded by his
parents in Aledo, Texas (more on this in chapter 9). Beyond history,
however, language, grammar, thinking, writing, mathematics, and
science all become exemplars of the way in which truth is grounded in
an absolute God. These are not, as they might appear to many, secular
subjects.

The second reason Reconstructionists see public education as irretrievably unbiblical is rooted in their commitment to theonomy and their
view of the structure of legitimate authority. The responsibility to educate
children is solidly placed in the hands of families, and when other institutions (namely the state) take on that responsibility they are violating
sphere sovereignty by usurping the legitimate authority of families.

Two Christian Schools: Then and Now

According to the National Center for Education Statistics, between 1993 and 2003 the number of American children enrolled in K–12 church-related private schools rose from 7.5 percent to 8.4 percent and rose again slightly to 8.7 percent between 2003 and 2007.[10] Because of the early work of Reconstructionists in publishing, helping establish Christian schools, and assisting the legal defense of parents' right to choose private school, Reconstructionists' influence extends beyond the numbers who identify with them.

Fairfax Christian School

Fairfax Christian School (FCS) was founded by husband and wife Bob and Rosemary Thoburn in 1961 and, as of this writing, is operated by their eldest son David and his wife. Several of their other grown children have established and/or run Christian schools.[11] At the time of the school's founding, Bob Thoburn was a minister with the Orthodox Presbyterian Church and an alum of Westminster Theological Seminary, where he had been influenced by J. Gresham Machen, Cornelius Van Til, and Rushdoony. FCS and the Thoburn family have not usually been included in studies of Christian Reconstruction, despite their place in the spread of Christian schooling.

The school began as an effort on the part of the Thoburns to teach their own children—all eight of them were educated there. In the process, the Thoburns developed an important early Christian school curriculum. Before taking ownership of the school, David owned Thoburn Press and Fairfax Christian Bookstore, which published and sold that curriculum, as well as many books by both Rushdoony and Gary North. David lived, for a time, in Tyler, Texas, when Gary North's Institute for Christian Economics and Dominion Press were based there. They both attended the same Reconstructionist church in Tyler.

FCS is an explicitly Reconstructionist school, independent of any church, and deals directly with parents to help them fulfill their biblical responsibility for educating their children. In his 1971 book on how to start a Christian school, Bob Thoburn includes lengthy annotated bibliographies on history and economics for Christian school students in a "special supplement" written by Gary North, whom he described as "the most brilliant young conservative on the scene today in the fields of history and economics."[12] Thoburn also credits Rushdoony for his work in developing a theology of the relationship between the Bible and law.[13] He writes:

> The education of children . . . is the duty of parents and the Christian school is an extension of the home. The training of children is not the function of civil government. Herein lies one of the chief differences between what is called public school and the Christian school. The public school in the United States ought more properly to be called a government school or a state school for it is owned and operated by the government. The government public school is based in the belief that the child belongs to the state and is to serve the state . . . Statist education is secular and humanistic. Man, especially, collective man in the state, becomes its focal point. The school exists as an extension of the state and its purpose is to glorify man and the state.[14]

The Thoburns have been an important influence. They claim to have to helped start over 200 schools across the country.[15] Bob, who passed away in late 2012, wrote three books, two of which pertain directly to Christian schooling: *How to Establish and Operate a Successful Christian School*, and *The Children Trap*, a volume in Gary North's *Biblical Blueprint Series*. Rosemary has developed extensive curricular materials that were disseminated through Fairfax Christian Bookstore. And David reprinted and sold the classic McGuffey Readers, a series of nineteenth-century reading books infused with the Calvinist values of their Presbyterian author. The books are still popular in Christian schools and homeschools across the country.

Like Rushdoony, the Thoburns believe in a biblical division of authority and reject public education (or government schools) as a usurpation of family authority. Though preferable to state-run schools, they believe that church-run schools also usurp the authority of the family. Ideally, Christian schools should be independent of churches and accountable directly to parents. Students need not necessarily be Christian (especially at first), nor do they necessarily come from Christian families.

FCS prides itself of the international character of its student body. This was true of the school from its earliest days, when many students were children of World Bank employees. It is still true, as evidenced by their website, which promotes special courses for international students.[16] The school touts its "classic curriculum," which begins with an emphasis on early (four- and five-year-olds) reading proficiency using phonics, and includes a foreign language requirement, a summer reading program, Latin, the "Great Books," and, of course, math, science, and the Bible.

Though there is a specific Bible class, in keeping with a Reconstructionist perspective, all courses are taught from a "biblical perspective." The school, which has resisted state accreditation as an intrusion of the government into the affairs of the family, has a strong academic reputation. The website also touts the children of well-known figures who have attended, including those of the late congressman Larry MacDonald; the late Howard Phillips, founder of the Conservative Caucus and former presidential candidate (whose son Doug we will hear much more about); Washington Redskins quarterback Joe Theismann; and former congressman Delbert Latta.

While the Thoburns are supportive of homeschooling, they argue that the biblical notion of a division of labor means that efficiency will dictate the rise of cooperative efforts that are, in effect, private Christian schools. Bob observes that as soon as two homeschooling parents share expenses to hire a specialist to tutor their children together in a specific subject, say art or music, they have, in fact, started a school. Still, the school in his view should not become a "total institution" but be seen as an extension of the family.

Bob claimed that if a parent wanted to take a student out of class for what the parent considered a valid reason, the school would not intervene. Things have changed significantly since then. There is now a student handbook, a rather strict dress code, and an attendance policy that parents are not free to violate. In a marked change from the old days when FCS understood itself as operating purely under the authority of parents, today the handbook says directly that parents should plan college campus visits so as to not conflict with school days.

Rocky Bayou Christian School

Rocky Bayou Christian School (RBCS) in Niceville, Florida, was founded in the 1970s after a crucial visit by the would-be founders to FCS. I happened upon their website in 2009 when their original superintendent, Bob Grete, retired and in celebration of his efforts at founding the school they had posted a story about its history that included the ties between Rocky Bayou and Fairfax Christian. I quickly e-mailed the new superintendent, Donald Lawson, to ask if I could visit the campus.[17] Lawson was very welcoming and agreed to meet with me for an interview and offered to put me in touch with the founders Bob Grete and Pastor Harold Thomas (who together had visited FCS all those years ago). The story of the founding of this school illustrates well the process by which Rushdoony's work spread, in this case through the work of the Thoburn family.

When I arrived on campus Grete took me to the library to show off some memorabilia from the school's founding era. As soon as we got inside, he walked directly to a wall of notebooks with old documents, pulled out the 1980 yearbook, opened it, and proudly told me "Dr. Rushdoony was our first commencement speaker." He had saved the announcements, the program, and some newspaper clippings from the event. He then walked to the other side of the room and pulled out a spiral-bound, self-published book that I immediately recognized as Robert Thoburn's *How to Establish and Operate a Successful Christian School.*[18] I knew of the book, but it was the only one of Thoburn's books I didn't own. When I marveled how, from my perspective, I had fortuitously fallen upon this perfect example for my work, he playfully yet seriously corrected me: "Providentially! We don't believe in luck."

Pastor Thomas had been convinced of the importance of Christian schooling since his earliest days in the ministry. Grete had not. But Thomas's larger theological system had evolved substantially over the course of his life, in large measure as a result of his exposure to the work of Rushdoony and the Reconstructionists and his involvement in the Christian school movement. Thomas was a seminary student at Dallas Theological Seminary, a school most renowned for teaching dispensationalism, a theological system that is seen as a direct competitor to the Calvinist postmillennialism of Christian Reconstruction. He had encountered the work of theologian J. Gresham Machen, which, he said, brought him into contact with Reconstructionist people. After seminary he had an opportunity to come to Niceville to establish a church, and he agreed under the condition that he also be allowed to start a Christian school. And while he was influenced by Reformed theology, he was still a dispensationalist and was "struggling theologically." Over time, as he worked to establish the school and then to run it, he found himself moving away from the dispensationalist camp and embracing the larger theological system he encountered in Rushdoony and Thoburn.

Thomas had met Bob Grete, an Air Force major, and had decided that Grete was the person he wanted to help him with the school. Grete was reluctant. Though he was a Christian, he was not a fan of Christian schools.

But Thomas convinced him to make the trip to FCS, where, Grete says, "Bob Thoburn changed my life." When they arrived on the FCS campus, Thoburn had them sit in on a chapel service in which Grete, in particular, was impressed by the behavior of the students. During a tour of the campus Grete came to think that the students were not just well-behaved but also extraordinarily engaged: "In every class I saw kids who seemed like they were interested in building a foundation." He compared those students to his own children and admitted "my kids just endured school." Grete felt "[my] kids have been cheated out of a basic skills education."

But more than the sound academic environment, it was what happened next that Grete said changed his life. It also sheds light not only on the underlying worldview in which the schools are based but also on the significance of opposition to evolution (see chapter 6) and the broader influence of Rushdoony and the Reconstructionist movement.[19] Thoburn asked him about creationism: "Is it a sin to lie to your children?" and "Is it a sin to hire someone to lie to them for you?" Grete had recently come "to the conclusion that Darwinism is simply antithetical to the Christian faith," and he saw this moment as providential. But what pushed him, he said, was the realization that the teachers teaching his children were doing so as his representatives. He was responsible to God for what they were teaching his children, and in public schools they were teaching evolution.

He explained this to me, all these years later, in terms of presuppositionalism. All worldviews depend upon presuppositions that are accepted on faith, the most basic of which is the question of whether God exists. In his view, Darwin's theory, like creationism, is essentially a religious explanation of observable fact. "Creationists have a different worldview to interpret the same facts," he said.

On the flight home the next day, Grete decided he could no longer put his children in public schools. He and his wife looked at the Christian schools available in the area and decided that none of them had the holistic biblical philosophy they wanted, so he finally agreed with Pastor Thomas that the two of them should start a new school. He continued explaining this to me in terms of what he understands as the providence of God. He pointed to his experience in the field of education which he understood, in hindsight, as God's providence acting in his life, setting him in places to acquire the skills and background for the task to which God would later call him. "I mean, it's just too much of the hand of God. You've gotta see it," he said emphatically.

But Grete wasn't the only one who needed convincing. The leaders in Thomas's church had just begun a building project and, according to Thomas, the church elders were afraid that he would be "spread too thin." In the end they voted against the school, pressing Grete and Thomas to move in a different direction. With the view that church leaders' authority comes directly from God, they would not start a school without the permission of their elders. But Grete asked if the elders would also object to a school that was independent of the church. The church elders agreed, so the school was established as a nondenominational independent school in rented space, just like FCS. RBCS was founded in September 1974, just over a year after their visit to FCS. Grete and Thomas relied heavily on Thoburn's book, which Grete told me cost $200 when he bought it in 1973.

They both insisted that what they wanted from the beginning was not a secular school "sprinkled with holy water." "It starts at a presuppositional level. I was more and more convinced that every area of life should be under the control of scripture. I wanted a Christian philosophy," said Thomas. Grete elaborated, "We didn't want to be throwing Christian darts into a secular curriculum but to start with the Bible and go from there."

Many Christian schools were founded in the wake of *Brown v. Board of Education*, and many people believe that support for segregation was a motivating factor. I asked Grete about this. He answered: "I'm sure some of them were not started for the right reason, but many others were started for philosophical reasons." I had noted that there was some racial diversity on the campus of RBCS, and I asked him how long it had been that way. He could not remember when the first black students were admitted or teachers were hired, but he was adamant that racial discrimination was wrong and was not the motivation for starting the school.

In 1973, with programs for three-year-olds through sixth grade, RBCS had twenty-two students, nine of whom were either Grete's or Thomas's. According to Thomas, they have had as many as 850 students at one time; when I visited there were about seven hundred in K–12. Over the years the school has developed an interesting structure and has thrived, in part, because of the way it has engaged certain challenges and opportunities. They have an advanced program, which is for students who have been in attendance for some time, and a regular program for students newer to the school. This is a model developed by FCS to address the fact that their students perform, academically, above students coming from other schools. Kindergarten students typically finish the year reading at a second-grade level, so a student coming into the school in first grade would be at a serious disadvantage. They also offer advanced-placement courses in their high school to keep students engaged and give them a leg up when they go to college.

Three other tracks at RBCS are, perhaps, most interesting. Rather than seeing themselves as being in competition with homeschooling, RBCS offers a program in which homeschoolers can participate in the school's services, courses, and activities, allowing homeschooling parents to customize their children's schooling. During my 2009 visit Lawson explained that there were at that time over one hundred students in this program. Part of what led Lawson to believe he was called to his role at RBCS—and he does see it as a calling and the path leading him there as directed by God—is his prior involvement in homeschooling. He worked to smooth over what he saw as competition between the school and the homeschoolers and to expand the interaction between the two.[20]

In addition to the options provided for homeschoolers, RBCS offers a "special services program" designed to meet the needs of students who learn best in a less-traditional classroom environment. Track Three, part of the special services program, is for students in grades seven to twelve with "average to superior IQ levels." Extensive testing helps the school develop a specialized program that allows these students to learn the same material as students in the regular and advanced programs, according to their own learning styles. Track Three Plus is a remedial program for students who are two or more years behind grade level. Finally, the special services program has a class for students who suffer from various learning disabilities called the Victors Class, focusing on "Biblical principles through life skills that are necessary for independent living."[21] RBCS also has a program designed to take advantage of Florida's school voucher plan. The plan, put into place by former governor Jeb Bush, permits students at "failing public schools" to obtain vouchers that can be used at any school. This has become such a significant revenue stream for the school that Pastor Thomas, who still works at the school in its IT lab, said that it would have a major impact on the school if the state were to decide to discontinue the controversial program, though at the time there was talk about greatly expanding it. Early in his term, Florida's Tea Party–supported governor Rick Scott had proposed a massive increase in the voucher plan, giving the parents of every school-age child a voucher, reportedly worth $5,500 to over $6,500 per student, toward tuition at any public, charter, private, or virtual school. Scott's initial attacks on public education in Florida took a toll on his popularity, forcing him to backtrack, but the conservative legislature took up the effort to expand the state's privatization of public education with vouchers and the expansion of charter schools. Florida's efforts mirror attempts across the nation to shift the delivery of public education to the private sector; a shift of tax money from a public endeavor intended to educate and foster a shared sense of what it means to be American to sectarian efforts, including efforts at schools like Rocky Bayou which seek to transform society according to biblical law. The longstanding goal of the Christian Reconstructionists to defund, and ultimately eliminate, public education has come as close as it has ever come to being a reality.

Lawson replaced Grete in April 2005 after a yearlong interview process. Insistent that education is "a parental responsibility," he is clearly Reconstructionist in his orientation. At the time he first expressed interest in the position, he and his wife were homeschoolers, and they attended Trinity Church (Christian Reformed Evangelical Church), which he says was "greatly influenced by Rushdoony."[22] The church has ties to the school and has many Reconstructionist members, including Archie and Marie Jones and Reconstructionist theologian James Jordan, who had been associate pastor of the Reconstructionist Westminster Presbyterian Church in Tyler, Texas. The pastor of Trinity had been pastor to Reconstructionist Greg Bahnsen in Jackson, Mississippi.[23] Lawson said:

> I was Air Force, and I had determined about five years prior to retirement that I was going to go into ministry in Christian education . . .Well . . . just about two years before retirement, Grete approached me and said, "I'm going to retire, we're looking for someone to take my place, I actually laughed at him . . . and then a few weeks later said, "Are you serious?" I'd always had a passion for Christian education. I used to cut out ads from *World* magazine . . . for Christian schools. Because my goal when I got out of the Air Force was to work in Christian schools."[24]

Schools like RBCS draw in Christians initially interested (or sometimes not yet interested) in Christian schooling and then, over time, foster in them an ethos that includes many aspects of the Christian Reconstructionists' biblical worldview. For example, when I arrived for my meeting with Lawson, he was briefly detained, so I spent some time talking with Beverly Foster, Lawson's administrative assistant. Foster had come to work at RBCS seven years earlier, and she spoke at length about the sense of calling people have for the school. She had not wanted to work at RBCS. She and her husband (who also works at the school) had worked in the moving industry and lost their jobs. She learned of an opening and applied because she needed a job, not because she had some vision about changing the world through Christian education. Foster had not sent her children to Christian schools (she said it didn't occur to her), but now she expressed shame over that fact. The transformation of her attitude about the importance of Christian schooling is illustrative of the way in which these institutions exert a subtle influence over time. Now Foster sees her displacement from the moving industry, the seemingly fortuitous way in which she learned of the job opening, and her being hired by the school as all part of God's providential plan. "It's amazing," she said, "to watch God calling on people who work and go to school here."

Government Intervention as Tyranny

Christian schools have resisted government accreditation in states where they are permitted to operate without it and worked to have the regulations changed in states where they aren't. They often prefer to hire uncredentialed teachers, as teacher-credentialing programs are seen as irretrievably humanistic. This has caused legal confrontations in several states, including California, Ohio, Nebraska, Kentucky, and North Carolina. The case in Nebraska was particularly noteworthy because it is an example in which the fundamentalists "won" and is cited by them as a reminder of the underlying conflict between their schools and the state, foreshadowing what is now a relatively widespread view, in this world, that any government involvement in education is tyranny. As the Nebraska legislature entertained discussion about school regulation in 2008, the twenty-five-year-old Sileven case still served as the backdrop to the debate.[25]

On Friday, September 3, 1982, a sheriff in Louisville, Nebraska, entered the sanctuary of Faith Baptist Church to arrest its pastor, Everett Sileven, as he preached to gathered schoolchildren. Just over one month later, the sheriff returned to physically remove a praying congregation and put a padlock on the church door. These events did not surprise the members of the congregation, as they had been involved in a three-year legal battle that began when the state of Nebraska passed legislation requiring private religious schools to hire state-credentialed teachers. Pastor Sileven and Faith Baptist refused, and in fact, the church had been padlocked once

before.[26] The church argued that the separation of church and state prohibited the government from regulating ministries of a church, including
its Christian day school. They also refused to comply on the grounds that
the church was God's property.[27]

Fundamentalists and evangelicals across the country followed the
case. *Christianity Today* carried images of the padlocked church and
Christians being carried away by authorities as they prayed.[28] Some three
hundred people, many of them pastors, had come to support Faith Baptist.[29] The pastors in the group vowed that, one by one, they would assume
leadership of the church and school. As soon as one pastor was arrested,
another would take his place.

A year later Pastor Sileven published a letter to the Nebraska legislature in the form of a small book entitled *Dear Legislator: A Plea for Liberty
in Christian Education*.[30] Sileven cited no sources for the perspective he
presented, and he did not identify himself as a Reconstructionist. Yet the
framing and the language of his argument closely follow Rushdoony. The
book begins: "By education, we mean the sum total of those processes
whereby a person is trained and formed in mind and character from a
philosophical base of truth . . . Therefore, all education is religious and
philosophical in nature."[31] In a later chapter he continues:

> Religion and education are inseparable. You control education and
> you control religion . . . Humanism has become the religion of the
> state and the state schools in the United States . . . A Christian
> cannot divide his life into religious and secular. The concept of Re-
> ligious vs Secular is a humanistic concept. God is the Creator of all
> Truth. All of life must tie to Truth. Math, Language, Science and
> History are all religious subjects with religious meaning. Knowl-
> edge is not a bunch of abstract facts, but an orderly arrangement of
> Truth from God with meaning.[32]

As if in anticipation of Gary North's *Biblical Blueprint Series* volume *Who
Owns the Family,* Sileven argues for a biblical family model in terms of the
"ownership" of children.[33] In the disagreement among Reconstructionists
over whether the church or the family is the primary social institution
ordained by God, Sileven aligns himself with Rushdoony: "the family is
God's first and central institution, even over the church."[34] He embraces
the view of biblical law for which Reconstructionists are most often criticized: "children who refused to be subject to their parents for training

were executed."[35] And with regard to why public education is, at its very essence, unbiblical, Sileven writes:

> It is a matter of the basic philosophical view of life. It is not a matter of co-existence. It is a matter of control . . . All of the goals of the humanist are a rejection of God and His authority. Man is god, man made government is final . . . [the] goals of the humanist are diametrically opposed to God and His order of things. Since, by law, the only legal philosophy of the government schools is secular or atheistic humanism, and since, by God's Law, Christians are mandated to train their children in a theistic philosophy, it is not possible for a true Christian to put their child in the government schools.[36]

That the Reconstructionists saw this case as exemplifying their viewpoint is evidenced by an essay Gary North later wrote. In "Why Churches Should Not Incorporate," North uses the Sileven case to explore the jurisdictional distinction between church and state and what he sees as the inevitable move on the part of the state to expand its power.[37]

The Sileven case was finally settled in 1984 when the legislature included an exemption for religious schools that provided "alternative evidence" that their schools were educating students properly. Legal scholar Neal Devins argued that this case was a turning point because the ability of Christian school supporters to mobilize as they did was a serious deterrent to other states considering regulations. The church's supporters forced the state of Nebraska into "a game of chicken," in which the state went to the graphic extreme of arresting a pastor and padlocking a church.[38] The fact that other states did not want to pay that price to regulate private Christian schools has allowed those schools (and homeschooling parents as well) to retain a significant degree of autonomy.

In addition to the degree to which this case established a legal and political turning point, it is also instructive in terms of understanding the essential incompatibility between the secular civil order and Reconstructionism. Why was the issue of submitting to state regulation so important to the supporters of Faith Baptist? The academic record of these schools is generally sound. In fact there was never a suggestion that the education being provided at Faith Baptist was inadequate. In all likelihood submitting to regulation would not have changed the school in any substantive way. So why did this controversy in Nebraska draw the attention of conservative Christians across the country, such that some of them, law-abiding middle-aged Christians, decided to risk arrest to stand in support of Faith Baptist? Finally, why did the sheriff relentlessly pursue arrest warrants and injunctions that escalated the battle to the point where it made sense to him to padlock a small Baptist church? This conflict was a flash point between two rival, irreconcilable, claims for authority; two versions of the proper ordering of the social world.

University of Chicago scholar of religion Bruce Lincoln provides a framework for interpreting the engagement of these rival claims by showing how myth, ritual, and classification—what he calls discourse—construct a social order. Rejecting the idea that society is constructed by consensus, he shows how competing hegemonies—that is, all-inclusive framing systems that order reality—vie for dominance. While initial dominance can be gained by force, Lincoln argues that force can serve only as a stop-gap measure, that it is discourse that ultimately establishes a reliably stable order. Both sides in this conflict invoke myth and ritual. While exercising force, civil authorities made use of what Lincoln calls spectacle and costume when they entered the sanctuary to place the pastor under arrest and again to remove the congregants who were praying. The state as sovereign, represented by the sheriff and his deputies, in uniform and in marked cars, asserted its authority by seizing the sacred space of the small group unwilling to submit its claim to sovereignty. They "desecrated" the church's sacred space by asserting the state as the ultimate authority.[39] Perhaps because force was unavailable to them, the supporters of Faith Baptist made even greater use of symbolic discourse. Rather than turning himself in to authorities, Pastor Sileven invoked the power of spectacle by strategically drawing them into his sacred space and forcing them to execute their warrant in a way that would produce the most symbolic capital for his side. In a society in which the overwhelming majority of people see themselves as patriotic, pro-family, Bible-believing Christians, he claimed the shared symbols and asserted the authority, as the representatives of a sovereign God, to invoke them:

Law enforcement will have to trample on the ministry of Christ, the flag, and the Bible and on the parents and members of this church, then enter the sovereign embassy of Jesus Christ to arrest me. If they choose to do all that, I will go without resistance.[40]

The same was true a month later when the sheriff returned to padlock the church. Supporters knew he was coming and had stationed themselves inside with plans to fall to the floor in prayer when they received word that he was on his way. This created a situation where authorities were required to carry people out of the sanctuary as they knelt in prayer, while others sang hymns and patriotic songs, and waved flags and Bibles at authorities. All this took place in front of cameras.

First and foremost it is clear that Pastor Sileven and his supporters considered Faith Baptist facilities sacred space. The sacredness of space and the control of it as territory cannot be understood apart from each other. The conflict here is over the space in question and who will be successful at appropriating the myths and symbols of America in order to control the contested territory. There is an important theme in Protestantism, in which all of creation is seen as sacred—all ground is holy ground, the "temple of the Lord" is in the hearts of believers. Nonetheless, the demarcation of some space as more sacred than other space persists. Church supporters balked at a proposed compromise in which they would move their school to another county.

At a second level this battle is about America as a symbol—the "new Jerusalem." At this level all of America is sacred space. The idea of America as a space chosen by God for the culmination of history can be traced back to the Puritans and is very much part of the worldview of these Christians. This was to be "the city on a hill, for all the eyes of the world to see." Through tears, church supporters sang, "God *save* America, land that I love" as they were being removed from the sanctuary. The sacred space of the church is seen as a bulwark protecting the larger space of America from the floodgates of Godless tyranny. When two competing groups share a symbol, their conflict often centers on attempts to rightfully claim that symbol. An exchange between a supporter of the church, Greg Dixon, and the sheriff who was seeking to remove Dixon from the church, illustrates the point. Ed Rowe, one of the pastors who came to Nebraska to assume leadership of the church until he was arrested, wrote of Dixon:

> With his Bible open, he aims a witness at the bullyish looking sheriff, warning of the judgment of God upon all who do not repent. "Oh now, don't try to scare me with that stuff," interrupts the sheriff . . . "I am a religious man myself. My grandchild goes to a parochial school. And it's a *certified* one, too." (Emphasis in the original)[41]

There is a ritual quality to this moment of conflict. It wasn't the physical presence of the lock that was powerful, it was the ritual in which the sheriff established symbolic authority over the church building. The actions of the pastors and supporters could be called rituals of defiance. On more than one occasion, before a crowd of people and numerous cameras, the padlock was cut in defiance. The sermon that Pastor Sileven was preaching when he was arrested is another example. There was no scheduled sermon or prayer meeting that night; both events were organized for the express purpose of dramatizing the significance of the sheriff's actions. The "men of God" were "standing firm" to "occupy" their sacred space.

But the conflict over symbols was not limited to these moments of engagement. Each side struggled to control the framing of the conflict in terms of the mythic dimensions of American patriotism as well. Myths and rituals create shared social identity. As a Jewish family gathers around the dining-room table at Passover to retell the exodus story, they each renew their identity as members of the community. They also demarcate the line between those who are in the group and those who are not (and even those who are enemies). When two competing groups share myths and rituals, the group that wins the right to interpret them and assign symbolic roles within them earns the power to say what the conflict itself means. In the case of the conflict between Faith Baptist and the Nebraska authorities, the sheriff and his deputies, as the representatives of American civil government, understood their work as the work of patriots preserving the civil order and the common good. Their reading of the shared myths did not go unchallenged, however.

Faith Baptist employed mythic narratives of its own. Ed Rowe writes, "Nebraska sought by force of the police state to accomplish what the lions of the Coliseum, the cross of execution, the sword . . . were powerless to accomplish long centuries ago."[42] The most frequent reference is to the fascist political efforts of Hitler and the Christians who challenged him. "State tyranny has reenacted the horrors of Nazi Germany . . . when uniformed men seized godly pastors in their churches, hauled them off, and locked them up," writes Rowe.[43] Sileven reread *The Rise and Fall of the Third Reich* in jail and argued, in a manner that seems hyperbolic but which presages future battles between conservative Christians and a government they have deemed "tyrannical," that there was "not much difference" between the education programs of Nebraska and of Hitler.[44]

Faith Baptist Church contested the right of the state to organize their sacred space by defiantly operating a Christian school without a state license and then "occupying" their sanctuary when ordered to evacuate it. It was a battle for power. In the effort to take control of the church building, the state sought to demonstrate the powerlessness of the church supporters. In this particular instance, the church supporters turned the tables. By using ritual to assert their authority over sacred space, they forced the state to back down, making it seem the state lacked power.

Pastor Sileven went on to serve a Baptist church in Texas County, Missouri. His website does not mention Reconstruction by name, but emphasizes "Biblical law found in both the Old and New Testaments" as well as all five points of Calvinism, and and numerous essays promoting Reconstructionist views he learned in the conflict with Nebraska.[45]

Conclusion

Rushdoony and Christian Reconstruction have had more influence on the Christian school movement than on any other aspect of society. The schools are important in terms of shaping generations of Christians imbued with a biblical worldview. While most people in our society see public schools as religiously neutral, Reconstructionists have a strikingly different viewpoint, and thanks in large part to their extensive writing on the topic, their framing of the issue has been embraced by a much larger, non-Reconstructionist, part of the conservative Christian world. In this view, all knowledge must start from presuppositions, and the only two possible places to start are biblical revelation or some application of human reason. Any system of knowledge not based in the Bible is, therefore, humanistic, defined as the presupposition that "man" is the measure of all things.

While many conservative Christians have worked to reform public schools and/or removed their children from them in favor of homeschooling and Christian schooling, Reconstructionists' critique of public education goes much deeper.[46] The Reconstructionist defense of Christian schooling is built on sphere sovereignty and presuppositionalism. There can be no long-term détente between those who are committed to the value of widely available public education and those who follow the extreme form of Reconstructionism; the two worldviews may well be mutually exclusive. Reconstructionists are unabashedly committed to the dismantling of public education, and their strategies and solutions have gained a hearing far beyond the boundaries of the small groups explicitly affiliated with them.

5

Homeschooling for Dominion

CHRISTIAN HOMESCHOOLING IS infused with the values of Christian Reconstruction and is seen by those in the movement as the single most important tool for the exercise of dominion. The theological, philosophical, and legal foundation for Christian education, based on the argument that the Bible gives authority over education entirely and exclusively to the family, was established, largely by Rushdoony, in the 1960s, 1970s, and early 1980s. Originally, such arguments were mustered in support of Christian schools, but by the early 1980s Christian homeschooling was on the rise and it is now the "gold standard" for Christian education. While most Christian homeschooling parents would not identify as Christian Reconstructionists, the views put forth by Rushdoony and his followers would be widely accepted. Christian homeschooling materials reflect this influence.

Because homeschooling regulations concerning reporting and credentialing vary from state to state, quantitative data on homeschooling are notoriously difficult to obtain. Some states have only minimal requirements and therefore have only general numbers, while other states regulate stringently, which results in some homeschoolers being "underground." But the US Department of Education estimated that in 2007 there were 1.5 million homeschooled students in the United States, representing 2.9 percent of the school-aged population.[1] This subculture has seen steady growth for over thirty years. There are now generations of homeschoolers who have become parents and are homeschooling their children. Moreover, there is now, for the first time, a critical mass of adults who, having grown up in homeschooling, are speaking out against examples of abuse and neglect. This has led to a series of resignations, lawsuits, and ministry closings.[2]

Christian Reconstructionists have been foundational to the homeschool movement and seek to expand their influence by using homeschooling to "reconstruct" society according to the model put forth by Rushdoony.

The Christian Homeschool Community

Christian homeschoolers have built a network of organizations providing resources, conventions, targeted travel opportunities, museums, a film institute in San Antonio (see chapter 7), and colleges especially for homeschooled students, such as Patrick Henry in Purcellville, Virginia, which capitalizes on its proximity to Washington, DC to train young homeschoolers for public service in government. Homeschooling appeared on the government's radar in the 1990s, and the Department of Education began surveys to track the numbers in 1999.[3] That year they found an estimated 850,000 homeschooled children (1.7 percent). Beginning in 2003 the study asked parents their most important reasons for homeschooling. They are given a list of reasons and asked to rank them. In some ways the options are unsatisfactorily vague. For example they are asked to rank "religious and moral instruction" (36 percent rank this option first), "concern over the school environment" (21 percent), and "dissatisfaction with the academic instruction" (17 percent).[4] While these three areas could be different for some parents, all three are decidedly religious concerns for many Christian homeschoolers. When allowed to choose three options, in 2003, 72 percent chose these three; in 2007 that number rose to 83 percent. Other concerns had to do with special needs children and other issues.

When people think about homeschooling they often envision an eighthour day at a kitchen table in which an isolated student does schoolwork. Homeschooling families, though, present a very different picture. First, the formal school day can be much shorter than it would be in a classroom where there are twenty to thirty children. There is no time spent maintaining an orderly classroom, lining up for lunch or recess, or waiting for other students to finish their work. Homeschooling families often attend churches where most of the students are homeschooled, and they get together for activities from field trips to show and tell. Some churches offer daytime programs for their homeschoolers, including Bible and physical education classes. We have seen how some Christian schools offer à la carte services that allow homeschoolers to take specialized courses and to participate in extracurricular activities such as sports. Homeschooling parents respond to concerns that homeschooled children miss out on socialization by securing opportunities for activities outside the home and by arguing that much of the "socializing" that occurs in school is not a positive influence on students.

The Christian homeschooling movement traces its roots to the Puritans and the Colonial period, but the contemporary resurgence dates to the 1960s. John Holt—author of a number of influential books that were critical of the structure, regimentation, and homogenization necessary for institutionalized schooling—led a movement that advocated nontraditional education. Gregg Harris, homeschooling leader and founder of Christian Life Ministries, explains in his 1988 book the limitations of Holt's work for Christian families. He writes, "John Holt's 'unschooling' moves far away from traditional schooling. Holt believed that children can learn by themselves and, thus, rejected most kinds of programmed instruction." Harris is critical of the fact that Holt undermined parental authority because he believed that children would learn everything they needed to know if they were just given freedom. Harris writes of Holt:

> In essence his theory eliminates teaching as a profession, or even a parental responsibility. Holt's books offer a few helpful insights into how children learn and what's wrong with public schools; for those views they're worth reading. However his basic assumptions about values and the nature of children, ignore the effects of the Fall and, thus, are saddled with an untenable secular humanism.[5]

Harris's book was published by Wolgemuth and Hyatt, a previously noted press with Reconstructionist leanings, and the book cites Rushdoony and other Reconstructionists throughout.

Home School Legal Defense Association

By the 1980s, the homeschool movement comprised mainly conservative Christians who had removed their children from public schools to give them an education that was rooted in what they see as a biblical worldview. In 1983 attorneys Mike Farris and Mike Smith founded the Home School Legal Defense Association (HSLDA). HSLDA offers families access to homeschooling resources, legal representation if they face challenges from authorities, and a network of other homeschooling families. HSLDA also serves as a lobbying organization opposing any and all oversight of homeschooling by authorities, presumably on behalf of homeschooling families.

Farris has moved on from HSLDA to found Patrick Henry College and serve as its chancellor. HSLDA is still focused on legal issues, and publishes a quarterly *Court Report*, tracking, state by state, the legal status of homeschooling, defending member families in court cases, raising constitutional challenges to laws limiting homeschooling, and lobbying on behalf of homeschoolers at the state and federal levels. The organization's unwavering defense of the notion that the state has absolutely no jurisdiction in the education of children has given rise to substantial criticism.

Like Christian schools, homeschoolers have faced government efforts to exert oversight authority. While this is manifested in myriad ways— ranging from certification laws to attempts to prohibit homeschooling altogether—commonly states require some sort of formal notification that parents intend to homeschool their children. Many also require some form of standardized testing, though given the widespread perception of government as at best an incompetent meddler but at worst an ungodly tyrant, there are also numerous stories of underground homeschoolers who go "off the grid" to avoid any oversight at all. HSLDA is proud of the fact that over the last twenty-five years homeschooling has become legal in every state. The organization monitors legislation potentially affecting homeschoolers' rights and even legislation having nothing to do with homeschooling specifically but which allows government regulation or oversight of family authority. HSLDA mobilizes member families to support or oppose relevant legislation. HSLDA brings lawsuits in support of parents' rights and defends member families in situations where their rights are challenged.

HSLDA played a central role in a recent skirmish on this front. From 2000 to 2008, California parents with valid teaching credentials could homeschool their children. Parents who did not have teaching certificates were permitted to homeschool their children by establishing their own private schools, making them exempt from truancy laws. In February 2008 the Court of Appeals for the Second Appellate District ruled that a homeschool is not a legitimate form of private school, effectively making most of California's homeschools illegal. One family put together a legal defense team made up of representatives of the United States Justice Fund (USJF), the HSLDA, and the Alliance Defense Fund (ADF) and was successful at having the ruling overturned in August 2008.[6]

According to HSLDA's *Court Report,* the greatest current "threat" to the freedom of families to homeschool is overzealous social workers who "don't believe they have to obey the Constitution":

When investigating child abuse and neglect cases (including educational neglect) social workers are bound to honor a family's Fourth

Amendment right to privacy unless there is "probable cause" to invade that privacy. But HSLDA routinely encounters social workers who have violated the constitutional rights of innocent homeschooling families. Today, HSLDA attorneys are dealing with more social worker situations than ever before.[7]

The *Report* encourages member families, when visited by social workers, to refuse entry on the basis of their constitutional rights against warrantless searches. They are instructed to call HSLDA and hand the phone to the social worker. HSLDA repeatedly warns parents to never give permission to social workers to enter their homes or to interview their children without first presenting a warrant. They warn of dire consequences to families that have done so—for example, losing custody of their children (or implying that families would have without the help of HSLDA). In a 2005 essay entitled "No Fear: Social Workers Restrained!," HSLDA's then-Senior Counsel Chris Klicka warned, "Social Workers [Are] Out of Control":

> There is a knock at the door. The homeschool mom answers and to her horror, a social worker is there! He simply informs the innocent mother that she has been accused of "child abuse." He will not tell her any more unless she immediately lets him in her house and interrogate the children alone.

He goes on to claim:

> Innocent families are routinely traumatized by child welfare agencies simply because an anonymous tipster calls the local child abuse hotline and fabricates a story or relays a suspicion. Parents who are subject to these "investigations" are told they must allow the social worker entry into their home and allow each of their children to be interrogated separately—before they will be informed of the allegations. In fact, most states in their child welfare code impose a statutory duty on social workers to enter homes and interrogate children separately from their parents. Unfortunately, since these state statutes often do not expressly delineate the constitutional limitations established by the Fourth Amendment, social workers "get away" with intimidating families into allowing them entry into their homes and interrogating their children.[8]

According to Klicka, the solution to this dire state of affairs is the work of HSLDA. They promote what they call "child welfare laws," which restrain child protective services agents, and fight against the child welfare system in court. Of course, the organization is funded by homeschooling families—something like a prepaid legal service—so much of their published material is deliberately designed to foster anxiety and suspicion of civil authorities. Founder Michael Farris's 1996 novel serves this function well. In *Anonymous Tip*, an innocent homeschooling mom is caught in a stranglehold of government bureaucracy and nearly loses custody of her daughter over an anonymous tip to protective services (made by her disgruntled ex) alleging child abuse.[9] "The most shocking part of all is," the book jacket alleges, "it really could happen to anyone!"

The Language of Homeschooling

In 1995, Chris Klicka published *The Right Choice: Home Schooling*, which includes chapters written by Greg Harris and was published by Noble Publishing Association, an arm of Harris's Christian Life Ministries.[10] Some twenty years ago, I interviewed Klicka and a nearby homeschooling family, Tracy and Kathy Johnson. Klicka was, at the time, an attorney and the executive director of HSLDA, and his views were identifiably Reconstructionist. He has since passed away, though he remained active in homeschooling circles through a long illness until his death in 2009. When I interviewed him, Klicka and his wife were homeschooling their own children, while the Johnsons were beginning the third year of homeschooling theirs.[11] The Johnsons were solidly middle class, and like many homeschooling families they owned a small business they ran out of their home. Neither had a college degree or any specific training as teachers, but they were involved in a court case with their county school board over compulsory school laws. Both families had chosen homeschooling for religious reasons. A comparison between the language used in a discussion of homeschooling by Klicka, a leader in the movement avowedly influenced by Reconstructionists, and that used by the Johnsons, a family more concerned with the practice itself than with developing a philosophical system in defense of it, is an interesting study in the way such ideas are popularized and make their way into the everyday lives of believers. Klicka explained his reading of the motivations behind conservative Christian homeschooling: "God has given the authority and the responsibility of educating children to the parents only. In other words, the state has no responsibility in education and has not been given that authority by God." I asked him if most of the members of HSLDA would agree with him and he told me that "a good three-quarters of them would believe that. A lot of their religious convictions are developing as they have to fight for the right to teach their children."

The Johnsons both grew up in what they described as liberal families, attending both Catholic and public schools. Their views about home-schooling had developed over time under the teaching of their pastor, though they did not claim the label Reconstructionist or communicate a sense that they had acquired this language directly from Reconstruction-ists. Kathy explained, "We're in a process ourselves . . . it wasn't one of those things where we said, 'boom! that's the way it is' . . . and we knew this all along before we had kids. We're in a process of finding out what God would have us do with our children." Kathy expressed the same con-cerns over education as other conservative Christians: "it's not so much that the public schools are 'anti-God,' it's just that God is plainly irrele-vant. That strikes at the heart of it. You can't be neutral with God. Either you're for God or against God." She then read to me the letter they had sent to the school board in support of their plea for a religious exemption to the compulsory education laws.

> The truth in God's word is relevant to every aspect of our life and cannot be excluded from any area of study. It would be offensive to our God to teach children the wonders of science and not tell them how God magnificently and wonderfully planned it all and spoke it into being. We cannot teach our children to count . . . and neglect telling them that God is the creator of order.

Still, the overriding concern of the Johnsons, which is the central concern of homeschoolers, is the issue of authority. Many homeschooling books begin with the argument that the government should have no control over education. Kathy explained how she came to believe that what was of con-cern to the school board in her case was ultimately who would have con-trol: "It was so offensive to the school board to think that they weren't going to get our children." She suggested that their attitude was, "well, that's the way everybody does it . . . That's what the law says—that we get your children now . . . give us your children," and then emphatically added, "we just couldn't get the point across to them: our children don't belong to you." Her point, framed in terms of ownership, was not that the children belonged to her (though she called them hers) but rather the real question was whether they belonged to the state or to God. These Christian homeschooling parents believe that parents may delegate that authority (or some of it) to specialists in a given area or even to a Christian school, but they believe that ultimately they are responsible before God; and that that responsibility is the most important responsibility God gives people, making delegation of it risky at best. They fear that even in a Christian school, they will not have sufficient control of their children's learning environment. Kathy Johnson explained, citing the Bible:

> God specifically addresses parents, by name, in the scriptures as the ones to do the teaching . . . Fathers, do not provoke your children to anger but bring them up in the nurture and admonition of the Lord. And, my son, observe the commandment of your father and do not forsake the teaching of your mother.[12]

I asked if they were opposed to anything *inherent* in public schooling. Kathy answered, "We don't think government has *any, any* say over children." When I pressed this point, asking if this meant that the government should not even supervise to make sure people learned to read, Kathy responded that her focus was on making the right choices for her children and not on the policy implications of her views. She said:

> I couldn't speak to that. Our quest is more along the lines of an offensive with what God has given us. We haven't sat down and said, "Well, this is what public schools are, and we're not going to do it that way—and this is what we feel about government . . . it really is that we are learning as we go along."

When asked about the legitimacy of taking tax money for something they considered illegitimate in the first place (what Rushdoony has called legalized theft) Kathy responded again, "We haven't pursued that a whole lot. We figure we're never going to be in public schools. We know why we don't want to be there." Even when discussing the issue of the legitimacy of the public schools as an institution, the Johnsons were still seeing it only in terms of their own actions and their own children. The seeds of the Reconstructionist worldview are clearly present but they are, just as clearly, not fully developed. Christian homeschoolers do not believe that the government has a legitimate role to play in education. Some of their leaders have developed a systematic worldview on these issues—even to the point of advocating the eventual replacement of the public school system with homeschooling, private schooling, and scholarships to help those who cannot afford either.[13] Klicka supported this view, admitting that charity might be unrealistic and some would go without education, but he countered by pointing to illiteracy rates, arguing that there are students who make their way through public schools yet still don't receive an education. Klicka and others see home education as serious competition to public schools and an effective tool to ultimately eliminate them. While this is clearly a minority view, it is the logical conclusion of the views held by many more. As Klicka observed, and the Johnsons illustrate, people become increasingly consistent in their views as they confront controversies over homeschooling choices.

Homeschooling Curriculum

The curriculum chosen by homeschooling parents varies tremendously, some of it explicitly Christian Reconstructionist; some of it subtly Reconstructionist; and some of it outright opposed to the influence of Rushdoony, theonomy, and dominion theology. Parents can choose completely self-contained home study courses, which may include standardized testing and diplomas. But they can also choose customized courses, tailored by parents to address the specific strengths, weaknesses, and interests of their children, or pick and choose materials to design their own curricula. Many of the books they use are the same books used in Christian schools.

Christian Liberty Academy School System (CLASS) in Illinois was founded in 1967 when the early Christian education movement was facing legal challenges. Originally called Christian Liberty Satellite Schools, CLASS, in effect, is a distance-learning Christian school. Parents enroll their children in CLASS and receive curricular materials, assistance, tests, and ultimately "legal cover" in terms of some state regulations for homeschooling. Parents can enroll their children in the full program, which includes everything from books to grading and testing, and students receive a diploma from CLASS. They also have the option of à la carte selection of products and services, allowing them to maintain their independence if they wish. Like most of the curricula used in Christian schools, the kindergarten program teaches students to read basic sentences using phonics; write the complete alphabet and basic sentences; and count, add, and subtract. Beginning in the fourth grade, CLASS emphasizes writing by requiring five book reports a year. By high school, these become research papers, in addition to classes on math, the Bible, creation science, literature, and a selection of electives.

While CLASS is not accredited, their promotional materials include an explanation for why they reject accreditation (as a violation of sphere sovereignty) and arguments that it has limited value. The materials also include a lengthy list of colleges around the country that have accepted CLASS homeschooled students. In addition to small schools and Christian schools, CLASS claims its students have attended several of the University of California and State University of New York schools, the University of Virginia, as well as Yale, Harvard, Dartmouth, and Princeton.[14] Homeschoolers emphasize the number of studies that have attested to the quality of education they can provide and publicize homeschooling students who win competitions such as the Scripps Howard National Spelling Bee and the National Geographic Bee.[15]

Reconstructionist influence on the understanding of Christian education is evident on the CLASS website:

> The fear of the Lord is the beginning of wisdom, not only in our educational philosophy, but also for each discipline of study. Education is not made Christian by merely adding a course in Bible or by beginning a class in prayer. If the course content or teaching method is humanistic, Christian supplements will do little to change the orientation. A Christian curriculum must derive its fundamental principles from God's Holy Word and work these out in a self-conscious manner. CLASS provides parents and students with these principles as well as the content and skills which enable them to develop a biblical worldview in each subject.[16]

In a statement that could have come directly from Rushdoony, or from the founders of Fairfax Christian or Rocky Bayou Christian, they explain their understanding of the relationship between the Bible and the rest of their curriculum:

> Because there is only one God and one Christ, there is only one truth. This truth is the center and criterion of Christian education. While the Bible is not used as the textbook in every subject, it is the foundational handbook for every course and the standard for teaching. As the foundational book, Scripture is the only infallible rule

for faith and practice, for grammar and literature, for mathematics and science, for health and physical education, for geography and history, and for social studies and the arts.

Likewise, with regard to the source of legitimate authority and the presuppositional nature of knowledge:

> In order for education to be consistently Christian the teacher must self-consciously teach all subjects in the framework of biblical authority . . . The most fundamental teaching of the Bible is the sovereignty of the Triune God. This truth is foundational for all Christian teaching. It alone separates Christian education . . . from all forms of humanism and naturalism . . . Because the Creator is the sovereign God, He is Lord of Heaven and Earth, and He speaks with absolute authority about all things. There is nothing in this universe which can truly be learned apart from Him.

And on the relationship between education and the exercise of dominion: "The purpose of Christian education is not primarily to meet human needs or develop human potential, but preeminently to labor to the greater glory of God, the honor of the name of Christ, and promote the development of His kingdom."[17] CLASS also subscribes to sphere sovereignty:

> In His infinite wisdom, God has instituted three governmental organisms for man in this world: the state, the visible church, and the family. He has ordained that these three are to coordinate in rights and functions with a mutual independence, so that the state or the church have no more right to invade the parental sphere than parents do to invade the state or church spheres.

Education, they claim, is an explicitly religious activity and a strictly a parental responsibility:

> God has committed to parents the high privilege and solemn responsibility of training and educating their children in the fear of the Lord. We further believe that they dare not surrender this God-given right to any other institution, such as the state . . . Education is religious, the Scriptures are the ultimate authority, and parents are accountable to God for the instruction and discipline of their

children. Therefore, we cannot in good conscience come under the control of either civil or ecclesiastical authorities with respect to the education of our children.

Though Reconstructionist-influenced Christians typically assert this biblical division of authority, CLASS lays out the ways in which they base this view in biblical texts in a particularly clear fashion, which helps shed light on the movement as a whole.

> God instituted the family before either the church or state had existence. Prior to man's fall into sin, the family exercised total responsibility over all aspects of God's creation (Genesis 2).
>
> God has in the fifth commandment granted only to the parents the adequate and prior authority commensurate with the discharge of this great responsibility (Exodus 20:12).
>
> The divine legislation given to Moses commands not the state or the church, but the fathers to see to the instruction of the children, that there might be faith and true knowledge in the race to come (Deuteronomy 6:4–7; Psalm 78:3–8).
>
> The inspired apostles hold fathers directly responsible for consistently bringing up their children in the nurture and admonition of the Lord, and exhort mothers to see to the godly upbringing of the daughters (Ephesians 6:4; Titus 2:4–5; 2 Timothy 1:5).
>
> In sacred history as recorded in the Scriptures, fathers such as Eli were condemned for their failure to instruct and discipline their children, thus bringing God's judgment on themselves and their house (1 Samuel 3:11–14; 2 Samuel 11; 12:10–11; 13; 14:21; 15).
>
> The Scriptures clearly state that failure to properly discharge this parental duty immediately disqualifies a man (i.e. the father) from the office of elder in the church (1 Timothy 3:4–5; Titus 1:6).
>
> The state, as a minister of God, is charged with the enforcement of the moral law in human relations, as a temporal ministry of justice among men, and is to protect the family and the church in the free exercise of all their God-given rights and responsibilities (Romans 13:1–10; 1 Peter 2:13–17; 1 Timothy 2:12).

Another widely used homeschooling curriculum comes from Bill Gothard's controversial Institute in Biblical Life Principles (IBLP) and Advanced Training Institute (ATI). Noted for the authoritarian character of his program, Gothard combines aspects of Christian Reconstruction, particularly an emphasis on biblical law and its applicability to all of life, with other components such as spiritual warfare and strategies to resolve life problems. In 1984 Gary North wrote approvingly of Gothard's program: "he is using biblical law to solve problems that only biblical law can consistently solve . . . [and he] is creating the foundation of a revolution in the world-and-life view of Christian pastors."[18]

ATI is intended to provide a Bible-based "cradle to grave, step-by-step systematized way to live." According to Gothard, "Every problem in life can be traced to seven non-optional principles found in the Bible. Every person, regardless of culture, background, religion, education, or social status, must either follow these principles or experience the consequences of violating them."[19] In an effort to relate the Bible to every subject, each of Gothard's "Wisdom Books" focuses on a topic that can be related to the Bible as well as to every other subject. The booklet on "light," for example, includes biblical passages on the subject, a "linguistics" section where students "learn words that describe how to be light in darkness," a history lesson on how "the light of scripture shine[d] in Europe before the Reformation," a science lesson on how "the speed of light illustrate[s] the consistency Christians should have," a lesson in law on how "the commandments of the father and the laws of the mother give light," and a lesson in medicine on lasers as illustrations of "the potential of unified Christians." These materials are characterized by a thoroughgoing hostility toward the medical community, especially, but not limited to, psychology and psychiatry. Gothard teaches that a majority of illnesses can be traced to spiritual problems, including demons. Gothard cites a Bible passage that indicates that envy "is rottenness in the bones," which he uses to conclude osteoporosis is the result of the sin of envy. The broader Christian Reconstructionist world would share his view that psychology and psychiatry are rooted in an unbiblical worldview and that many mental health problems result from sin, disobedience, and rebellion. Reconstructionists, however, would not share his views of traditional medicine and physical illness.

Unlike other homeschool curricula that parents can buy and implement as they see fit, ATI includes regular travel to training sessions and ongoing participation in the Gothard world. There has long been extensive criticism of ATI as spiritually abusive and, as one might imagine, much of the criticism of Gothard's program is aimed at its extraordinarily poor educational value.[20] More recently, though, stories surfaced alleging sexual impropriety on the part of Gothard, involving multiple young women serving at the organization's headquarters over many years, which resulted in his resignation from IBLP in March 2014.[21]

Homeschooling and Christian Reconstruction

Though most homeschooling families would not identify as Christian Reconstructionist, the movement is an ideal illustration of the way in which Reconstructionist influence shapes the underpinnings of the conservative Christian subculture. That influence is broader than its numbers might indicate and is traceable in ways that require a fluency in Christian Reconstruction to hear. This is true of both homeschoolers, whose endeavors are shaped by Reconstruction in ways they do not see, and scholars studying homeschoolers, who may miss the influence of Reconstruction. Robert Kunzman's excellent *Write These Laws on Your Children: Inside the World of Christian Homeschooling* draws on fieldwork to outline, document, and analyze the homeschool "world."[22] Kunzman discusses homeschool curricula that includes Reconstructionist materials but mentions Reconstructionism only once.[23] Kunzman is interested in the way in which Reconstructionism provides an opportunity for homeschoolers to think through challenging arguments for positions they don't hold. He presumes that Reconstructionists are marginal to homeschooling and wonders about the results should homeschoolers read Reconstructionist works and come to agree with them. Yet I would argue that, in addition to helping lay the legal foundation for homeschooling, many of the overarching themes he finds in homeschooling are taken directly from Reconstructionists. One has to be conversant with Christian Reconstruction to recognize it.

By far the most common theme that has Reconstructionist roots is the argument that education is solely a parental responsibility and that the government has no right to regulate it or be involved in any way. Kunzman writes:

> The right of parents to raise and educate their children—and the complete lack of government authority in that regard—is perhaps *the* foundational conviction in homeschooling. For conservative Christian homeschoolers, this clearly has theological underpinnings.[24]

Examples of this view appear in nearly all the families he interviews, but one of the most clear is "Alan," who says:

> I don't believe that the child has a "right" to education . . . Rights aren't things that the government is responsible for providing. The government's responsibility is to ensure that somebody else doesn't infringe on my God-given rights to life, liberty and property.[25]

This is clearly formulated along the lines of Rushdoony's early work on the absence of children's rights, sphere sovereignty, and the specific obligations and limitations of each sphere. For example, this critique of the notion of rights, especially as applied to children and education, was developed by Rushdoony in 1963.[26]

The Reconstructionist commitment to philosophical presuppositionalism is present as well. Kunzman cites his homeschooled respondents:

> "Public schools are quite simply humanist churches," one student writes . . . Some students seek support in their Scriptures, such as one who argued, "The Word of God says that parents are to raise their children in the 'nurture and admonition of the Lord.'" what does this mean? It means that it is a sin for Christian parents to submit 20,000 hours of their child's childhood to an influence which teaches them that there is no God. Another puts it quite simply, "Children are not spiritually strong enough to attend a humanist church five times as much as a Christian church."[27]

In this world neutrality is philosophically impossible. One starts with the revealed God of the Bible and reasons from this, or one does not and enshrines human reason as the arbiter of truth. Rushdoony laid out this argument in detail in *The Messianic Character of American Education,* and it remains an important focus (with Rushdoony cited as its source) among the self-identified Reconstructionists in the homeschool movement today.

Kunzman notes "pro-homeschooling retailer Vision Forum," and its focus on restoring godly families and distinctly gendered homeschooling materials, without recognizing the organization's Reconstructionist roots. He mentions also the preference among homeschoolers for the McGuffey Readers and the *Blueback Spellers* without noting that Reconstructionists promoted their use in the 1970s and that Reconstructionist Thoburn

Press was one of the main sources for reprinted versions of both. Kunzman discusses numerous resources that are difficult to track down because he often does not give their titles, but one source he does cite is *Biblical Economics in Cartoons*, though he mentions it only in passing.[28] It's unlikely that Kunzman is conversant with Christian Reconstructionism, but to anyone who is, the influence is undeniable. The book is a cartoon version of Gary North's views of economics. It embraces the continued relevance of God's law as contained in the Old Testament, the notion of sphere sovereignty or jurisdictional authority, and a third component that is unique to Christian Reconstructionism as promoted by North: the "five-point covenantal structure." Developed by Reconstructionist Ray Sutton, North took this model as the fundamental structure for his economic commentary, and David Chilton used it in his development of Reconstructionist postmillennialist commentary on the book of Revelation.[29] Moreover, Kunzman's respondents echo Reconstructionist themes and language (probably without knowing that they are doing so) when they refer to public schools as "government schools."[30] When a respondent argues for "getting rid of public schools" or when another argues that public schools are "Marxist-socialist" or still another argues that charity is the responsibility of churches rather than government, it is possible that these respondents have not been influenced by the longstanding Reconstructionist arguments on these issues, but it is also reasonably likely, given the specific phrasing of the arguments and the circles in which they travel, that Reconstructionism is exactly the source of these viewpoints.[31]

Even the title of Kunzman's book, *Write These Laws on Your Children*, points to the influence of Reconstructionists' emphasis on the Old Testament and their commitment to biblical law. The title is an allusion to Deuteronomy, in which God admonishes the Israelites to take his laws and "teach them diligently unto thy children . . . write them upon the posts of thy house, and on thy gates." Thus, in Reconstructionists' view, parents are responsible for education. Few contemporary forms of Christianity other than Reconstructionism make much use of Deuteronomy.

From the 1960s through the 1980s, the Christian school movement was the most important strategy in the Christian Reconstructionist effort to eliminate public education and raise generations of children imbued with a biblical worldview who could transform all of culture. That emphasis has slowly shifted, such that Christian homeschooling has become much more important. But the two efforts together remain central. Any discussion of Christian Reconstruction in homeschooling inevitably leads to cries from homeschoolers about the variety of perspectives found among them. That is undoubtedly correct, yet the influence of Christian Reconstruction is broad and deep, such that some non-Reconstructionist homeschoolers, even many who are conservative Christians, are increasingly concerned, especially as they identify specific efforts on the part of Christian Reconstructionists to dominate homeschooling as a movement and an industry. Blogger Julie Ann Smith explained to me that, in most states, homeschooling families who want to connect with the homeschooling community must choose between secular homeschooling associations and conventions, and the Christian ones that are dominated with a "Reconstructionist agenda." She draws a helpful distinction between homeschoolers and what she labels the Homeschooling Movement. John Holzmann, cofounder of Sonlight, the Christian homeschooling curriculum, is another such blogger. He expresses concern from within the movement about the efforts of Reconstructionist-oriented homeschool leaders to exclude other viewpoints.

These bloggers were already worried about the influence Reconstructionists have in the homeschool world, but they grew more alarmed when information surfaced about the 2009 Men's Leadership Summit, which was hosted by the Christian Home Educators of Colorado (CHEC) at a Bill Gothard Institute for Biblical Life Principles (IBLP) facility in Indianapolis. Though hosted by a state homeschooling organization, the Leadership Summit had a national focus, and the speakers were identified as Reconstructionists: CHEC Director Kevin Swanson; Vision Forum President Doug Phillips; Senior Counsel to HSLDA Chris Klicka; pastor, author, and regular speaker at American Vision Conferences Voddie Baucham; and National Center for Family Integrated Churches Director Scott Brown.[32] The irony that a movement made up mostly of women would hold a conference of self-appointed leaders that were all male was not lost on critics.

While it is sometimes difficult to find hard evidence of the Reconstructionist strategy for influence in movements such as home schooling, this is one of the rare cases in which they laid out the plan in explicit and documentable terms. The goal was to capitalize on changing attitudes in the general public toward the increasing privatization of education (attitudes they have worked tirelessly to change):

The time has come to define the vision. With the explosion of school choice and the increased accessibility of state-funded options for home educators, the time has come to define the vision that characterizes the Christian Home Education movement, thus unifying both national and state leadership and solidifying the vision for generations to come.[33]

Swanson set the stage by making clear the lineage of the homeschool movement, from the 1960s, through the 1980s and into the twenty-first century, as those leaders would have understood it.

> Let's give credit also to the men [and] the women that founded this movement, the homeschooling discipleship movement. I spent the last number of weeks reading the great books written by the R. J. Rushdoonys, the Gordon Clarks, of the 1950s, 1960s . . . the Cornelius Van Tils, the men who were framing the ideas we are using today, and moreover I also read some great books by guys like Gregg Harris, Chris Klicka . . . I'll tell ya what . . . Mike Farris . . . these guys were writing things in the 1980s that we are saying today. We're standing on the shoulders of the guys that went before us . . . We're just their progeny. We would not be sitting here today if it weren't for the men that went before us and started what I believe to be the Reformation of the twenty-first century.[34]

The purpose of the summit was the development of a "Christian Education Manifesto." John Holzmann preserved a copy of the manifesto, which he shared with me.[35] The lectures were available for sale, for a time, but they have since been removed, as have the references to the summit on the various websites that once promoted it, though I was able to acquire recordings of twelve lectures. The goals are clear: the elimination of public education and any government regulation of "parents' rights," including dismantling of child welfare agencies, departments of children and families, and child protective services. Ultimately, they seek the transformation of homeschooling to reflect the values of biblical patriarchy, including placing it completely under the authority of fathers and limiting the education of girls to that which prepares them for homemaking and motherhood.

Challenges from Within the Homeschooling Community

On the various blogs populated by former homeschoolers, there are numerous attestations to the widespread sense of embattlement and persecution at the hands of social welfare officials. While the fear may seem ginned up by those who benefit from it, it's clear from the postings that to those inside this community the fear is very real. These critics argue that this is a key component of a larger cultural system that enables abuse.

While most former homeschoolers insist they do not oppose home-schooling in general, they also insist that the current legal state of home-schooling, built in large measure by HSLDA—and, as we have seen, on the arguments made by Rushdoony half a century ago—creates a sce-nario in which the abuse of children is far too easily hidden. Blogger Libby Anne is one of the most cogent, relentless, and systematic critics of the HSLDA. Libby Anne is a pseudonym; she feels she must use one because the material that she writes about would damage her relationships with her family members. In a series of posts, she accuses HSLDA of enabling child abuse by fighting any legislation that allows social services or law enforcement to effectively investigate accusations, even in cases unrelated to homeschooling.[36] There are, she writes,

> four primary ways that HSLDA is complicit in aiding and abetting child abuse and educational neglect: (1) They work to minimize the reporting of child abuse; (2) They seek to stall the investigation of child abuse; (3) They defend the legality of excessive corporal pun-ishment; and (4) They oppose any homeschooling regulation what-soever, even when it is merely intended to ensure that learning is actually taking place.

In one case she cites, HSLDA opposed legislation banning "excessive" cor-poral punishment, the language of which, she argues, would have effec-tively provided legal recognition of any and all "reasonable" corporal punishment. In another case she takes HSLDA to task for allegedly de-fending a homeschooling parent who admitted to locking his children in a cage.[37]

Observers often perceive a division between "liberal" and "conserva-tive" religion in America, sometimes also called modernism and funda-mentalism or progressivism and orthodoxy. But these labels don't really tell us what is *different* about these two camps. Bruce Lincoln has offered a helpful alternative; he frames the two camps "minimalist" and "maxi-malist."[38] People who are grounded in the modern secular world, even those who maintain a commitment to religion, do so in a minimalist way. That is, they tend to see religion as a private concern, focused on certain spiritual issues but largely separate from the rest of life. Lincoln calls those who oppose this compartmentalization "maximalist." To maximalists religion is all-encompassing; there are no aspects of life that are "secular" (i.e., outside the realm of religion's influence).[39] Minimalists, those for whom religion is but one influence, encounter competing perspectives. Maximalists, however, withdraw into exclusivist, mutually reinforcing, totalistic enclaves, and maintain a worldview that seems bizarre to those outside it. In parts of the homeschooling movement, the rejection of any outside influences on the family's educational obligations and authority fosters maximalist religion, sometimes to the detriment of the more vulnerable members of the community. When conservative Christians remove their children from public schools, and even from Christian schools, they eliminate one of the most important ways in which children and their families interact with the larger world. They become absorbed in an intertwined network of fellow believers. The ideas with which they engage are filtered through and mutually reinforced by that social group. This is partly why, for example, broad swaths of American Christians believe in a literal six-day account of creation and a version of history intended to show God's plan for America, despite the fact that scientists and historians agree that the believers are inaccurate or wrong. The religious culture at issue here is characterized by extreme dualism resulting in a profound suspicion of outsiders. In presuppositionalist terms, there are really only two possible perspectives: biblical Christianity and everything else. All religions, philosophies, and ideologies not rooted in the Bible are rooted in rebellious human reason that seeks to be autonomous from God.

The homeschool world, even the Christian homeschool world, is diverse. And the fact that Rushdoony did much to establish the view that Christians should not turn their children over to "government schools" for a humanistic education does not meant that most homeschoolers are on board with the Christian Reconstructionists' agenda. There is a growing cohort of homeschool parents and former homeschooled students who work to oppose what one called the "Reconstructionist agenda" of many of the big names in the homeschool movement.

Beyond critiquing cases in which zealous protection of parental prerogatives in education creates a space in which abusive parents can operate outside the reach of the authority of civil government, many other former homeschoolers raise concerns about the practices of more mainstream Christian homeschooling. Julie Ann Smith is one such critic.[40] Smith and other homeschool movement critics charge that homeschoolers within the

movement too often reach adulthood without adequate educational prepa-
ration, especially in science and history. Smith draws a helpful distinction
between the practice of homeschooling (which she supports) and what she
calls the "Homeschool Movement," which she says is broadly influenced
by a core group of authoritarian men with a "Reconstructionist agenda."
Indeed, for a movement whose work is overwhelmingly performed by
women, there is a striking gender imbalance in the leadership.

Kevin Swanson, who is, as mentioned, president of CHEC, is a regular
speaker at both broadly construed Christian homeschooling meetings
and explicitly Christian Reconstructionist venues such as Vision Forum
and American Vision conferences. As Smith told me, for parents looking
for resources and support to teach their children at home, there are only
two choices: the secular associations and the Christian ones dominated
by people like Swanson and Doug Phillips. These Reconstructionist-
oriented leaders plan conventions, choose speakers, and tightly regulate
the exhibitors allowed at homeschooling conventions. It was Swanson's
CHEC that sponsored the 2009 Men's Leadership Summit where they
sought to lay out a Reconstructionist-oriented patriarchal vision for homeschooling, urged the elimination of public schools, and proposed a strategy to implement that vision in Colorado and then replicate that effort
across the country.

6

Creationism, Mythmaking, Ritual, and Social Formation

IN THE EXHIBIT hall of the annual meeting of the Florida Parent Educators Association, I struck up a conversation with Joanne, a representative from the Creation Studies Institute of Fort Lauderdale.* Founded in 1988, Creation Studies Institute operates a creation museum, publishes educational materials, and offers workshops and training sessions designed to "retrain" believers, replacing the evolutionary worldview that pervades contemporary America with the "biblical truth" about human origins. Joanne is an intelligent woman who can explain, in detail, creationist arguments about fossil records and genetics. I asked at one point why, if all the evidence really supports a biblical account of creation in six days as she believes, so many scientists interpret that evidence differently. She then outlined for me a vast conspiracy on the part of atheists to suppress the truth and to silence anyone who doesn't fall in line with evolutionary orthodoxy. I marveled at the detail and apparent internal coherence of her view and left wondering how it is that creationists of this stripe come to see their view as so obviously true that they struggle to comprehend how one could believe in evolution. There are lots of ways in which conservative Christians' beliefs collide with the modern secular worldview. Yet no issue seems more important to those Christians than the conflict between evolution and creationism. We see what appear to be two mutually exclusive positions: atheistic evolution and a uniform commitment to a reading of the book of Genesis that demands a relatively recent, literal, six-day creation from nothing. Why does this matter so much? Gender roles, homosexuality, contraception, education—all have real impact on people's everyday lives, not so for theories of human origins. And yet, somehow, this fight becomes the proxy for the others. One reason is its function in mythmaking and social formation.[1]

Christian Reconstructionists were an important force in the rise of contemporary creationism, and of course I'm not claiming that all creationists are Reconstructionists. But the story of that involvement is an excellent illustration of the subtle ways in which they have impacted contemporary conservative Protestantism and beyond. In 2010 Gallup reported that four in ten Americans believe in "strict" creationism, which Gallup defined as "the view that God created humans as is 10,000 years ago."[2]

Equally important is that seeing the creationist movement through the lens of the work of Reconstructionists helps elucidate what is at stake in the battle. The creationist movement has been extraordinarily successful at convincing conservative Christians that their "young earth" readings of the stories of the creation and the flood are the only possible biblical readings, such that those conservative Christians think that there are two possible views (and only two): evolution for atheists and young earth creationism for Christians. As we shall see, this was not always the case, and while alternative versions of creationism persist, among Reconstructionists young earth creationism is understood as the only biblical version of creationism.

This may seem like a debate about science, but it isn't. It is, as the Reconstructionists argue, a clash of worldviews based on different presuppositions. The conflict seems, on the surface, to be about arguments and evidence, when in reality no argument or newly discovered evidence would change the debate at all. People talk past each other, speaking from such different frameworks (with different assumptions and metaphors) that they may as well be speaking different languages. Their fundamental assumptions—and their goals—are completely at odds.

Creationists have a network of mutually reinforcing institutions that allow their worldview to become a pervasive reality, to construct a social reality that comes to seem self-evidently true. The network of institutions includes schools at every level, books, magazines, newsletters, churches, and conferences. Creationists can take family vacations to Answers in Genesis's now well-known Creation Museum (and planned Ark Park) in Kentucky or other creationist museums such as the one in Arcadia, Florida, that organizes fossil hunting trips and educational cruises. The following will explore how creationism became fully integrated into the conservative Christian world and what cultural purposes it serves.

Outside of creationist circles, the rejection of the theory of evolution is considered absurd. Creationists are dismissed as naïve (at best) or idiotic simpletons, who deny basic scientific principles in defense of a childishly simple version of Christianity. Outside the creationists' world, it seems as bizarre to deny the theory of evolution as it would be to deny the theory of gravity. But from within that world, it all makes perfect sense.

What Is at Stake in Creationism?

The story of creation is as important to conservative Christians as the story of the crucifixion. Naturalistic evolution is nothing less than the denial of the authority and sovereignty of God in favor of the supremacy of human reason. It is an alternative faith; an idolatrous faith. Rushdoony argued that the Bible should be understood as a coherent whole, a singular narrative revealing God's plan for his glorification in history. That the various books contained in the Old and New Testaments were written at different times in different places and by different people is overridden by God's involvement in their production. All scripture is "God breathed." It is inerrant, infallible, and the only source of true knowledge.

In *The Mythology of Science*, first published in 1967, Rushdoony develops a presuppositionalist position on the relationship between evolution and creationism. He begins by asserting that Christianity does not challenge science itself; in fact Rushdoony understands science as an exercise of dominion. But like other disciplines in today's academy, according to Rushdoony, contemporary science in not true science because it is held hostage by its naturalistic, humanistic assumptions. Rushdoony argues that evolution presupposes the supremacy of human reason and the sufficiency of the natural world. In his view it does so to free humans from the authority of God and the requirements of biblical law, so it is inherently atheistic. He argues that it is incoherent because it relies on the order and predictability of creation while at the same time, schizophrenically, asserting randomness and chance.

> The theory of evolution requires a belief that somehow all things arose out of chance . . . Science thus *wants* a universe of law and of causality without God, and it would rather ascribe all the magnificent order of the universe to chaos rather than to God, because the scientists are *fallen* men, men in rebellion against God and bent on suppressing their knowledge of Him. Men will either presuppose God, or they will presuppose themselves as the basic reality of being. If they assume themselves to be autonomous and independent from God, they will then wage war against God at every point.[3]

These themes in Rushdoony's early work are foundational to contemporary creationism. The view that young earth creationism is the only biblical view and that creationism and evolution are mutually exclusive; the view that this reading of creation is totally interrelated with the resurrection and the meaning and purpose of history; the view that those who reject it are in denial and rebellion and that they know the truth but suppress it because the alternative is submission to God—all are common among young earth creationists.

The Rise of Young Earth Creationism

This particular "literal" reading of Genesis developed in the not-so-distant past. It did not predate Darwin, nor was it an immediate response to Darwinism. Even the set of pamphlets that gave the fundamentalist movement its name, *The Fundamentals*, was divided over the issue of Darwinism. The essays included a number of views on evolution or as Ronald Numbers writes in his definitive history of creationism, "the entire spectrum of evangelical opinion . . . as a whole lacked the strident attacks that would soon characterize the fundamentalist movement."[4]

Indeed, *The Fundamentals* were intended to combat what was perceived as a much greater threat to the Bible: higher criticism. The intellectual architects of fundamentalism in the 1920s, and interestingly the Princeton theologians whom Reconstructionists consider their theological forefathers, were divided on the issue. In *Darwin's Forgotten Defenders*, David Livingstone argues that in the decades following the release of Darwin's *Origin of Species* evangelicals actively participated in naturalistic science and exhibited widespread disagreement about evolution on both scientific and theological grounds.[5] But, as Livingstone argues, the real division between Darwin's supporters and those who would become the forebears of his opponents was not, as many have presumed, just a doctrine of scripture. It was philosophical in character and "sprang from Darwin's challenge to the Victorian understanding of the character of the universe and 'man's place in the natural order.'"[6] Princeton theologians, including the architect of contemporary biblical inerrancy, Benjamin Warfield, rejected Darwinism for its perceived atheism but, to a man, they believed that Darwinism and evolution were not synonymous, that evolution did not require atheism, and even that evolution was compatible with biblical inerrancy.[7]

Others in this period who did oppose Darwinism and/or evolution on the grounds that it was incompatible with the Bible did not necessarily believe in a literal six-day recent creation. William Jennings Bryan, who defended a biblical account of creation in the Scopes Monkey Trial, held that the "days" described in Genesis were geological "ages" and that the Bible did not preclude evolution "so long as it did not impinge on the supernatural origin of Adam and Eve."[8] Gap theory, which reconciles claims of scientists that the earth is very old with biblical inerrantists' claims that human history is relatively short (based on the listings of "generations" that appear in the Bible) by positing a gap between the original creation of the earth and the cosmos, and the creation of Adam and Eve, was the most prominent challenge to Darwinism at the time. According to Numbers, gap theory was dominant among conservative Protestants through the middle of the twentieth century. The earliest creationist organizations were beset by divisions and conflict and, according to Numbers, up through the middle of the twentieth century "organized creationism in North America appeared to be all but dead."[9]

The view that the earth is a few thousand years old, was created in a literal six days, and was destroyed by an epic flood that created the fossil record scientists hold as evidence of evolution was promoted initially only by George McCready Price, a Seventh-day Adventist. Adventists, even today, are saddled with the label "cult" by some fundamentalists. They developed out of the controversial millennialist movements of the mid-nineteenth century led by William Miller, who repeatedly set dates for the end of the world, leading to a series of failed prophecies and then a new denomination of Christianity. Adventists draw much of their tradition from the ecstatic visions experienced by Ellen White. They observe a Saturday Sabbath, tend toward holistic health practices, and hold what some consider unorthodox views on the nature of Jesus.

Adventists' defense of the literal six-day creation account is rooted in their particular view of the Sabbath, which is central to their distinct identity within Christianity. But in the 1960s, the publication of *The Genesis Flood,* by John C. Whitcomb and Henry M. Morris, brought this view, once controversial among conservative Christians, from obscurity to hegemony. Numbers attributes the current near-unanimity in support of young earth creationism to the popularity of *The Genesis Flood* in Christian schools and Christian homeschools.[10] In *The Anointed: Evangelical Truth in a Secular Age,* Randall J. Stephens and Karl W. Giberson concur on the significance of Whitcomb and Morris's book. Citing its influence in court cases, on Christian schools, and on the now-vast creationist literature, they write, "It greatly influenced evangelicals, perhaps as much as any text on any topic in the second half of the twentieth century . . . it's hard to imagine any other book with anywhere near its cultural impact."[11] *The Genesis Flood* argued for an interpretation of the flood that, in Whitcomb and Morris's view, explained the fossil record. "Catastrophism" became the dominant view such that today it seems to be the only view. Indeed, when I asked one of the creationist curriculum representatives in the exhibit hall at a Florida homeschool convention whether there were materials at the convention that were based on day-age creationism or gap theory creationism she said there was not because all the exhibiters at the convention "taught creationism from the biblical perspective."

There are three ways in which Rushdoony's influence helped make this version of creationism interchangeable with the Genesis story. He helped ensure publication of *The Genesis Flood*, he integrated young earth creationism into the systematic presuppositional apologetics of Christian Reconstruction, and *The Genesis Flood* was disseminated by virtue of the Christians schools and Christian homeschool movements solidly rooted in his work. Rushdoony was one of the early readers of Whitcomb and Morris's manuscript when it was under contract with Moody Press. Moody withdrew its agreement to publish the book, and Rushdoony helped Whitcomb and Morris secure a contract with his own publisher, Presbyterian and Reformed. *The Genesis Flood* is still in print, is still a standard work on the subject, and is still widely used as a textbook in Christian schools and Christian homeschools across the country. Furthermore, there are untold numbers of public school teachers who have been trained at Christian colleges who see this work as the foundational text for biblical creationism.

It is helpful to think about creationist works in terms of two categories: those that seek to challenge and develop what they claim is scientific evidence and those that seek to develop a philosophical and/or theological argument about the significance of evolution and creation to any given worldview. Stephens and Giberson describe *The Genesis Flood* as "two arguments woven together, a logical double helix, part of which was an assault on a 'compromised' biblical interpretation."[12]

It is exactly this assault that is rooted in Rushdoony's presuppositionalism and that gives the current creationist movement its uncompromising character. The influence of Rushdoony's thinking, especially in terms of presuppositionalism, is even more apparent in Whitcomb and Morris's more apologetic writings, including Morris's 1974 work *Scientific Creationism*.

If the system of flood geology can be established on a sound scientific basis, and be effectively promoted and publicized, then the entire evolutionary cosmology, at least in its present neo-Darwinian form, will collapse. This, in turn, would mean that every anti-Christian system and movement (communism, racism, humanism, libertinism, behaviorism, and all the rest) would be deprived of their pseudo-intellectual foundation.[13]

Also a standard text in Christian schools and homeschools, *Scientific Creationism* was published in two versions: one intended for Christian schools and the other, said to be devoid of the theological material, for public schools. But even in the 1970s Morris was clear that the key to the promotion of creationism was the Christian school movement:

Real understanding of man and his world can only be acquired through a thoroughgoing creationist frame of reference. True education in every field should be structured around creationism, not evolutionism. Most Christian schools are, therefore, committed to Biblical creationism as a basic premise in their philosophy of education.[14]

The Conference Circuit

I spent a weekend in the middle of October 2009 at a conference sponsored by the Institute for Creation Research (ICR) called "Demand the Evidence." ICR was founded in 1970 in San Diego, California, by Henry Morris, coauthor of *The Genesis Flood*. Today ICR is run by Morris's sons Henry Morris III and John Morris and is perhaps best known for its graduate school, which teaches creationists and credentials them with doctoral degrees.

John Morris was one of the main speakers at the conference I attended. One of the organization's staff members told me that there were several "teams" doing these conferences around the country and that there were some thirty-seven scheduled between then and the end of November. This conference was held at First Baptist Church in Jacksonville, Florida, one of the largest Southern Baptist churches and home to former president of the Southern Baptist Convention (and the congregation's former senior pastor) Jerry Vines. This church is at the physical center of downtown Jacksonville, taking up several city blocks and housing schools of every level, missions buildings, administrative buildings, parking garages, and, of course, a main sanctuary.

The church is at the center of the city metaphorically speaking as well. It is widely recognized as the seat of local political power: political leaders, media elites, and corporate officers attend. Many Jacksonville residents attribute the struggles to revitalize downtown to the ability of the church to limit nightlife options. When the Jacksonville City Council voted, in 2013, to exclude LGBT citizens from the city's Human Rights Ordinance, First Baptist invited those members of the council who fought inclusion to stand and be recognized during the service.[15] The city council members stood and were introduced one by one with their families as the congregation applauded in appreciation.

So as I drove on campus and parked in one of the church garages, I did not have the sense that I was about to enter a world of marginalized people; quite the opposite really. The garage was filled with SUVs and relatively new cars, pointing to the general middle-class status of those in attendance. The conference attendees were almost uniformly white and varied widely in age. There were about three hundred people present, about half of whom indicated, when a speaker asked for a show of hands, that they were from the Jacksonville area, with most of the rest coming from various parts of the Southeast.

In this world, the earth is only a few thousand years old; Adam and Eve are literal people from whom we all descended; God created all of it in six twenty-four-hour days; and the scientific evidence from geology, biology, physiology, genetics, and every other branch of science proves this to be true. In this world it seems entirely plausible that the vast majority of those in the scientific community are covering up evidence that is contrary to their theory because it undermines their more fundamental commitment to a science without God and that there are many more legitimate scientists whose careers are derailed because they depart from evolutionary orthodoxy.

These people were not simpletons. While many middle-class Americans were shopping, doing yard work, or watching college football, these folks were settling in on Saturday morning for a full day of intense instruction in history, philosophy, biblical interpretation, molecular biology, physiology, human reproduction, and genetics. And if the lines at the cashiers can be taken as an indication, many were buying books and DVDs to continue their study when they returned home.

The strategy at the conference is not unlike what I saw in numerous other contexts. At Demand the Evidence a series of speakers created a framework that supports a worldview in which evolution seems absurd; the components of that framework appear again and again in the literature and at these events. One might think that the purpose of the conference was the presentation of evidence in favor of young earth creationism over against evolution. But one would be wrong. There were no skeptics there weighing evidence. The conference goers were already convinced of the "truth" of creationism and that young earth creationism is the only biblically legitimate interpretation of the Genesis account of creation.

Instead, the conference served as an exercise in social formation; the building of a community though myth and ritual. The "myth" at issue is more than the creation narrative itself. In retelling the Genesis story, describing the fight to defend it, identifying the enemies of God, and ridiculing them as sinister and ungodly, the storytellers mark the boundaries of who is inside the group and who is not. The "myth" in question is the story of an embattled but faithful remnant, holding fast to God's truth in the face of persecution. The ritual is the public enactment of the identity through storytelling.

The Stakes Are High

For creationists, the battle against evolution is an all-encompassing one. This is a dualistic world in which they are the faithful remnant, maintaining faithfulness over against the enemies of God. This means that being in opposition to "the world" is, to them, itself proof of the validity of their claims. Moreover, criticism and even ridicule from "the world" becomes further evidence confirming their position. This temperament is part and parcel of much of American religion, and varieties of it are present today in marginal religious groups as well as those with significant power and influence. This "oppositional identity" is part of conservative Christians' sense of who they are. To be authentically Christian, for them, means to be in tension with the surrounding culture in some significant sense. When tension does not exist in socioeconomic terms, it can be manufactured in ideological terms. In all these discussions of creationism, a basic form of presuppositionalism is assumed. There are those who begin with what they take to be the authority and sovereignty of the God of the Bible, and there are those who reject this as a basis of knowledge and rely on human reason, naturalism, and ultimately atheism. As one conference speaker said, "Does man decide what God meant, or does God dictate what you'll believe?" Or as another put it, "Who is the boss here? That is what is really at stake."[16]

Morris explained it to the Demand the Evidence audience: "[There are] only two faith answers: we're all a result of inanimate energy or created by an omnipotent and omniscient being. You can't prove either one. Genesis refutes atheism, polytheism, materialism, dualism, humanism; it refutes everything that is out there." He concluded, "'They' are in denial about both creation and God, and often they reject creation *because* they are atheist, and it allows them to escape God." For creationists, the battle between creationism and evolution is nothing less than a battle between theism and atheism.

Joanne at the Florida Parent Educators Association meeting explained to me that if Genesis is not taken literally, then all of Christianity crumbles because without the Fall there is no need for redemption, thus there is no Jesus.[17] The whole of the Bible is understood to be one coherent, consistent narrative. As Morris explained:

> The big version of the Gospel, the "everlasting Gospel," references back to the Creator . . . It's the clear teaching of scripture: the Gospel messages entwined with who Christ is, part of what makes the Good News good. Jesus as Creator. [If there is no] creationism [there is] no Jesus; no creationism, no kingdom; no creationism, no Gospel. The Gospel isn't merely a central piece, it's the beginning as well as the end and everything in between . . . It's woven throughout, God is identified as Creator.

So, for example, despite their claims that creationism is "science," creationists' studies of evolution are typically considered, by creationists themselves, as part of apologetics or the philosophical defense of faith. ICR graduate school is actually a school of apologetics.[18] Morris explained at the conference that his motivation in promoting creationism is evangelism and many of the creationist conference speakers include in their talks rather typical conversion narratives explaining how they came to see the truth about creationism despite their evolutionary training. These narratives serve to explain the change of heart regarding evolution (I once was blind but now I see) and also to erect a social boundary between the insiders and the outsiders. They then build community among the insiders by making them feel as though they are part of something important.

One of the conference speakers, Gary Parker, shared just such a story: "God opened my eyes. When I came to know Jesus my IQ didn't jump twenty points, my friends thought it dropped two hundred points. I just saw what was there." The congregation applauded enthusiastically, and the woman sitting next to me nodded so empathically she caused the church pew we shared to rock.

You Don't Need to Pay Attention to the So-Called Authorities

The creationist narrative includes widespread ridicule of scholarly knowledge in favor of "common sense," laying the groundwork for the epistemological basis of the whole message: your understanding of this material is adequate to evaluate the validity of science. It is rooted in broad-based American populism and more specifically the Protestant notion of the priesthood of all believers. The apologetic dimension of the fight against evolution is the sacred responsibility of all believers; the responsibilities of the priesthood require that the necessary knowledge be accessible to all. Or, as a conference speaker said, "You can assess this for yourself, and you have a Christian duty to educate yourself." Another conference speaker said, "Don't let someone tell you the Bible needs special expertise; this violates the first commandment by getting between you and God." But more derisive examples had the added benefit of ritually delegitimizing opponents, including "you don't have to get a PhD to be that dumb" and "[it's a] good thing God's Word is eternally protected: can you imagine if God wrote his Word and then relied on scholars to protect it?"

Ironically, this strategy also depends on a heavy emphasis on the claimed academic credentials and accomplishments of the creationist speakers. Every one at the Demand the Evidence conference sported the title Dr. before his name and in each case there was an effort to foster the implication that the speakers were scientists with doctoral-level credentials, when in fact for the most part their advanced degrees are in other fields, mostly ministry, apologetics, and education. Promotional materials indicated, for example, that Gary Parker has been at ICR for thirty years and that he is a "former evolutionary biologist" with undergraduate and graduate degrees in biology, chemistry, and education, but the materials do not indicate which degrees are in which subjects. He represents himself as a scientist and repeatedly makes reference to his "time as a college professor," implying that he taught science. It turns out, though, that his doctoral degree is in education, and he is a science educator of sorts (though by the standards of science education this would be inaccurate as well). He teaches Christian high school teachers to teach creationism. Speaker Randy Guiluzza began his talk by explaining that he had "tried to work for ICR for years" before he was hired. Duane Gish (a well-known creationist debater) told him he "needed more degrees," though he had degrees in public health from Harvard and in medicine from the Air Force. Guiluzza is a rather impressive MD, but he's still not a research scientist working on issues related to evolutionary biology or genetics, despite the fact that he cultivates that misperception. The other two speakers' doctoral degrees are ministerial seminary degrees, though they make it difficult to know that they hold doctorates in ministry rather than in scientific fields. They go to great lengths to cultivate the impression that they are scientists by using the title and saying they have degrees from particular schools, without being clear about what those degrees are and which ones come from which schools. Deceptive? Undoubtedly. But also, perhaps, puzzling, given the emphatic claims about the worthlessness of academic credentials. The controversial graduate program at ICR is actually a program in science education for Christian teachers. According to Morris's description at the conference, they offer a "Creationist Science Worldview" online professional diploma program that includes some thirty-three courses "in apologetics [and] life sciences fulfill[ing] the Dominion mandate . . . in education, politics, law and all of our culture."

Because Our Experts Are Just as Good: Parker and Guiluzza

Though the conference was called "Demand the Evidence," the presentations were not about demanding any evidence from evolutionists but rather practicing the story of who "we" are—constructing, embodying, and enacting that identity. Gary Parker's presentation had two foci. In opposition to secular-atheistic evolution, he argued that the order in the universe could not have developed by chance. In opposition to those who try to combine evolution and theism, he argued that the requirements of evolution are incompatible with the character of God.

Parker suggested that accepting evolution by chance is like saying "Wow, that's a great book; where can I buy some of that ink." Of course, this isn't an argument, it is a group-building, boundary-marking exercise. The audience laughed with him at this idea that the complexity of life makes it patently absurd to think that life could exist without an intelligent creator. It is an idea they have embraced long before they arrived at the conference. His PowerPoint presentation belabored this point by suggesting other examples, such as a tornado passing through a junkyard resulting in an airplane. The audience laughed at each, and the result is that evolution looks preposterous while creationism looks like sophisticated science.

Parker continued with a discussion of genetics, using models of DNA, proteins, and amino acids. It was all very complex, with lots of scientific language that is impossible to unpack without some background in science, which many laypeople do not have. The whole presentation can be very convincing and certainly assures attendees that "our team has scientists too." The other part of his presentation was actually a critique of theistic evolution, a category into which these young earth creationists lump every other version of creationism, thus developing a taxonomy designed to delegitimize them. He referred to his teaching days and said that he used to have students who "tried to believe evolution and creation." He said, "I thought, 'Now I've got them. Who would want to believe in a god like that?'" Parker characterized evolution as being in opposition to God's basic character: "millions and millions of years of struggle and death" as opposed to "a world made correctly from the beginning . . . How could a God of love and power allow so much struggle and death to occur? Evolution is dead things, dead things, dead things, everywhere in its path."

Later in the day Randy Guiluzza, a medical doctor, gave the most scientifically sophisticated presentation, though it was still interwoven with theology, apologetics, and even worship. The various themes I have outlined were all present in his talk. His "hypothesis," he said, was that in the "complexity of the human body, design is clearly seen; such that 'they' [those who claim not to see it] are without excuse." After citing Psalm 139, he continued, "If you don't see design it's because the scientists are not doing their job. Worship is the normal, proper response to science." Guiluzza characterized popular science documentaries like those presented by NOVA, National Geographic, and the Discovery Channel as, at the same time, elitist and watered-down science: "In trying to persuade everyone that evolution is true, they make everything sound simple to make it believable . . . Nothing in biology is simple. Simplicity is the hallmark of evolutionary thought. Complexity is the mark of biological reality." While other speakers claimed that anyone can evaluate the claims of science, Guiluzza's goal seemed to present material so detailed as to overwhelm anyone's ability to evaluate it. His point, though, was that the components of the human body are so sophisticated that they could not have evolved one at a time, that there are dimensions to physiology that illus-trate "irreducible complexity." Evolutionists have to ignore this fact be-cause it is contrary evidence to which they can't answer. But the presentation was so complex that it was overwhelming. It demonstrated that he is familiar with a lot of science, which perhaps he intends as an argument that his view of creation is reliable against evolutionists who, he says, try to make their explanations so simple they are inadequate. The changes "just appear" over time, he says sarcastically. According to Guiluzza, this explanation is no explanation at all. The simplicity of the evolutionary explanations, as they are presented by Guiluzza, seem ridic-ulous, and the audience laughed.

Persecution and Conspiracies

The fact that an overwhelming numbers of scientists affirm the evolution-ary model is explained in terms of the "narrowness of the path of righ-teousness." The Bible promises that believers will be persecuted for their faith. Creationists charge evolutionists with the intentional misrepresen-tation of evidence, hiding evidence contrary to their theory, and perpetrat-ing a conspiracy to shut creationists out of academia. While this trope was invoked at the Demand the Evidence conference, it was much more explic-itly in play at the American Vision Worldview Conference in Powder Springs, Georgia, in the summer of 2009. There I met author and lec-turer Jerry Bergman. Bergman made a name for himself in apologetics as an outspoken opponent of Jehovah's Witnesses and now participates in debates over the teaching of creationism. Bergman writes for Answers in Genesis's "research magazine" and the AiG website indicates that he is a psychologist.

> Jerry Bergman has taught biology, genetics, chemistry, biochemis-try, anthropology, geology, and microbiology at Northwest State College in Archibald, Ohio for over 17 years. Now completing his 9th degree, Dr. Bergman is a graduate of Medical College of Ohio, Wayne State University in Detroit, The University of Toledo, and Bowling Green State University. He has over 600 publications in 12 languages and 20 books and monographs.[19]

His talk at the Worldview Conference was entitled "Killing Careers of Cre-ationists." He is the author of *Slaughter of the Dissidents: The Shocking*

Truth About Killing the Careers of Darwin Doubters.[20] His lecture and book outline a vast conspiracy against academics who are creationists, charging that they are regularly fired or not promoted on the basis of nothing more than religious discrimination. He began his talk with a lengthy recitation of a series of difficulties he had endured that he believes "derived" from his "coming out of the closet" as a creationist. "My advice to you," he said, as though he were talking to an audience of academic creationists: "stay in the closet until you get tenure." Yet he holds out hope that "truth" will prevail.

> Atheists push evolution because it's the key to atheism. So you can see when you send your kids to college or grad school what world-view they're going to get. The goal seems to be to get students to drop Christianity and become atheists. Both evolutionism and creationism are theories of creation. Truth will come out. Darwinists will prove themselves wrong. [But for now] we're locked out of science; [we] can get degrees [but] can't get jobs, can't get grants . . . We would just get there sooner if we weren't locked out of science.[21]

Bergman indicated he was working on his ninth graduate degree and gives the impression that he is a university professor. Because the fluid invoking of academic credentials (while deriding their value) is common in the creationist world, it seemed worthwhile, in terms of evaluating his claim to be a creationist scientist who has been discriminated against for his religious views, to look at what credentials he has. Bergman earned a PhD from Wayne State University. He claims the degree is in measurement and evaluation, which, according to Wayne State University's website, is an education degree in leadership.[22] He claims, also, a PhD in human biology from Columbia Pacific University in San Rafael, California, which was an unaccredited distance-learning institution that was closed by the state of California in 1997. This institution's articulation of its "vision of integration, health and lifelong learning [was] consumer centered, providing an opportunity to pursue interdisciplinary studies without soul-crushing politics" in no way indicates that it includes a top-notch science program. While, according to Columbia Pacific University, its closure was unfair—based on mistakes and possibly fraud—it is clear that Bergman's doctoral training is not as a research scientist at a mainstream institution.[23] Furthermore, the publications he lists are not peer reviewed, are published via obscure presses, and include magazine articles on creationism and numerous textbooks, none of which contain original research. In a highly competitive academic job market, it is just as likely that his lack of formal science credentials and his academic training in other areas at marginal or questionable institutions are better explanations for his career path than systematic discrimination because of his religious views. (If he had sought a position in an education program, the field in which he is credentialed, he may well have succeeded.)

But Bergman's lecture at the Worldview Conference, and his book that was on sale in the exhibit room, created the perception that this brilliant scientist (he lists MENSA membership in his bio) with numerous degrees and multiple PhDs has been frozen out of academia because liberal, atheist academics are desperate to preserve the illusion that science supports evolutionary theory. In this narrative, those atheists are stalling the inevitable crumbling of evolution because it is the only way for them to maintain autonomy from the demands of God's law.

Christian Reconstructionism and the Creationist Movement

It is not my point here that Rushdoony, specifically, or the Reconstructionists, in general, are responsible for the contemporary creationist movement, only that Rushdoony and his work helped shape what became the dominant view. He joined early—supported the work of flood geology, participated in developing the philosophical underpinnings and drawing out the philosophical implications of creationism, and led the fight for Christian schooling and homeschooling that have made this, young earth creationism, the dominant reading of Genesis among conservative Christians. Reconstructionist influence is evident in the way in which six-day young earth creationism is woven so tightly into the worldview of these conservative Christians. The breadth of the contemporary movement has been aided extensively by Reconstructionist work in homeschooling and Christian schooling and by the promotional work of groups that explicitly embrace the Reconstructionist influence, such as Vision Forum and American Vision.

The Creation Model in the Catastrophic Flood

Lunchtime at Demand the Evidence was as informative as the presentations themselves. I walked into the crowded lunchroom and spotted a half-empty table. The older couple and the young man sitting there didn't seem to know each other so I asked if I could join them. As is my practice in such situations, I do not make a point of explaining who I am and why I am there (any more than other attendees do), but I do not hide it either. These are public events with no admission criteria; I pay the registration fee and register under my own name.[24] I introduce myself and when asked what I do, I explain that I teach about religion and always answer questions honestly, including in this case explaining that I teach about "all religions."

I learned that the young man sitting next to me was a high school student hoping to apply to West Point. The couple, Stan and Sue, were from south-central Florida and had come to First Baptist often for pastors' conferences.[25] While neither was a pastor, Stan had worked in prisons and found the conferences helpful. They exemplified the way I have described this world as insular and self-reaffirming. They made many assumptions about me, by virtue of the fact that I was a seemingly sane person at their conference. Sue spoke to me like an insider, explaining how bothered she was, when Stan worked in prisons, by the fact that those prisons had to order different food for "Muslims and kosher Jews." They both communicated that they felt concerned about "not being allowed to witness and speak the truth" at the state prison. Sam wondered aloud if it was hard to be in my job. When I asked what he meant, he responded, still assuming that I was a fellow-believer, "At a public school, you can't witness, can you?" I answered, "That's not really what I do," and I was rescued from continuing the discussion when another young man joined us and explained that he was on the ICR staff. John was a special events coordinator, and, in the course of conversation, I learned that he was a former gang member who spent five years in prison for attempted murder.

As the conversation continued, I shared that I was at the conference doing research for a book. My standard short explanation of the book project was that it's a book on the "legacy of a theologian named Rushdoony." At the lunch table, John chimed in after recognizing Rushdoony's name. He mentioned his "friend Doug Phillips" (of Vision Forum) who "talks about Rushdoony," then ran through the names of several of the groups in the network, including the National Center for Family Integrated Churches (NCFIC), a Reconstructionist-oriented network of churches founded by Phillips and Scott Brown.

According to John, Phillips used to do conferences with ICR, and Phillips and Morris are friends. In fact, Phillips and Morris had just returned from a trip to the Galapagos to make a DVD that ICR and Vision Forum were in talks to do joint conferences to promote. This is a great example of cross-fertilization between these groups. It's also an excellent example of the way in which Reconstructionists like Phillips and his organization Vision Forum are at the forefront of developments in the broader conservative Christian world. In the fall of 2009, Vision Forum released *The Mysterious Islands*, a documentary filmed in the Galapagos Islands to debunk the conclusions Darwin drew from his research there. Phillips and his adventurers (including his sixteen-year-old son Joshua and John Morris of ICR) retraced Darwin's steps and came to "different conclusions." By early 2010, Vision Forum was organizing screenings of the film on the 40th anniversary of Earth Day, "an event that is," according to Vision Forum, "characterized by a host of wrong worldview perspectives on the cosmos, including the idea that man is an unwelcome interloper, rather than the pinnacle of God's creation, and that the creation itself should be worshipped and elevated above the Creator."[26] This film led to the launch of the Mysterious Islands Campaign, a presuppositionalist effort to frame environmentalism as an anti-Christian pantheistic religion that is profoundly dangerous to human life. This effort has a distinctly Reconstructionist tone:

> Without a proper understanding of the biblical doctrine of creation, man, the animal kingdom, dominion and sovereignty, our children may well fall prey to the vision-destroying false worship and spirit of the age—environmental pantheism. Environmental pantheism is a direct attack on the biblical family because it devalues human life and seeks to obliterate the mandate that men through their families take dominion over the earth. Most importantly, it substitutes the worship of the creature, for the worship of the Creator.[27]

In a parallel development, a twelve-part DVD series was released by the Cornwall Alliance for the Stewardship of Creation, which also characterizes environmentalism as an alternative (and dangerous—even deadly) religion that has captured our youth and permeated our culture. The Cornwall Alliance Board of Advisors includes Christian Right activists, some with Reconstructionist and/or dominionist ties (such as David Barton and George Grant) and other more mainstream evangelicals. The series blends criticism of global environmental efforts with an affinity for conspiracy theories. Most of the media focused on the ominous tone and the over-the-top claims presented in the series; many wondered if it was a parody. Far from it. By early 2012, the view that environmentalism is an alternative religion made its way from the narrow world we have been discussing into the Republican presidential primary. Then-candidate Rick Santorum, a Catholic with deep ties to the homeschool movement shaped so profoundly by Reconstruction-ism, claimed that President Obama was promoting a "phony theology." Initially it seemed he might have been returning to conspiracy theories that insist the president is a Muslim; then it seemed he might have been referring to Glenn Beck's assertions a year earlier that "progres-sives" embrace unbiblical "liberation theology." Other observers argued that the subtext was a racialized suggestion that the president is "not one of us."

In an effort to explain, Santorum insisted he was not questioning the president's religion but was referring to the president's commitment to environmentalism. To many, this distinction seemed incoherent. What could it mean to question the president's theology but not his religion? But for those familiar with presuppositionalism, widely held in the Chris-tian homeschool movement for which Santorum is an important advo-cate, it is clear what he meant. The rejection of the creation account is thought to lead to a distorted understanding of the relationship of humans to creation. Santorum elaborated that he was referring to "this idea that man is here to serve the Earth, as opposed to husband its resources and be good stewards of the Earth . . . man should be in charge of the Earth and have dominion over it." Moreover, Santorum connected this religious cri-tique of environmentalism with the view that environmentalism is no more than an opportunity for civil government to overstep its biblically appropriate jurisdiction, thereby claiming ultimate authority and leading people to look to the state for salvation.

Rushdoony called this the messianic state. In a quote that could have easily come from Rushdoony, or Gary North, Santorum said, "When you have a worldview that elevates the Earth above man and says that we can't take those resources because we're going to harm the Earth . . . this is all an attempt to, you know, to centralize power and to give more power to the government." While these views are by no means limited to Christian Reconstructionists, Reconstructionists are important in the development and dissemination of them.

In his 1967 work *The Mythology of Science*, Rushdoony characterized biblical Christianity and environmentalism as "two rival faiths." In the earliest years of the Reconstructionist movement, this critique was the basis for the opposition to population control (in 1975 Rushdoony wrote *The Myth of Overpopulation*). By 2000, in his *Systematic Theology*, Rushdoony was concerned that environmentalists were transforming the relationship between "man" and creation from the biblical emphasis on dominion to an antagonistic relationship in which "man" is understood as a destroyer. Santorum is no secret Reconstructionist.[28] That this framing made its way from the small world of Rushdoony to the Christian homeschool movement and then to the campaign for the presidency is an example of the degree to which Reconstructionists have been successful at shaping the discourse of the conservative Christian subculture in the half-century since Rushdoony began writing.

Conclusion

The influence of Reconstructionists in the contemporary creationist movement was evident from its inception. Rushdoony was an early proponent of young earth creationism. He developed a philosophical-theological system in which creationism is both plausible and necessary to the larger tradition, and then it played a key role in the growth of the institutions that helped disseminate it. The newer generation, including Doug Phillips, John Morris, Henry Morris III, and other leaders of Christian Reconstruction, continue to play a central role in the creationist movement. Creationism is a powerful mythic narrative about human origins, a narrative that creates profound meaning, order, and purpose in the conservative Christian worldview. The plausibility of creationism is maintained by a careful strategy that both promotes the legitimacy of creation and undermines the plausibility of evolution. Creationists explain away opposition from evolutionists by claiming that the truth of creationism is "obvious" and that evolutionists deny it not because it is bad science but because it is atheism's bulwark against God and his authority. They do this through a mutually reinforcing set of institutions that allow believers to divide the world into "us" and "them," rarely engaging with opponents they must take seriously. This all-inclusive worldview is, in many ways, the result of the influence of Reconstructionism and the legacy of Rushdoony.

Moreover, the contemporary battle to "protect" creationism becomes a site for ritual enactment of community and social formation through narrative. It inculcates believers with a connection to a group and a sense of identity, telling them they are at the center of an important conflict, a conflict in which defeat is both intolerable and impossible. The willingness to look absurd and to defy the outside world becomes a badge of membership and of honor. Participation in the persecution narrative becomes a ritual way of demonstrating loyalty to God, which is, as Durkheim argued, loyalty to the group.

7

Building a Family Dynasty: Doug Phillips and Vision Forum

We're part of the story of the unfolding Gospel! . . . Our quest this week is dedicated to this mission: remember the past so we can stand in the present and move forward to the next generation.

—DOUG PHILLIPS at the opening session of Reformation 500

AN IMPORTANT CONTEMPORARY expression of Christian Reconstruction, Vision Forum sought to reshape all of culture in terms of the biblical worldview developed by Rushdoony half a century ago. The core of Vision Forum's strategy was to promote biblical patriarchy as the model for families, especially within the homeschool world but also in the family integrated church movement and a Christian film industry. Powerfully framing homeschooling as part of a grand view of history, family legacy, multigenerational faithfulness, and vision, the organization's influence extended far into the homeschool movement, bringing a version of the dominion mandate to many who never heard of Rushdoony or who would reject it if it were more explicitly framed in Reconstructionist terms.

My first in-person encounter with Vision Forum came at the Florida Parent Educators Conference in Orlando, Florida, in May 2009. Founder Doug Phillips was one of the speakers at the conference, and Vision Forum had a large booth in the exhibit hall. Phillips made his way around the conference with an entourage that included his wife, some of his children, staffers, and several attendees who seemed star struck. Within five years of this convention, where Phillips and his family moved about as homeschooling royalty, Phillips would resign amid a scandal that rocked the homeschool world. Vision Forum would crumble, its resources sold off in a "fire sale," and a lawsuit would be filed against Phillips, Vision Forum Inc., and Vision Forum Ministries.[1]

Vision Forum materials were widely promoted and distributed through conferences, its websites, and its catalog. Vision Forum Ministries reported $2,253,905 in gross receipts for 2012 and $3,392,988 for 2011.[2] All of the materials were geared toward building families that exemplified a very specific structure, character, and purpose—families with a role to play in the unfolding of God's plan. "Faith and Freedom Tours" were especially important, but for those who could not afford these expensive trips, books and DVDs (lectures, documentaries, and feature films) sent the same message. Classic works such as *Pilgrim's Progress* and the "providential history" series *The Hand of God in History* encouraged the type of visionary history promoted by the organization. The movement's commitments to free enterprise and autonomous, patriarchal families came together in books and DVDs that encouraged and promoted entrepreneurship. Providing an alternative to what is seen as our "shortsighted, hyper-individualist" culture, *The Entrepreneurial Bootcamp for Christian Families* sought to foster "freedom in Christ and multigenerational faithfulness, communicating hope by offering practical teaching that explored various business models in light of God's Word."[3] Numerous products promoted "family vision" by focusing on parenting, marriage, family worship and devotions, and worldview training. All of this material was profoundly patriarchal. Children's literature promoted heroism, chivalry, adventure, and evangelism for boys and true beauty and femininity (defined as submissiveness and dependency) for girls. There was a homeschool curriculum that included Noah Webster's *Dictionary* and *Blueback Speller* (widely used in the Christian school and homeschool worlds), and Vision Forum's own "prelaw" course for homeschoolers. Creationist materials included "science and technology kits," ant farms, and earthworm nurseries. You could also buy iPods preloaded with Vision Forum MP3s, including a "family creation adventure radio drama" called *Jonathan Park*, and you could buy a replica of the young hero's communicator watch.

San Antonio–based Vision Forum Inc. and the nonprofit charity Vision Forum Ministries were founded by Doug Phillips. The tax-exempt organization "minister[ed] to Christian families by emphasizing apologetics, worldview training, home education, multi-generational faithfulness, bold manhood, and creative solutions whereby fathers can play a maximum role in family discipleship."[4] Every element of its vision derived from a Christian Reconstructionist worldview. In fact, taken as a whole, Vision

Forum, its affiliated ministries, and the Phillips family give us a window into how a reconstructed culture might look. Phillips, according to his late father, Reconstructionist and Constitution Party founder Howard Phillips, was "raised on Rushdoony." Chris Ortiz of Rushdoony's Chalcedon Foundation has written:

> For a good many years, the Chalcedon Foundation, and the Rushdoony family, have enjoyed a mutually edifying friendship with Doug, his personal family, his father [Howard], and many of the fine staff at Vision Forum. Doug Phillips was a featured speaker in 2005 at our 40th anniversary conference and is a vocal endorser of the ministry of R. J. Rushdoony.[5]

When the elder Phillips passed away in 2013, the Chalcedon blog was one of the first venues in which his passing was announced. In Chalcedon's "remembrance" of him, Phillips is described as a "longtime colleague, supporter and personal friend of Rushdoony." Phillips contributed to a collection of essays published in honor of Rushdoony and joined in a podcast series named "Remembering Rush." Doug Phillips attended Reconstructionist Fairfax Christian School, worked for six years as an attorney at the Home School Legal Defense Association, and taught adjunct courses for Henry Morris's Institute for Creation Research. In short, Vision Forum was a thoroughly Reconstructionist organization.

In the summer of 2007, I spoke with the elder Phillips. He described meeting Rushdoony in the 1970s and hearing what he thought was the best critique of "socialized medicine . . . entirely based on the Bible." He attributed his conversion, in part, to Rushdoony, and spent much time with him in the subsequent years. It's hard to overstate Phillips's influence in the transformation of the more secular midcentury conservatism of Barry Goldwater and William F. Buckley into today's religiously inflected conservatism. In the 1980s Phillips played an important role in the Reagan revolution as president of the Conservative Caucus, founding member of the Council on National Policy, and a senior editor at the *Conservative Digest*. By the 1990s, finding the Republican Party's shift to the right inadequate, Phillips turned his efforts toward building a viable third party, founding the U.S. Taxpayers Alliance, then the United States Taxpayers Party, later renamed the Constitution Party. The Constitution Party's goal is to "reestablish" biblical law as the foundation for American society. In the interview, the elder Phillips excitedly told me about Doug, his family, and the work he was doing. Doug's family includes his wife Beall and their children Joshua, Justice, Liberty, Jubilee, Faith, Honor, Providence, and Virginia. Howard Phillips was especially enthusiastic about the successful family conference Vision Forum had recently held in Jamestown and the annual Christian Film Festival, with filmmaking seminars for homeschoolers, they had hosted in San Antonio.[6]

Family Legacy and Providential History

In his convention speech before the Florida Parent Educators, Phillips rarely used the word "dominion," but this is exactly what he was describing. He encouraged families to develop a "200-year plan" to foster multi-generational faithfulness. He taught homeschoolers to see themselves as part of an ancient legacy beginning with Adam and Eve and their descendants in the Old Testament, through the incarnation of Christ and the revelation of the New Testament, and up through the Reformation to the present day. Their day-to-day activities at homeschool are transformed from mundane tasks to small acts of profoundly meaningful obedience and faithfulness to God by virtue of Phillips's ability to situate them in the context of God's plan for eternity. Phillips imbued homeschooling families' every moment with meaning and purpose rooted in God's vision; vision revealed in history. This sense of history was the linchpin of Phillips's influence, and it came directly from Rushdoony.

Perhaps few listening to the lecture recognized this influence, but had members of the audience made their way to the Vision Forum exhibit booth they might have been told (as I was) that it comes from Rushdoony's *The Biblical Philosophy of History.* In his 1979 work, Rushdoony presents a unified theory of history, bringing together creationism, infallibility of scripture, and presuppositionalism. Humanist history, he claims, requires naturalistic explanations: "the humanist faces a meaningless world in which he must strive to create and establish meaning." The Christian, according to Rushdoony, understands history as the unfolding of God's plan. "The Christian accepts a world which is totally meaningful and in which *every* event moves in terms of God's predestined purpose."[7] Creation is not something that happened in another time. Creation and history are only artificially distinguished. The transcendent force present in creation remains present and active in history, uniting both in the revelation of God's plan. Time and history are "the arena of man's dominion."[8] Rushdoony compares this biblical view of history with

agnostic and atheistic historiography [that] begins with a fundamental act of faith, the faith that God has nothing to do with history.
This assumption has nothing to do with science or history: it is a
pre-theoretical axiom with which all factuality is approached . . . By
this act of faith, history is declared to be man's area of operation exclusive of any divine determination or operation.[9]

Phillips shared Rushdoony's appreciation for the work of Southern
Presbyterian theologian Robert L. Dabney. In 1997 Phillips's Vision
Forum published *Robert Lewis Dabney: The Prophet Speaks,* a collection of
apparent quotations from Dabney's work edited by Doug Phillips.[10] Phillips extols Dabney's "prophetic" voice on the evils of contemporary society,
from public education ("the ultimate problem with government schools
would be that they exist") to women's equality. Phillips writes, in characteristic dramatic style, "Once or twice in every generation a prophet
emerges who challenges with devastating accuracy the reigning cultural
paradigm . . . He boldly states what many know to be true but few are willing to say." Phillips shows Dabney praising home education and calls him
"refreshingly virile" in his antifeminism. "One must not forget," he
writes, "that Dabney wrote in the last great period of American history in
which men were proud to be men, and to call someone a 'patriarch' was to
pay him a compliment."[11] The book introduces a sanitized Dabney to a
homeschool audience, on issues with which they will agree. Phillips hints
at Dabney's strong defense of the South but includes no quotes or references to it, to slavery, or to Dabney's deeply problematic views on race.

History, like every other aspect of culture, becomes a conflict between
two diametrically opposing worldviews, based on mutually exclusive presuppositions, one or the other embraced by faith. But it also becomes, for
the Christian, meaningful in every detail. Thirty-five years after Rushdoony wrote *The Biblical Philosophy of History* its vision informed Doug
Phillips's ministry to homeschoolers. Homeschoolers came to imbue
their educational choices with a sense of purpose and calling, even when
they are unaware of Rushdoony.[12]

Much of the work of Vision Forum was in service to this goal of transforming the way Christians understand history and their place in it. "Faith
and Freedom Tours" were some of their most elaborate efforts, all exhibiting Phillips's characteristic heady sense of drama and destiny. In July of
2009, they hosted a gathering called Reformation 500. Co-sponsors included a who's who of Reconstructionist and Reconstructionist-influenced

organizations: Chalcedon Foundation, Tolle Lege Press, Coral Ridge Ministries, the Center for Family Integrated Churches, Answers in Genesis, the Mayflower Institute, the Foundation for American Christian Education, Generations with Vision, and Samaritan Ministries, among others.[13] The attendees were almost all homeschooling families. Vision Forum was "graduating" its interns, all of whom were male homeschool graduates. There was lots of talk about "College Plus," a program homeschoolers use to get through college without having to attend: taking advanced-placement exams to minimize the amount of time needed to get a college degree and fulfilling most of the remainder of the requirements online and/or with sympathetic colleges. This is a subset of the larger homeschool movement, but it was the part of that movement most explicitly influenced by Rushdoony and the Christian Reconstructionist movement. Reformation 500 gave me an opportunity to document the ways in which that influence developed.[14]

Reformation 500 occurred over four days and included lectures, tours of the Boston area, a children's parade, historical reenactments, and even a "debate" between actors playing Charles Darwin and John Calvin. Vision Forum employees and volunteers were dressed as historical figures in an effort to "make history come alive" for the children in attendance. Children were encouraged to meet the historical characters, listen to information about each, and get their signatures in autograph books they carried around. Children who obtained signatures from all the "Reformers" won specially minted "coins of remembrance."

The opening ceremony was packed with families. Thousands of homeschoolers had descended on the city to celebrate the Reformation (in its Calvinist incarnation) and its influence on American history, and to renew and strengthen their sense of themselves and the place of their families in the unfolding of God's plan. A significant number of attendees—adults and children alike—were in costume, dressed as Colonial patriots, frontiersmen, Native Americans, and European Reformers. Tricorn hats were quite popular. Joe Morecraft, pastor of a Reconstructionist Atlanta church, gave the opening prayer. Then Phillips gave a welcome lecture and introduced the speakers who would address the gathering over the days ahead. Phillips invoked the "spiritual wealth that has been bequeathed to us as part of an unfolding legacy."

> Boston was a place directly impacted by Calvin . . . it was the city of the Reformers. Though that light has been forgotten; we're here to wake them up. We're here to remember; we're here to proclaim . . .

It's important to do this because God commands us to remember the Ebenezers. We forget. But this week is about remembering so we can do important things with our lives for the Kingdom of God. HAZZAAHH!![15]

Phillips gave a brief historical outline of the last two thousand years, touching on what he believes to be the most significant events from the first and second centuries, in which the Christian fathers "secured orthodoxy against Gnosticism, Arianism and so forth," to the period most "fundamental to the development of Western civilianization: the sixteenth century and the seventeenth century" that brought about the "application of those theologies . . . to all the nations." While many see John Calvin's Geneva as anything but religiously tolerant, Phillips attributes the very notion of religious freedom to Calvin. The way in which he does this highlights just what Reconstructionists mean when they refer to "religious freedom." They do not mean that other religions should be tolerated, let alone that having religion and having none should be treated as equivalent in a religiously neutral society. No; Calvin was "the author of religious freedom" in the sense he understood the limitations placed on the role and authority of the state by the Bible. Religious freedom is not a freedom possessed by individuals, it is the freedom of religious institutions from the influence of the civil government. In other words it is sphere sovereignty.

Phillips focused on the role of the city of Boston in an integrated march of history, directed entirely by God. Sitting in this ballroom, convention goers learned to see themselves as central to that story, as heirs to the tradition and protectors of it for the future. They learned that remembering and honoring those who came before, and teaching their children to do the same, is a sacred obligation; an obligation that creates, over generations, a legacy of meaning. Phillips concluded:

For us to forget this legacy would be to condemn our children to hopelessness. We celebrate; we study. We march . . . and we will do it to prepare our sons and daughters for battle. We still have freedom we are enjoying; thank you, John Calvin and the Reformers. Thank you to those who came to America, knowing that those who greeted you would as soon fill your sides with arrows as shake your hand. *Sola de Gloria,* to God be the glory. Amen!

Vision Forum's biblical philosophy of history (history is God's unfolding plan) comes together with postmillennialism (Christians are to make the Kingdom of God an earthly reality) in this celebration of the Reformation and the principle *Semper Reformanda* (always reforming). This gives rise to a Reconstructionist variation on this classic Reformed notion that the reformation advocated by the Reformation is an ongoing process. Throughout the conference we were told that Calvin and the Reformers brought the faith more in line with a biblical worldview, but they were limited by their culture in ways they couldn't see, so there remains work to be done.

Bringing this to bear on the issue most central for the homeschoolers in attendance, Geoffrey Botkin said that Christians are charged by God to raise "little reformers; there's too much to do in one generation." "Men teach sons," he continued. "I didn't think my daughters would be reformers changing America, but having been exposed to this early on, they, within their appropriate limits, have changed many lives." Botkin's daughters had coauthored a book published by Vision Forum. His intense pride in the accomplishments of his daughters, with the obligatory articulation of the women's limits, brings into focus how intensely gendered Reconstructionism is. I suddenly remembered being on the edge of this world, within reach of something that seemed big, something that seemed, at the time, important, and yet being excluded. The ever-present careful policing of the boundaries of power and authority, ensuring that women remain on the outside, takes a much more powerful and pervasive form than the articulation and assent to the rules. The subtle yet powerful social norms that also police the boundaries are illustrated by the fact that this most popular of public speakers ended his talk by inviting participants to chat one on one—he said he could stick around for a bit, and he welcomed conversation. I watched as a crowd gathered—all male. After twenty-five minutes, he was still talking and the crowd was smaller, but not one woman had approached him.

As an example of a realm still in need of reformation, Phillips focused on art and culture. Giving a quick critical assessment of specific works of art at the time, Phillips then showed a slide of Michelangelo's David (carefully cropped to obscure the genitalia).

In a very real sense this sculpture represents all that is wrong with the time: [it's a] homoerotic piece of art, in the Greek form emphasizing the human body . . . Art was thought to be a "get out of

modesty free" card. Naked super boy Greek god David . . . it's technically perfect; the best ever; but it's unlawful.

He continued his critique of both medieval and contemporary art with
a focus on music. "Of all callings one we know is still in heaven is
music . . . The Bible says that when he was an angel, Satan was the
leader of the choir. Don't be surprised that he can take music and use it
to his purposes." Phillips reflected on the power of music to shape the
way we think and feel and critiqued contemporary music specifically in
terms of gender: "Music [should] strengthen us in our manhood . . .
[But] our boys are listening to feminized music, singing in falsetto.
Bach is the pinnacle of reformation of music [reflecting] God's design:
the complexity of God in music."

But the call to continue the Reformation is the call to apply the contributions of the Reformation to contemporary art and culture. "*Sola scriptura* applies to aesthetics; the Bible must give us our theory of beauty,
work, worship: all captive to the Glory of God." And, of course, Phillips's
effort to bring an ongoing reformation to the arts was the impetus behind
his efforts to develop the Christian film industry.

The Reformers, he said, "sought to develop a systematic theology of aesthetics," but the arts "are the least reformed in the Reformation." According
to Phillips, the Reformers' culture limited their ability to effectively reform
the arts: concerns over idolatry, a mistaken division of the world into sacred
and secular, perceived ties between paganism and the arts, and the distinction between the clergy and the laity in worship. While the Reformers would
say that every lawful calling was a holy calling and a ministry of God, their
application of that principle was incomplete. God's revelation becomes increasingly clear in history as Christians seek to consistently apply his law to
every area of life. It is the calling of contemporary Christians to continue to
apply the insights of the Reformation, to be always reforming.

Lest those present think that the task of the cultural transformation, the
task of always reforming, was for great historical figures alone, Joe Morecraft
asserted, "we are blinded by our culture in ways we don't understand but
that will be clear in 200 years." Thus, the principle of *Semper Reformanda*,
which makes the actions of today's Christians just as important as those of
the past. Marshall Foster whose Mayflower Institute has always had strong
ties to Rushdoony and the Reconstructionists offered examples of trusting,
faithful believers repeatedly overcoming great odds to further the Kingdom:
"History is not run by great men, it is built on the sovereignty of God

and a motley crew with their trust in him. The Magna Carta resulted from preaching in the pulpits against the tyranny of the king . . . Pagan Scots running around in skirts" transformed Scotland. "Have every father read the Geneva Bible to his children every night . . . you'll get rid of your Queens, or Kings, or whatever you have."[16] When faithful Christians find their place in history, it gives their lives meaning and fulfills God's vision for transforming the world.

Patriarchy and Material Culture

My visit to the Boston conference was cut slightly shorter than I had intended. I had registered for the conference in advance and paid the full registration fee. I had listened to the lectures, visited the book exhibit, taken some pictures of attendees in costume who happily posed for me, and chatted with a young man who was a volunteer and a homeschool student. At one point I went to the registration desk to ask about buying an extra ticket to the evening event. When the staff member said I should probably talk to media relations, I turned in the direction in which he gestured and the media relations person was standing so close that, had I taken a step back, I would have stepped on him. He said, "I understand you are writing a book. All media inquiries are supposed to come through me." I apologized and offered him my business card. He asked several questions, which I answered. As I did, he wrote in a notebook that, I noticed, already had my name at the top of the page when he first approached me. He said that he would "check some things out" and that if I didn't hear back from him I was fine. I was sitting in a session on biblical law when he slipped into the row where I was sitting and said, "I'm going to have to respectfully ask you to leave." I was really quite stunned, though I guess I shouldn't have been. He said he had looked up my previous book on the Internet and read some of the introduction and "it wasn't something [they] wanted to support." When I looked at him, confused, he clarified: "the gender studies." I said that this was an entirely different project, knowing that that would make no difference. He reminded me that I was free to buy the recorded lectures online.

They refunded my registration fee ($200), and he stood nearby to make sure I left. The whole thing seemed so strange. It did give me a first-hand reminder of the way in which, in this world, a closed circle of men are in charge, and only those willing and able to fit within the structure deemed by those men to be appropriate are allowed to be present. Or, as

Bruce Lincoln writes of the women in his study of authority, "Gatekeepers and potential audiences judged them, because of their gender, to be 'wrong' speakers and denied them access to authorized and authorizing spaces."[17]

Doug Phillips and Vision Forum were strong advocates of biblical patriarchy, a movement to reshape Christian families. The notion that the Bible teaches that women should submit to their husbands is present, in one form or another, in most evangelical and fundamentalist churches. But there is also a significant "biblical feminist" movement that argues for gender equality in both the home and the church. The biblical patriarchy movement has developed in direct response to the influence of biblical feminism.[18] Biblical patriarchy, however, promotes gender relationships that seem extreme even by traditional standards of fundamentalist churches.[19] Often, these writings echo Rushdoony. While many versions of Christianity hold that God is neither male nor female (or that the characteristics of masculinity and femininity are both included in God, who is beyond anthropomorphism), biblical patriarchy asserts that God is male and that the human male is the "image and glory of God in terms of authority, while the woman is the glory of man." With regard to family authority, the "husband and father is the head of his household, a family leader, provider, and protector, with the authority and mandate to direct his household in paths of obedience to God." And while men have a calling to exercise dominion in the world, women's calling is to assist their husbands by serving in the home. Women in the "exceptional state" of being unmarried may have "more flexibility" in their exercise of dominion but it is not the "ordinary and fitting role of women to work alongside men as their functional equals in public spheres of dominion." Patriarchal authority requires that fathers retain responsibility for the education of their children, primarily in the home. Grown sons may leave their father's home, but daughters should not do so until they are married. Sons may choose their wives (with parental counsel), but daughters should look to their fathers to find a suitable spouse for them.

This is driven home in a recorded lecture by Geoffrey Botkin from Vision Forum's father-daughter retreat *Preparing Your Daughter for Marriage*.[20] Drawing on the division of legitimate biblical authority, Botkin outlines the relationship between the family and the church. Individual families are to be submitted to, and under the discipline of, a local church, with the church being made up of patriarchal family units. Leadership in these institutions is precluded for women and, according to Botkin, "a

God-honoring society will likewise prefer male leadership in civil and other spheres as an application of and support for God's order in the formative institutions of family and church."

In her book *Quiverfull* Kathryn Joyce traces how these tenets play out in the daily lives of men and women connected through churches, the homeschool movement, and the biblical patriarchy movement. Joyce found women who were expected to ask their husbands about every detail of household management, even to the point of complicating church efforts to provide food for church members who were ill. In the communities Joyce studied, the women were silent in church, were discouraged from speaking in the company of men, and were typically blamed for marital difficulties, most of which are attributed to women's lack of submission. While women's submission is taught as something that women do willingly in a godly family when husbands fulfill their obligations, Joyce found that women who failed to submit faced sanctions ranging from criticism, to the denial of communion, to outright excommunication and shunning.[21]

Each year Vision Forum produced an elaborate catalog, designed to evoke old mail-order catalogs, from which one could learn about almost every aspect of the ministry.[22] Vision Forum's strict notions about gender roles, family, and authority are present, explicitly and implicitly, in everything they do. It's easy to conjure a nostalgic scene in which a biblical family gathers excitedly together when the Vision Forum catalog arrives in the mail. The parents are excited over the variety of homeschool materials available, as well as the books and DVDs that encourage parents as they struggle with family life. The family might, together, look at the events offered throughout the year and imagine the possibility of traveling on the "Faith and Freedom Tour" to see historic places, learn from godly leaders, and find fellowship with families like their own. But clearly the children will be most interested in the second half of the catalog, which reminds me of the old Sears Christmas Wish Book. It is divided into two sections—*The Beautiful Girlhood Collection* and *The All American Boy's Adventure Catalog*—each filled with costumes, toys, and books designed to foster very specific gender identities. Each section is introduced with a "letter" signed by "Doug Phillips, ESQ., President" and each item listed for sale is eloquently described in such detail that the catalog itself becomes a way of inculcating gender identity.

The girls' section begins with Phillips reflecting on "what a privilege it is to be the father of four precious daughters and husband to the greatest wife in the world." He goes on to explain the mission of Vision Forum in terms of the "restoration" of the family and the "rebuilding of the culture of virtuous womanhood." "Beautiful Girlhood" is defined in terms of six pairs of values: Faith and Fortitude; Purity and Contentment; Femininity and Grace; Enthusiasm and Industry; Home and Hospitality; and Joy and Friendship. Each item in the girls' catalog has been chosen to foster these virtues. Page after page of dolls help girls prepare "to be a mommy someday." Some are traditional baby dolls, and many are character dolls depicting "pilgrim" girls, "patriotic" girls, "frontier" girls, and "American Indian" girls. The dolls come in many varieties of skin color as do the catalog photographs of the girls playing with them. Pewter scissors with a matching needle case, and a kit for making doll clothes, matching mother/daughter aprons, an ice cream maker, and a wooden baking set all foster domestic skills. The catalog notes that the one symbol that most captures "the essence of a girl's dreams of marriage and motherhood" is the hope chest, and it promotes a book detailing what such a chest should contain.

The catalog also includes "American Patriot dresses" and even "Titanic dresses" (the Titanic has a mythic place in Vision Forum's world for the chivalry shown by courageous men who allegedly put "women and children first"). The books tell stories of faithful women, God's providence, and appropriate roles for Christian women. They include "Young Ladies Classics" such as *Heidi* and *Black Beauty*, the advice-oriented *Feminine by Design: Helping Them Choose* (a marriage partner), *Raising Women of Virtue*, and *Before You Meet Prince Charming*. There is no *Nancy Drew* here, not even *Little Women*; nothing that teaches independence, self-sufficiency, or autonomy. On the contrary, submissiveness, purity, and contentment are valued. The 2007 catalog includes *The Journey of Daughterhood*, a DVD for fathers; *Story Time with Daddy*; and other resources (including a discipleship retreat) encouraging fathers to focus on their daughters as well as their sons. The catalog description of the recording from the 2003 father-daughter retreat encapsulates the values that run through the entire catalog.

> A father's most sacred duty is his daughter's protection and preservation from childhood to virtuous womanhood. He leads her, woos her, and wins her, with an affection unique to the bonds of fathers and daughters. Success in a father's mission is directly related to his ability to raise his daughter as an industrious child-loving woman of God, secure in her worth and vision. When these

relationships are realized and cultivated the generational mission of the Christian family is secure.

As alluded to previously, Anna Sofia and Elizabeth Botkin have embarked on their own efforts at restoring biblical womanhood. In work their father proudly lauds as appropriate to their gender, they have written *So Much More* and released a DVD entitled *Women of Vision: The Return of the Daughters* and a CD called *How to Be Your Father's Ambassador, Arrow and Princess*. In these materials the Botkin daughters promote "Stay-At-Home Daughters," the notion that their purpose as young women is to learn to assist their future husbands as helpmeets in their exercise of dominion by practicing that role in their relationship with their father. Critics charge that this model creates an unhealthy family dynamic that borders on emotional incest, and Phillips's assertion that a father's job is to "woo" his daughter seems to support such criticism.

A letter from Phillips also begins the section of the catalog promoting items for boys. Boys are expected to "rescue damsels in distress" and "explore America with Lewis and Clark." "Courageous boyhood" is the goal. Phillips writes that "every toy, tool, and book has been carefully selected and designed to inspire boys to dream big dreams for the glory of God." While contentment is a quality to be prized in a girl's character, it is not so with boys.

> One of our goals is to demonstrate that the skills and experiences which historically made up the life of a boy were God-honoring vehicles for preparing him to be a man. He learns to explore because he is called to take dominion over the earth. He learns to emulate the lives of heroic Christians because he, too, is called to leadership. Scripture is clear. "Where there is no vision, the people perish." Boys need vision.

The values that make up "courageous boyhood" are Vision and Honor; Faith and Fortitude; Dominion and Scholarship; Loyalty and Patriotism; Virtue and Duty; Adventure and Evangelism. While one might imagine that many of the virtues listed for girls and boys respectively might be prized by either gender, not so in this world. The boys' books for sale are a mixture of adventure and "providential history," and there are far fewer of them than there are for girls. Without attempting to gauge the substance of the volumes in each category, in the 2007 catalog there were twenty-one CD/DVD offerings for girls and forty-seven books (some paperback and some hardback). For boys that same year there were only eighteen CD/DVDs and fewer than half as many books as for girls (nineteen). Two years later the catalog was similar, with thirty-two CD/DVDs for girls and thirty-three books, and twenty-five CD/DVDs for boys and only eleven books. And yet "scholarship" is a virtue for boys but not for girls.

Playing dress-up, however, is not regarded solely as a game for little girls. There are costumes for the boys too: Revolutionary War attire, including a George Washington costume, and a WWI Sergeant York uniform. Parents can buy, for their boys, a "Commando Beret," a Civil War hat, a WWII helmet, or, the one costume option that is not war attire, a cowboy outfit, complete with gun. There are swords, daggers, tomahawks, guns, slingshots, hand grenades, miniature tanks, and crossbows; nearly every page promotes a weapon of some sort (all but the detective page and the treasure hunter page). Even the "tree house page" includes an *Encyclopedia of Survival Techniques* and a book on *Backyard Ballistics*. Without a doubt, boys are more inclined to play games like "cops and robbers" and "army," but the aggressive quality of these toys, to the near exclusion of anything else, is remarkable. Furthermore, not a single toy or book for boys focused on families, aside from the toy weapons with which Phillips teaches his son to "protect his little sister." Many of the articles in the catalog are "modeled" by the Phillips children, as is the case in the "Boy, Defend Your Sisters" shield and sword. In a characteristic entry, Phillips writes:

> When my daughter (Liberty) was born, I took her with my son Justice [both pictured] to the United States Supreme Court and read them the words etched on the back of the edifice of that great building: "Justice Guardian of Liberty." Since then, it has been one of my missions as a parent to train my sons to view themselves as protectors of womankind. Sometimes we pretend that Justice is a knight and his sister a princess. These nicely crafted wooden swords and shields make the game great fun.[23]

Family obligations for boys, as they are portrayed in the material culture of Vision Forum, become almost entirely about machismo. They create helpless women and then defend them. Boys are told to study and explore as part of their exercise of dominion, but those activities take a back seat to the adventures of war. If the girlhood collection fosters "child-loving" women, then the boyhood collection fosters, almost exclusively, violence-loving men.

Both catalogs include sections on science and technology and creation adventure that are not explicitly gendered, but these sections are at the end of the boys' catalog, and the children depicted are all boys. Presumably for the whole family, the "family creation adventure radio drama" *Jonathan Park* reinforces patriarchal gender roles in a way that is not the slightest bit subtle. *Volume 1: The Adventure Begins* is a fictional account of a "reality" show in which a team of evolutionary scientists (which includes a female scientist) and a team of creationist scientists face a challenge in which they encamp at a chosen site and compare their explanations for the geological evidence found there. The creationists are all men, but they travel with their wives and numerous children. Jonathan Park is the son of one of the creation scientists. When the wives run out of diapers, they ask their husbands what to do. The women hike miles back to the car to drive to town to buy more after they have been directed to do so by their husbands. Jonathan's sister wanders off and gets trapped. She calls to her brother, who comes to rescue her, but the female scientist comes along and ends up falling into the gulf with the sister. Jonathan, the hero, is left trying to figure out how to rescue both his little sister (who is appropriately remorseful for wandering off without checking in) and the adult scientist with a PhD, who is now dependent on a small boy. Cleverly, Vision Forum has Jonathan make explicit use of his "communicator watch," with two-way communication, which they sell for $55 a pair.

The clear demarcation of gender roles carries through from the children's sections of the catalog to those intended for adults. Women's titles include *Why and How to Honor Your Mother, Stand by Your Man: A Wise Woman's Guide to Blessing Her Husband's Vision, Who Controls the Womb: Be Fruitful and Multiply*, and *A Vocation of Victory: Passionate Housewives Desperate for God*. The titles for men are far more numerous and varied. A whole section on "entrepreneurship" includes Rushdoony's *Tithing and Dominion* as well as a book on *Preparing Sons to Provide for Single Income Family*. One of Phillips's many products promoted in the catalog is *The League of Grateful Sons*, a DVD designed to "leave you grateful for America's heroic fathers and motivated to surpass their legacy." The 2007 catalog included a four-page section on "Biblical Patriarchy" that celebrates "Manliness." Phillips's DVD *MANLINESS* is a recording of his presentation at Vision Forum's Christian Boys and Men's Titanic Society Anniversary Celebration. Phillips argues that masculinity is in a state of crisis because of the social and political gains women have made. "The twentieth century, with its emphasis on feminism, a co-ed military, and mothers leaving the home for the workforce, wreaked havoc on the doctrine of manliness," he said. Other titles in this section of the catalog include *Manly Men Write Manly Letters, Manliness though Fatherly Discipleship, Biblical Patriarchy Made Simple,* and *Multi Generational Victory: Fathers and Sons.*

Clear lines of gender demarcation exist across Vision Forum's products. Fathers are to have vision, exercise dominion in culture (including business, the arts, and the law), and lead their families in understanding their place in providential history. Mothers are to bless and support their husbands' vision, being a "helpmeet" and always playing a dependent and secondary role. This is an interesting reading of the dominion mandate, since in the Garden of Eden dominion was given to both Adam and Eve. Yet the interpretation of dominion as being first the calling of men, who are assisted by their helpmeets, is taken directly from Rushdoony. In his *Revolt Against Maturity,* Rushdoony argues that woman's task is to assist man in *his* dominion, an essential component of which is reproduction.

"Fertility is an aspect of man's dominion," Rushdoony argues, quoting Psalm 127, the very text from which the contemporary Quiverfull movement takes its name.[24] Kathryn Joyce's book, *Quiverfull,* draws on extensive field research to trace the contours of the biblical patriarchy movement, providing the most thorough available account of it. In two sections she draws the explicit connections between the movement and Christian Reconstruction but barely elaborates on Reconstruction itself. Yet the Phillips family, their ministry, their followers, and their church play central roles in the narrative she weaves and, in very real ways, that narrative is a window into a reconstructed world as Reconstructionists envision it.

Family Integrated Churches and Ecclesiastical Discipline

As postmillennialists, those associated with Vision Forum and the Quiverfull movement anticipate an eventual worldwide conversion to Christianity that will transform every dimension of culture, bringing all of it under the lordship of Jesus. Family, church, and civil government are distinct spheres of authority, each with its own responsibilities and jurisdiction. Each also, importantly, has limits on its authority and jurisdiction. The families are patriarchal; they understand themselves to be part of a multigenerational effort for dominion in submission to biblical law, and the homeschooled children are plentiful. Quiverfull families homeschool because God delegated responsibility for educating children to families and because there is no such thing as a religiously neutral education. Every aspect of education is understood in terms of the Bible, whether that be science (dominion and creationism), math (dominion and God's revealed order), history (dominion and God's providential plan), art (dominion and worship), or philosophy (dominion and seeking God's wisdom after him). Gender norms are nurtured and strictly enforced. Many families build home businesses, often in addition to a full-time job for the father. This practice has been advocated by Gary North for years, and how to do it is a frequent and popular topic at conferences and in books and DVDs. Such businesses are intended to provide a level of economic self-sufficiency, which brings with it a level of autonomy from all manner of social institutions for the patriarchal family unit, as well as a way to develop skills and work ethics among the children.

On a day-to-day basis patriarchy is enforced and gender boundaries are policed, in the subtle ways we have already explored, but there are also social structures that perform this function.

Many of those who are now former employees of Vision Forum attended churches that identify as family integrated churches. In September 2001, Vision Forum Ministries hosted a summit on "Uniting Church and Family" at their headquarters in San Antonio. From that meeting developed the National Center for Family Integrated Churches (NCFIC). The NCFIC reflects the values and vision of Vision Forum, including the emphasis on "multigenerational faithfulness," patriarchy in the church and family, and the notion that church is a family made up of families, headed by men, and should be organized as such. More than a decade after its founding, NCFIC, led by Scott Brown, a frequent speaker at Vision Forum events, maintains a nationwide network of churches. NCFIC does not require that churches ascribe to their views to be listed, but NCFIC makes its views clear in the "Confession," which reflects Vision Forum's positions on issues such as the sufficiency of scripture; presuppositionalism; jurisdictional authority; church discipline; and biblical qualifications for ministry, including being the "husband of one wife," limiting leadership to men. There is no mention of Rushdoony or Christian Reconstruction but the underpinnings are there.

It is impossible to get an exact count of affiliated churches, but there are thousands of them. The NCFIC is located in Wake Forest, North Carolina, and is affiliated with Hope Baptist Church. Each summer the center takes applications from young men from age eighteen to twenty-five to serve as interns. In the summer of 2010, NCFIC sponsored a national road trip during which they conducted conferences from Maine to Washington state. Family integrated churches are focused on bringing members of the family together and reinforcing the patriarchal structure: husbands as leaders, wives in submission (literally being silent and saving any questions they have for when they get home, as they believe the Apostle Paul commanded in his letter to the Corinthians), and children in obedience. Leadership in the church is almost entirely male, though women are allowed some leadership roles in groups composed of women and young children (when they reach a certain age, boys should not be taught by women). One of the more interesting dimensions of Reconstructionist ecclesiology is the establishment of "church courts" to adjudicate certain kinds of conflicts. Rather than take their troubles to civil court (Christians are prohibited in the book of Matthew from suing one another), church members bring them before ruling elders who have authority to issue punishments, demand repentance and restitution, and threaten excommunication.[25]

Joyce's *Quiverfull* has been criticized by supporters of Vision Forum and biblical patriarchy because it includes what they charge are uncritical, and undocumented, accounts of the stories of two women in the homeschool movement who found themselves in conflict with Phillips. In both cases, marital difficulties led to church courts, which concluded that the women were being unsubmissive or rebellious (to both their husbands and to church authorities) and were therefore responsible for the problems. According to the women's stories, even when charges of abuse were raised, they were still blamed. Joyce's analysis focuses on the ways in which biblical patriarchy serves to protect men from criticism and keeps women isolated from one another; they are afraid to talk about their problems lest they be charged with "gossiping" or "rebelling against church authority." Regardless of the merits of these particular women's charges, Joyce provides a striking look at just how the ecclesiastical judicial system Reconstructionists envision might work.

Indeed, Phillips has a law degree (from George Mason School of Law) and says that an important dimension of his father's discipleship when he was young was teaching him constitutional law. Another of the Vision Forum projects, the Witherspoon School of Law and Public Policy, focused on preparing leaders to play godly roles in politics and law. The "school," which aimed to teach "Biblical Principles of Law," was a four-day course open only to men. It was clearly rooted in Rushdoony's teachings about the connections between the Bible and the American Republic.

> [Witherspoon was] designed to equip students, attorneys, lawmakers, pastors, and fathers with a Reformation understanding of the Scriptures as the source book for law and liberty and the only sure foundation for addressing the challenging ethical questions of the twenty-first century. The Witherspoon School is especially designed for young men who desire to influence our nation for righteousness and who recognize that, to do so, they must communicate an entire world and life view as dictated by Holy Scripture. Witherspoon students will be exposed to distinctively biblical training under leading Christian attorneys and historians. They will study the Scriptural foundations for property, tort, and contract law; the influence of Christianity on the Constitution; the relationship between the case laws of Exodus and the Common Law; and the writings of Sir William Blackstone.[26]

The relationship between religion and law, as outlined by Rushdoony and embraced by Phillips, takes on real significance when a person is brought before the church leadership to respond to formal charges in the way that they might in a civil court.

While this is unusual in contemporary America, the *Wall Street Journal* has reported that the "use of ecclesiastical courts is on the upswing in American churches."[27] Church discipline goes back at least as far as the Middle Ages and played an important role in Calvin's Geneva. It still exists in a modified form in contemporary Catholicism and in some Protestant churches. Contemporary church courts tend to focus on issues of orthodoxy and leadership. So, for example, a priest might be disciplined for ordaining women, a political leader might be denied communion for supporting abortion rights, or a pastor might discipline a member for being vocally critical of the church leadership. But rarely would two church members bring a "private" disagreement before such a body. First, modern notions about what issues fall appropriately under religious authority have changed: if I hire a carpenter who also goes to my church to build a deck, and he does a shoddy job, I'd be unlikely to go before the church elders and ask them to address it. Second, Protestantism has led people to think of the church they attend as a choice, which has contributed to the decline of these institutions (or our freedom from them, depending on one's perspective). For church courts to be effective, churches must have mutually supporting networks of affiliated churches, such that a member disciplined by one church cannot easily go down the road and join a similar church. This is exactly the type of ecclesiastical discipline envisioned by Reconstructionists. Some 10–15 percent of American Protestant churches, and churches associated with Vision Forum, now follow this model.[28]

In *Law and Society: Volume II of the Institutes of Biblical Law* Rushdoony outlines this practice, rooted in the writings of Paul in I Corinthians. Paul condemns Christians who take their disputes before "unbelievers." In the Roman Empire, Jews were permitted to adjudicate their own internal conflicts according to their own law, free from Roman interference.[29] Rushdoony uses this to argue that, while in a godly society civil law is rightly applied by civil courts, in a humanistic society, Christians should not take their disputes before unbelievers. "They must resolve their conflicts within their Kingdom courts . . . [or] suffer wrong rather than go to ungodly judges."[30] Rushdoony explains that going outside "the circle" to settle a dispute undermines the cohesiveness of the group and places the adjudicating institutions in a position of higher authority. Believers are called both "saints and brothers"; the church is, by analogy, like a family.

> The strength of family government is that the godly family, which having numerous problems and disputes, settles these within its own circle. The family is an institution of strength. To go outside the family is to deny the family and to break it up. When a husband and wife, or parents and children, or brother against brother, go to an outside court, the family life and government is in most cases dissolved or at least shattered. The state is then declared the greater agency, and the family denies its own power and the basis of its existence. So too the Christian denies the reality and power of the Kingdom of God if he seeks justice outside the Kingdom. The only real Kingdom for him then is the other agency.[31]

Kathryn Joyce reports on the case of the Epsteins, who were members of Doug Phillips's church, Boerne Christian Assembly (BCA). Jennifer Epstein had approached Phillips and his wife Beall for marital counseling. Over a long period of time, through many counseling sessions, and through many tense and often public exchanges, the situation escalated. It began with demands that Jennifer repent for failing to submit to her husband

and church leaders, gossiping, and criticizing church leaders. Then both Jennifer and her husband were denied communion. Ultimately, they were excommunicated and shunned by the other members of the church. As Jennifer reports to Joyce, the process had a decidedly legal character. "Charges" were read in public before the congregation, and they were asked to "enter a plea." As Joyce writes:

> Phillips acted as the lawyer he'd trained to be for the Home School Legal Defense Association, and turned his church into a court-room, trying Jennifer with briefs and witnesses testifying to the state of her unrepentant heart. Jennifer responded in equally litigious fashion, charging that Phillips didn't follow proper methods of Biblical conflict resolution as detailed in Matthew 18 and that the structure of BCA didn't follow Presbyterian guidelines and so couldn't constitute a fair court.[32]

The excommunication of the Epsteins was supported by other churches in the area. The way in which these groups construct internally reinforcing, consistent, and interdependent meaning systems and social networks makes them very strong. This is what makes them appealing for those who adhere to them and also makes them potentially devastating for those who find they no longer can. It's striking how the weight of this structure falls most heavily on women. Women are disproportionately vulnerable in these cases in that they often have no financial resources or work experience they can take with them. With the husband as patriarch, it is considered reasonable for the assets to be in his name. Because of the way in which submission teaching is understood, marital problems are frequently blamed on women, and the men in authority close ranks around the husbands. If a husband is unfaithful, questions arise as to the wife's submission to her husband's sexual desires. In a widely reported example, pastor and well-known author Mark Driscoll responded to the scandal in which Ted Haggard admitted to an extramarital homosexual relationship by saying that "too many pastors' wives let themselves go."[33] If a husband has anger issues, his wife is likely to be met with demands for a level of submission that is inevitably unattainable. In the Epstein case, for example, Phillips demanded that Jennifer assent to a list of points on which she should submit, a list that ultimately precluded her from questioning their assessment of the situation. The reverse situation is rarely the case: that is, if a woman has an

adulterous relationship she is denounced as a "Jezebel," and it is rare
that her failing is attributed to some inadequacy on her husband's part.
Furthermore, these judicial processes are administered entirely by men,
who have a vested interest in preserving the male privilege afforded by
patriarchy. Men have all the church authority, and even when pastors'
wives participate in "counseling," they do so in the context of a submission doctrine that precludes them from disagreeing with their husbands. The women facing charges, furthermore, are risking additional
charges of "gossiping" and insubordination to church authorities if they
talk openly to anyone about the case.

Moreover, biblical patriarchy teaches that any effort to limit one's
procreation is sinful rebellion, so women who leave or are forced out of
the community often have numerous children dependent upon them.
In 2010, in response to the fiftieth anniversary of the release of "the
pill," Vision Forum's Baby Conference "celebrated the blessing and
preciousness of life amidst a culture of death." According to Vision
Forum's statement, the conference "featured encouraging messages on
the blessing of children and the culture of life, special lectures and
panel discussions for mothers, forums on child-training, and presentations for the whole family that explored the wonder of God's creation
through the intricacies of the womb." At the conference they honored
Michelle Duggar as Mother of the Year. Duggar has given birth to
nineteen children and she is lauded by Phillips, Vision Forum, and the
biblical patriarchy movement as someone who "has encouraged many
women to embrace the blessing of children and rejoice in the high calling of motherhood." She is also the star of the hit reality series *19 Kids
and Counting*. The event, the award, and the show are excellent illustrations of how a Reconstructionist worldview has trickled into the broader
American culture in ways that are not always obvious. On the show,
the Duggars are portrayed as a wholesome American family who just
happen to have a lot of kids; in one episode we see their resourceful-
ness as they shop for baby clothes at a thrift store. Absent from the
screen, and smoothed over in the public representation of the Baby
Conference (as well as in much of the homeschool movement in which
the Duggars worked with Phillips and Vision Forum), is the extreme
position on women's roles and women's rights, promoting patriarchal
male authority and framing any activity outside of motherhood on the
part of women (especially limiting the numbers of children in any way)
as promoting "the culture of death."

The Scandal

Beginning in January 2013 Phillips's life began to unravel. Details alleging an inappropriate relationship with a young woman began to trickle out of this tightly closed community, and Phillips was removed as an elder of his church.[34] He eventually made a public confession of sorts and resigned from Vision Forum Ministries.[35] By early 2014 the woman had filed a lawsuit against Phillips, Vision Forum Inc., and Vision Forum Ministries alleging that in his role as her pastor, counselor, and employer, Phillips was guilty of various sexual improprieties, emotional damage related to that impropriety, and even fraud.[36]

Lourdes Torres worked as the Phillips family's nanny and assisted in the work of Vision Forum Ministries and Vision Forum Inc. According to her legal complaint, Phillips began grooming her for their relationship when she was fifteen years old. While Phillips has admitted to the relationship, he has claimed that they did not, strictly speaking, have sex.[37] The complaint alleges that between 1999 and 2006 Phillips fostered increasing emotional intimacy between them and that their sexual involvement (which began in 2007 and stopped just short of intercourse) was one-sided. The complaint details years of pursuit on the part of Phillips in the form of phone calls, e-mails, and text messages. It alleges that Phillips said his wife would die soon, promised he would marry Torres, and at one point moved her into his home. According to the complaint, as the relationship grew more intimate, Torres became increasingly uncomfortable, asking Phillips repeatedly to leave her alone.

Finally, Torres told her parents and, according to the complaint, sought their help in keeping Phillips away. Then, in January 2013, after Phillips allegedly attempted a late-night visit to the Torres family home (by knocking on her bedroom window), her parents brought the situation to the attention of the church elders. In early 2013 Phillips was removed from authority in his church, but he remained at the helm of Vision Forum Ministries until near the end of the year, when a confrontation with a handful of friends and colleagues forced his resignation. At the end of 2013, Vision Forum Inc. sold off its assets and closed its doors, though Phillips appears to still own the company.

Key to Torres's claims of abuse is the issue of consent. Her accusations span the age for legal consent, but the cultural context of biblical patriarchy (much of it designed and established by Phillips himself) raises issues even when Torres was legally old enough to consent. The form of

women's submission, the intentional cultivation of dependency and shel-
teredness, the self-conscious efforts (of which Phillips has been a part
since his early work at HSLDA) to ensure that the homeschooling world
is legally autonomous from government oversight, and the system of
church courts that discourages independent evaluation of claims, all miti-
gate against a young woman being able to make real choices in a situation
like this.

The church and its affiliated churches require that members bring
legal disputes before church elders (all male), and, at least initially, Phillips
would likely have been one of those elders. The prohibition on gossip
would probably have made it difficult for a confused young woman to seek
advice from anyone outside this circle. A young woman in this community
is usually carefully kept from outside influences and marginalized from
inside sources of power and protection, potentially rendering her incapable of confronting abuse or giving real consent to a sexual relationship.

Regardless of the legal outcome, Phillips has admitted to scandalous
behavior.[38] His personal influence seems to have come to a halt and part
of his empire has been dismantled. And while apparent contrition and a
period of absence from public life can powerfully remake a leader in this
world centered on forgiveness (at least for the men involved), much of the
work Phillips has done to insert a version of Christian Reconstruction
into the very fabric of the homeschool world remains. Phillips promoted a
view of the world infused with Christian Reconstruction, though before
the scandal some Reconstructionists (including some at the Chalcedon
Foundation) had distanced themselves from Phillips and his views. Moreover, several other homeschool leaders who have been his long-time
brothers-in-arms, such as Kevin Swanson (Generations with Vision) and
Scott Brown (NCFIC) share Phillips's worldview and remain in positions
of authority and influence.

Conclusion

Vision Forum illustrates the manner in which Christian Reconstruction
is, and is not, about politics. Vision Forum was focused almost exclusively
on ministry to homeschooling families, reforming churches through the
NCFIC, and transforming media to reflect godly values. Phillips has been
involved in Tea Party activities in his home state of Texas.[39] According to
Kathryn Joyce's sources he has strongly endorsed the Constitution Party
(founded by his father) and its candidates, not just as an individual or a

homeschool leader but also in his role as elder/pastor at his church. Phillips has opposed, in writing, women serving in leadership positions in civil government as a violation of biblical qualifications for leadership. He even opposed Sarah Palin's vice presidential candidacy on these grounds. Pointing to John McCain's advanced age, Phillips wrote:

> At this point, Americans must consider the real possibility that the United States may have a mother of young children serving ultimately as commander-in-chief of the military and chief executive over one of the most influential nations in the world. Today, our friend Janice Crouse of Concerned Women for America offered a press release in which she declared: "Here is a woman of accomplishment who brings a fresh face to traditional values and models the type of woman most girls want to become." . . . I respectfully disagree with part of that statement. I am confident that Mrs. Palin is a delightful, sincere, thoughtful, and capable woman with many commendable virtues. But in fairness, there is nothing "traditional" about mothers of young children becoming career moms, chief magistrates, and leading nations of three hundred million, nor is this pattern the Biblical ideal to which young women should aspire.[40]

Phillips's detractors also charged that Vision Forum opposed women's suffrage on the grounds that there is a "Biblical assumption" that husbands and/or fathers represent their families so that individual votes by women are unnecessary. In the event that women wished to vote differently from their husbands this would be evidence of a lack of submission. It is an argument that I heard Reconstructionists make thirty years ago and that can still be found on a Vision Forum–affiliated website, *Persevero News.* Vaughn Ohlman writes:

> Some denominations, nowadays, have made it a rule that churches must send one man and one woman to ruling conferences and the like . . . But surely this must be a denial of either Biblical doctrine or simple logic. If the woman is obeying her husband "in everything" then this includes, obviously, her vote and the opinions she expresses . . .
>
> So what is the point of the woman at the meeting? . . . Our society has put this in place with the woman's vote . . . The woman who

votes is either voting in agreement with her husband or father, or in opposition. And if in opposition, then this system denies the very authority that God has put in place for families . . . Or if an agreement then what is the point? Adding to the vote of successful patriarchs?[41]

Little of this is explicitly "political" in the narrowest definition of the term: pertaining to efforts to shape the structures of civil government. But of course, no one can miss the profound political implications of every dimension of what Phillips and Vision Forum did. They sought to promote a very specific worldview that governs every dimension of life by promoting biblical law, dominion, and patriarchy.

8

American Vision and the Repackaging of Rushdoony

WHILE THE INFLUENCE of Rushdoony and Christian Reconstruction is often subtle and hidden, that is not always the case. One organization that explicitly identifies with Christian Reconstruction is American Vision. Examining this group gives us a chance to see what Christian Reconstruction looks like in organizational form.[1] The leaders of American Vision believe that they are building on the framework established by Rushdoony, equipping Christians in the effort to make "every thought captive to Christ"; to exercise dominion over every aspect of life; and to make the family, the church, and the civil government conform to the dictates of biblical law.[2] Their ties, as we shall see, extend well beyond the world of Christian Reconstruction to the nexus of states' rights, patriot, gun rights, and Tea Party groups.

Located just outside Atlanta in Powder Springs, Georgia, American Vision was founded in 1978 by Steve Shiffman. In 1981 American Vision hired Reconstructionist author Gary DeMar, who became its president and chief public face in 1986. Gary North has relocated to the greater Atlanta area, and though he has no official role at America Vision, they have a close relationship. North is involved in American Vision events and, according to DeMar, he is a frequent presence at the organization's offices, where he is seen "a couple times a week."[3] Perhaps the most prolific among a new generation of Reconstructionists is Joel McDurmon, American Vision's research director, whose in-laws are Gary North and Rushdoony's daughter Sharon. American Vision's staff included Brandon Vallorani, who was executive vice president until late 2012, at which time his name dropped off the website's staff page. Formerly executive vice president of Answers in Genesis, Vallorani is also cofounder of Tolle Lege Press and Liberty Alliance, a network of websites that includes the Tea Party–oriented Patriot Update, Patriot Depot, and Zionica.

The goal of American Vision is to return America to its biblical foundations "from Genesis to Revelation." The organization functions as a think tank supporting the writing and publication of books, websites, podcasts, blogs, and, until recently, an active community discussion forum. DeMar and other staff members speak at church conferences across the country, and American Vision sponsors its own "national" annual "Worldview Conference" each summer as well as regional conferences throughout the year. Held in church facilities, the conferences draw 150–400 people who are largely familiar with the speakers and Christian Reconstructionism, but who come to advance their understanding and be invigorated by the fellowship of like-minded believers. In addition, Christian Reconstructionism often spreads through committed small groups who promote it in their churches, which may be sympathetic to aspects of Christian Reconstruction but don't identify with the movement. American Vision's work is key to these efforts.

Gary DeMar and Joel McDurmon

DeMar established his credibility as a Reconstructionist author and his niche in that small circle with his three-volume *God and Government* series, published between 1982 and 1986. DeMar is not a technical theologian pushing the boundaries of Christian Reconstruction like Rushdoony. He is, rather, a popularizer. Reconstructionists' leading apologetics theologian Greg Bahnsen called him the "finest" of Reconstructionist authors in terms of his ability to gain a wider audience than many of the more technical thinkers and writers.[4] *God and Government* is not a new analysis of the application of a biblical worldview to government. It is an articulation of Rushdoony's ideas in workbook format, accessible for use in Christian schools and homeschools as well as in Bible-study groups. These volumes laid important groundwork for the later promotion of Christian American history by people such as David Barton. Originally published by American Vision (1982–1986), the series has been released in several editions and remains in print.

In the second half of the 1980s, DeMar turned his attention to the challenges to Christian Reconstruction from within fundamentalism, specifically from dispensationalist premillennialists. Dave Hunt, a popular fundamentalist writer, argued that Reconstructionism is a "deviant theology" that is "dangerously" tied to the New Age movement. At the time, fundamentalists exhibited tremendous concern over New Age religion and the rise of witchcraft and Satanism (they often conflated these three strains of American religion into one) and feared that those demonic influences were infiltrating the church. Hunt argued that Reconstructionists erred in presuming that humans could bring about the Kingdom of God and that such a narrative, rooted in a progressive view of history, derived from New Age theology rather than biblical Christianity.

In 1988 DeMar responded, in a work coauthored with Peter Leithart. DeMar and Leithart agree that the New Age is a threat, but insist that Hunt mischaracterizes Reconstructionists' understanding of the spread of God's Kingdom. Hunt's pessimistic theology, they claim, "denies God's victory in history" and is an inadequate response to the New Age movement.

Bahnsen also described DeMar's work as "the best presentation of the transformational world-and-life view known as 'Christian Reconstruction.'"[5] And indeed, presenting this "transformational world-and-life view known as 'Christian Reconstruction'" is an apt summary of DeMar's work and the mission of American Vision. American Vision retains its emphasis on the importance of postmillennialism.

American Vision's research director Joel McDurmon has written eight books (and edited two more), all between 2007 and the end of 2012. The books vary in topic but are mostly in the broad category of apologetics. Reconstructionists often complain that scholars fail to engage their work, but (as with every other example that comes to mind) McDurmon's work is not peer reviewed and is essentially self-published by American Vision, the one exception being a volume published in 2011 by Reconstructionist Tolle Lege Press. McDurmon can exhibit the same acerbic style as the writers who preceded him, but he also cultivates a hipper persona, eschewing conservative Christians' notions about appearance and behavior that he argues are extrabiblical. Sporting a full beard and elaborate tattoos, images of him smoking cigars and drinking beer abound on the Internet. He revels in the rejection of American Protestant sensibilities about alcohol and has authored a book entitled *What Would Jesus Drink?*[6]

Perhaps most interesting is McDurmon's recent project on county rights, which has become a centerpiece of American Visions offerings.[7] As we saw in chapter 1, Rushdoony argued that the founding fathers envisioned a weak, decentralized federal government and a loosely affiliated collection of independent Christian republics, with most power localized in county governments. McDurmon builds on this position, thinking through what it would mean on a variety of issues in ways that resemble an updated version of North's *Biblical Blueprint Series*. The project includes a book, (*Restoring America One County at a Time*), articles on the American Vision website, a series of videos that present the material in a lecture format, and public lectures that have included a stop at Michael Peroutka's Institute on the Constitution.

Peroutka was a member of the Board of Directors for the League of the South, which along with other neoconfederate groups shares McDurmon's sensibilities about localism, decentralization, and American history.[8] McDurmon is involved with a group of young men in Georgia with ties to American Vision, homeschooling, and Vision Forum who have become activists in local and state Republican Party politics. Their efforts are reported on the website PerseveroNews.com, which is owned by Nathaniel Darnell.[9] Darnell worked at Vision Forum before joining the staff at American Vision as the director of ministry advancement. As one might expect from a young man mentored by Doug Phillips, Darnell is a Christian filmmaker and fiction writer. His novel *Glory, Duty, and the Gold Dome* is published by Vision Forum in their Sires & Sons Adventure Series.

In April of 2013 PerseveroNews.com reported that "a coalition of new small-government, constitutional conservatives appeared to have captured a large number of leadership positions across the state on both the district committees as well as the state committee."[10] This coalition included McDurmon and Darnell, who were both elected to the Georgia GOP state committee. In June of 2013, the conservative coalition spearheaded an effort to change the state party nominating process from a primary system to a caucus system, which tends to favor the more hardcore grassroots activists. A co-author of the resolution was Brant Frost V, chairman of the Coweta County Republican Party, a homeschooler, and, even at the age of twenty-three, a long-time Republican activist. In August of 2013 the Georgia Tea Party hosted an event to explore the caucus nominating proposal, and Darnell appeared in support of the plan.[11] If one wanted to assess whether a generation of homeschoolers raised on Christian Reconstruction have any influence, the Georgia State Republican Party might be a good place to start.

Self-described "small-government, constitutional conservatives" came out in large numbers in support of Cliven Bundy, the Nevada rancher who refused to pay the required fees to allow his cattle to graze on federal land. In April of 2014 the Bureau of Land Management sought to seize his cattle when his armed supporters confronted them in an antigovernment standoff. Observers puzzled at why he thought it was legitimate to refuse to pay these fees (in fact, he offered to pay them to his county government). Bundy asserted that he did not recognize the "existence" of the federal government and called on his county sheriff to "disarm the BLM." These views, promoted by Rushdoony and popularized in Tea Party circles by McDurmon, were played over and over in coverage of the confrontation, until Bundy made even more controversial assertions about African Americans being better off under slavery (a view also promoted by Rushdoony and popularized in some far-right circles by Reconstructionist Doug Wilson in his book *Slavery as It Was*). This is not to claim that Bundy is a Reconstructionist or that Reconstructionists are the only ones to have ever made these arguments. Yet the arguments are currently popular in this nexus of the religious right, the Tea Party, patriot groups, and gun groups where American Vision and its affiliates are situated.

Today, American Vision reaches beyond self-identified Reconstructionists, participating in events that include the broader community of "Reformed" Christians, such as the study cruises sponsored by Alpha and Omega Ministries. Perhaps more important are American Vision's political ties to the far-right wing of the conservative movement, in part by virtue of Gary DeMar's participation in "patriot"-oriented events. DeMar offered a study cruise called "The Patriot Cruise," which featured such Tea Party regulars as William Federer, Alan Keyes, and Victoria Jackson.[12] Indeed, many of the concerns that have become widespread in the Tea Party movement have long been promoted by Reconstructionists. Christian American history, the critique of public school teachers, and the rise of Islamophobia were all on Reconstructionists' radar before becoming more mainstream. Before the end of the first decade of the twenty-first century, DeMar and American Vision were playing a key role in what would soon coalesce into the Tea Party movement.

Like many tax-exempt nonprofit groups, American Vision has a companion organization that can legally raise money and promote candidates for elected office: Vision to America. Vision to America focuses on promoting conservative Tea Party politics and exhibits very little clear affiliation with American Vision or Christian Reconstruction. Its website says it is a "private organization dedicated to promoting conservative values and restoring our Founding Father's [*sic*] vision for America as a Christian Republic." Vision to America has promoted the full range of Tea Party issues, from the conspiracy theories about President Obama's birthplace, to the fight against health care reform, the effort to defeat Nevada

Senator Harry Reid and then Nancy Pelosi, opposition to environmental regulations on the grounds that global warming does not exist, support for eliminating the Federal Reserve and returning to a hard money standard, opposition to the congressional vote to raise the debt ceiling in the spring and summer of 2011, to spreading fear about Muslims in a fight against "creeping Sharia." Yet ties to Christian Reconstruction are not immediately obvious unless one looks in the "Frequently Asked Questions" section under "Who is behind Vision to America," or in the links in the online store to "popular brands" that include many Reconstructionist groups. Even then, one has to recognize the names to make the connections.

President Obama, Inauguration Day 2009, and the Faithful Remnant

Though I have followed the work of American Vision for decades, I really began to plunge into its world in January of 2009 at a precruise study conference in Fort Lauderdale. As I drove south from Jacksonville the day preceding the conference, I listened to National Public Radio's coverage of the inauguration of Barack Obama. Even that day there were bits of evidence of the persistent religious divide. President-elect Obama had angered many when he chose Pastor Rick Warren to give one of the official prayers at the inauguration—Warren had been active in fighting against marriage equality in California. The NPR commentator set up the prayer, telling us to listen for whether Warren prayed "in the name of Jesus." The commentator explained that, previously in such situations, Billy Graham dropped the phrase in an effort to be more inclusive, but that more recently his son Franklin had included it. I thought about the fact that the people I study question whether Warren is even a Christian—he's too liberal, too tolerant, too postmodern, they think.

As has happened repeatedly, pundits and scholars alike came to believe, with the elections of 2008, that the religious right would disappear. They would be proved wrong. The religious right was already remaking itself, again. The seeds of the Tea Party were present immediately after the 2008 election, as Republicans debated whether the Democratic landslide could be attributed to the failure of conservatism or the failure to be consistently conservative. But as conservatives remade conservatism, the core group of conservatives whose views are rooted in religion—and in some measure Christian Reconstruction—would remain an important force.

Only two years later, in 2010, the 2008 "sea-change" was reversed when the Tea Party led the Republicans to election victories across the nation at every level. Several of the leaders of the national Tea Party groups insisted that the movement was exclusively about taxes (and free-market economics). Yet at the grassroots level, many Tea Party events were explicitly religious, organized by churches and often held in church facilities. As I watched those midterm campaigns, Reconstructionist influence could be seen everywhere: from Kentucky's Rand Paul, who won his bid for the US Senate, to Nevada Tea Partier Sharron Angle, who lost hers. In the first half of 2009, American Vision presented decades-old Christian Reconstructionist arguments that have become central to Tea Party rhetoric.

The day after the inauguration, as I got ready to leave for the conference, I listened to CNN and thought about how absolutely giddy the news anchors were. Driving, I turned on the radio and the commentator said, "It's been less than one full day, and it's a whole new world!" It seemed as if everyone was celebrating. I wondered how this would impact the conference I was about to attend.

Sovereign Seas is an arm of Alpha and Omega Ministries that organizes cruises as study vacations for conservative and Christian groups. The cruises range in price from approximately $500 per person to as much as $1,500, making them affordable vacations for many middle-class Christians. Typically short, they depart from Fort Lauderdale. An example is the January 2009 cruise "God's Faithful Word in an Unbelieving World," which brought together people from several distinct ministries. Some identified as Christian Reconstructionists—like American Vision, the Mayflower Institute, and D. James Kennedy's Coral Ridge Ministries. Others, such as Ligonier Ministries and Samaritan Ministries, were on the periphery of Reconstructionism but are often found at Reconstructionist conferences and are supported by website links and the like. These ministries are all Reformed in character; that is, they understand themselves as being rooted in the Calvinist wing of the Reformation and as distinct from both the larger culture of American evangelicalism and from fundamentalism. Michael O'Fallen, a Reformed Baptist, is president of Sovereign Seas.[13] He explained to me that, though there were differences between Reconstructionist groups and the other groups represented—he specifically mentioned the controversial Reconstructionist commitment to theonomy, or government by biblical law—the people present at the conference, he said, were "all brothers in Christ." Many were young couples and seminary students.

The cruise itself was preceded by a daylong conference which culminated in a debate between James White, the director of Alpha and Omega, and Bart Ehrman, professor of religious studies at University of North Carolina at Chapel Hill, called "Did the Bible Misquote Jesus?"[14] Though there were 150 people registered for the cruise, the conference drew as many as fifty people during the day and probably seventy at night for the debate. The crowd was largely male but diverse in terms of age. There were many people in their sixties and also a significant number of young people—several of whom could be overheard talking about seminary. One young man was studying at Reformed Seminary in Mississippi, and several others were at Reformed in Orlando and Knox Seminary (D. James Kennedy's school) in Fort Lauderdale.

There were five speakers whose presentations lasted for about an hour each, the first and last based explicitly in Christian Reconstruction. Marshall Foster spoke first. His book *The American Covenant* has been an important text used by homeschoolers and Christian schools to teach "Christian American history." When I told him I was working on a book that would explore the "legacy of Rushdoony," he smiled broadly and exclaimed, "He changed my life!" Foster's talk offered material he has been presenting for more than twenty years. But he made it newly relevant by placing it in the context of the current political realignment and the seeming widespread enthusiasm about Obama. Noting wryly the "coronation of a king yesterday,'" he asked, "how many of you are down . . . looking at our future? It appears that there is little hope." A few in the audience made noises, but it was clear that everyone agreed. While the rest of the world was celebrating, this core constituency of the conservative movement was struggling to make sense of it all. Where was the promised victory of postmillennialism?

But postmillennialists take the long view, and Foster reassured the crowd that understanding history, and God's intervention in it, is the key to optimism. Foster's point was that the contemporary church was becoming less and less relevant to the issues of the world, mostly because they have forgotten the lessons of history; the implication being that if Christians would just wake up everything would turn around. This is a temporary situation that has repeated itself over and over since Genesis; people have forgotten how to build a Christian civilization. The problem will be solved when we Bible believers get back to the word of God, live it, and take it to a fallen world.

Foster's sweeping narrative stretched from sixteenth-century Europe to the present. It was a narrative in which God's blessing and victory are made visible. He described how, repeatedly, a "small band of the faithful," seeking reformation, was blessed by God. He traced the history of the Puritans from England to Holland and then to America: a "glorious beginning for a reformation." He doesn't call it American exceptionalism, but within a year this view would be at the very heart of the Tea Party emphasis and its critique of President Obama. Within two years I would be watching Foster on "the big screen" in Kirk Cameron's Christian American history film *Monumental* at an event hosted by my local Tea Party group. Foster refers to a common thread in the "Christian American history" narrative in which the Puritans initially established a community in which they shared their resources communally and failed to thrive. He ties this narrative to the immediate political situation, labeling President Obama a socialist. This critique would also become widespread among conservatives within a year: "They [the Puritans] left for America against all odds when there was no hope. Well, they starved for the first two years until they turned from Obamanomics . . . oops—I mean socialism—to free enterprise." Foster's message is clear: we can see from history how people who are obedient to God's law have prospered and people who are disobedient have not. "When people fear the difficulties (wars, economic crises . . .), they need to be taught to fear God instead." When that happens, revival will come and those "who have studied the Word of God and remember how God works in history will be ready to build a Christian civilization."

In each of the examples, Foster shows how a small group of faithful Christians persevered against great odds, maintained their focus on the Bible and the law of God, and were blessed by God with victory and prosperity. "Standing in faith against all odds is the Christian faith." It was a message of encouragement, fitting for the day when a despised Democratic president was inaugurated. It was also a familiar trope to these Christians who have long seen themselves as the embattled faithful remnant maintaining God's truth against the onslaught of humanism. Indeed, seeing themselves as the few who know the truth and are willing to be obedient to it only serves as confirmation that they are right. The insistence that Christian Reconstruction is not primarily a political movement made the defeat of conservatives and the election of President Obama much less disheartening to followers; it fostered a sense of hopefulness that things are still on track, despite how it seemed.

One of the speakers sandwiched between Foster and DeMar, who was not identifiably Reconstructionist, was David Wheaton, a commentator on Christian Worldview Radio and author of *University of Destruction,* a book intended to "prepare" Christian young people for the challenges they will face in college. Wheaton spent one year in college at Stanford and then became a professional tennis player. While most of the speakers had an academic quality to their presentations, Wheaton's talk resembled a corporate motivational talk: simplistic and drawn from his background as an athlete. He began by arguing that "universities are designed to bring together and isolate youth for the purpose of indoctrinating them in liberal socialist and sexual values." According to Wheaton, the threats are sex, alcohol and drugs (because they lead to sex), and humanism. He charges that the "college campus is [the] most sexually immoral environment in America; students are forced to live in coed dorms." The concern over coed dorms was repeated over and over again. Wheaton cited two graphic examples of the "dangerous sexual" climate on college campuses: the "Exotic Erotic Party" from the Stanford University school paper (intended, he says, to remove the taboo on masturbation) and "sex week" at Yale. Wheaton quoted the website for this event, describing it as an "interdisciplinary exploration where renowned professionals from a wide variety of industries will convene to challenge students' conceptions about sex and question the way sex is presented in our society." He did not explain that "sex week" is not an event sponsored by the university at all but by an independent student group. Moreover he presented it as though such events are commonplace on college campuses. They are not. Nonetheless, Wheaton claims that universities' goals are to "desensitize" young people to issues related to sex and undermine their faith in favor of humanism, "the new faith on campuses." There was really nothing new in Wheaton's critique; it could have been lifted word for word from the work of Tim LaHaye more than twenty-five years ago, a popularized version of the work of Rushdoony.

Gary DeMar, president of American Vision, was the final speaker of the day. DeMar's basic thesis was that in the war between believers and skeptics, the theological problems inherent in premillennial dispensationalism give too much ammunition to the skeptics. He framed his talk as a "microcosm of the coming night's debate." DeMar claimed that "one of the things that led Bart Ehrman to be skeptical of the Bible is eschatology." DeMar pointed to the verses in Matthew 20 that promise that all the things discussed would happen before "this generation passes away" and explored longstanding disputes about what this verse means. DeMar's underlying point is that, for those who claim to take the Bible literally and see these promises as future prophecies (as premillennialist dispensationalists do), these verses make no sense. "Part of the problem we have is that we have evangelicals who want to hang on to an end-times theology and tweak their Bible interpretation to fit. Skeptics will take advantage of that," he said. DeMar's talk was a lengthy defense of postmillennialism, framed both as a critique of premillennial dispensationalism and also as a bulwark against the criticisms of "skeptics" like Ehrman.

Most of the speakers at this conference were promoting materials their organizations had for sale. DeMar noted that his talk was taken from his new book, *Why the End of the World Is Not in Your Future*. Foster had a new twelve-part DVD program called *From Terror to Triumph: Proven Strategies of History to Triumph over the Terrors of Our Times*. Reformed apologist James White, as director of Alpha and Omega Ministries, was the "draw" for the precruise and postconference evening event. The conference ended, and the attendees went to dinner, to reconvene in an hour and a half for the debate between White and Ehrman. As people waited outside the conference room before the debate, there was excited chatter, and I heard a couple of people say they were "nervous" about the debate. This was clearly not a debate in which both sides were to present arguments in an effort to decide who had the stronger ones. On the contrary, the "buzz" in the hallway, as well as the daylong prep session, revealed an audience that was sure it already knew which of the debaters was "right." The event seemed designed to demonstrate the strength of the "Truth," by showing the "skeptic" to be the weaker debater. I wondered why Ehrman, who had received much attention for his book *Misquoting Jesus*, appearing on Jon Stewart's *The Daily Show*, Stephen Colbert's *Colbert Report*, and several interviews on National Public Radio, would subject himself to an event like this. Yet, Ehrman seemed to know he had been set up. He began by cleverly pointing to the elephant in the room, "How many of you hope I get creamed in this debate." But in the end it wasn't really a debate.

This conference (and the cruise that followed) was a perfect case study of the way in which, as I have argued, Christian Reconstruction has influence far beyond those who identify with it. This cross-fertilization was apparent in the presentation of David Wheaton. His framework and underlying assumptions have become part of this subculture and are no longer identifiable as Reconstructionist. One woman I met shared with me the extent of the friendship between her husband, herself, and Marshall Foster. When I told her about my project, she had not heard of Rushdoony or Christian Reconstruction. Yet, for years Foster had shaped their way of thinking, and Foster attributes his worldview to Rushdoony. I met another couple at dinner who had been friends with David Wheaton's mother for years. They knew nothing of Reconstructionism. I asked them if they knew what Wheaton's millennialist views were, and they did not. Yet they attended four days of workshops (on the cruise) in which the underlying framework was postmillennial and largely theonomist. I am not suggesting that they came to embrace postmillennialism and theonomy, merely that they were influenced by days of teaching that was based in those ideas, whether they knew it or not. This is exactly the way Reconstructionists had long spread their views in churches, how they had influenced the early religious right groups in Washington, and how they continue to make inroads into the evangelical-fundamentalist subculture.

American Vision's Worldview Super Conferences

American Vision holds an annual Worldview Super Conference, as well as a number of regional conferences. Each year the national super conference has a different theme.[15] The July 2009 conference was held at Midway Presbyterian Church (PCA) in Powder Springs, Georgia. Lectures were held in the church sanctuary, and the event included an exhibit hall of booksellers and affiliated organizations such as Samaritan Ministries, Tolle Lege Press, and Patriot Depot. The program boasted an impressive list of speakers on a variety of topics. Ted Baher of *Movie Guide* and Joseph Farah of *World Net Daily* would speak on the media. Voddie Baucham, who writes about marriage, family, and biblical manhood and womanhood; David Goetsch, vice president of Northwest Florida State University; and home education advocate Kevin Swanson would speak about education. Gary North and Joel McDurmon would discuss economics, and Gary DeMar and Herb Titus would address politics.

When I arrived, the parking lot was full, and I noted that while many of the cars had Georgia plates, others cars had come from as far away as Connecticut and also from Florida, Iowa, Kentucky, Louisiana, and North Carolina. Everything about this conference felt different from the Vision Forum conference I had attended earlier in the month. There were fewer big families and the crowd was somewhat older. While there were a few teenagers, there were almost no children in the sessions (there was child-care available and the sessions were targeted toward adults). With registration fees ranging from $99 per person or $299 for a family, and accommodations at local hotels for about $100 per night, this conference was significantly less expensive than Vision Forum's at the swanky hotel in Boston. It was also much more casual; attendees were dressed in jeans, T-shirts, and sneakers; and there wasn't a single costume to be seen. The crowd was almost entirely white and made up about equally of males and females.

Joel McDurmon was at the registration table when I arrived, and he greeted me. We had met at the conference in Fort Lauderdale, and it was he who suggested I come to American Vision's conference. We talked, and he asked about my university, how many conservatives teach there, and whether I was "persecuted." He said, "We don't get many professors, es-pecially professors of religious studies who are followers of Rush." I had described my project as I always did, "a book examining the legacy of Rushdoony," but he had taken that to mean I was a follower.[16]

Though this conference occurred only months after the first stirrings of Tea Party discontent, the influence of Christian Reconstruction on Tea Party rhetoric was already present, most explicitly in the presentations of Gary North and Herb Titus. By most accounts, the protests now known as the Tea Parties originated with a video of former futures trader turned cable news reporter Rick Santelli on the floor of the Chicago Mercantile Exchange in late February 2009. Santelli launched into a rant about the Obama administration's plans to assist homeowners in mortgage trouble, inviting "capitalists" to join him in dumping derivatives contracts into Lake Michigan.[17] Tea Partiers and others argued that the movement was about taxes, spending, and government power, and for many it certainly was. But others saw early ties to the religious right and explicitly to Chris-tian Reconstructionists. Indeed, Christian Reconstructionists were in-volved in the very early framing of Tea Party issues and rhetoric, illustrating both their persistent influence and challenging the view that the Tea Party is exclusively concerned with fiscal issues.

The sanctuary was packed for Gary North's session on the gold stand-ard; the room sat several hundred people and it was standing room only. With his distinctive and familiar voice, North told us that he was quite pleased that this was his first ever PowerPoint presentation: "I thought of it this morning while walking the dog, wrote it up and e-mailed it." While, he said, "everyone can remember where he was when he first heard about the Kennedy assassination," North explained that there was "a second date as clear" to him. It was August 15, 1971, when he was told, during the bluegrass radio show for which he was a disc jockey, that Richard Nixon "had just announced wage and price controls" and the elimination of the gold standard. "On that Sunday afternoon the economic system that had been in operation internationally had been destroyed . . . The Western world was off the gold standard and has never recovered . . . and it won't ever," he said ominously. When North predicted that "Islam" would inherit the wealth of the West, the audience gasped: "We have lost the religious and philosophical standards out of which the gold standard came." We are seeing, he argued, the conflict between the presuppositions of Christianity and Darwinism "and their relative effects on the economy."

North's presentation made the case for a hard money standard with arguments organized around the five-point covenantal model that has become the central framework for his version of Christian Reconstruction.[18] According to North the model is based on Old Testament treaties. The five points are (1) Transcendence/sovereignty, (2) Hierarchy/authority, (3) Ethics/boundaries/dominion, (4) Oath/judgment/sanctions, and (5) Inheritance/continuity. Applying the model to contemporary economics, North argues for the *sovereignty* of God as the source of all law. Citing Rushdoony and highlighting all five points, North explained that the way to identify the god of a society is to identify the authority upon which it bases its laws (its *sovereign*): "the *hierarchy* of the covenant that demands human obedience to God's *authority* . . . an *ethical* structure . . . built into the universe" "characterized by self-government . . . final *judgment*, and the *inheritance* of believers." North compares this to the "doomed humanism of Darwinism," in which "Nature is autonomous, unplanned, meaningless until man appears." These are, in his words, "rival worldviews: and the comprehensive Christian, biblical worldview . . . is based in private ownership . . . self-government under God's law, money as a free market development moving society from barter to a division of labor . . . a limited civil government and stable money over time."[19]

Within a year Tea Party activists would be calling for the elimination of the Federal Reserve and championing Ron Paul's economic views, which are rooted in his long history with Gary North and the Constitution Party. Those views would suddenly gain respectability on Capitol Hill, and Paul himself would be made chairman of the congressional committee that oversees the Federal Reserve.

The *New York Times* has called the Tenth Amendment the "Tea Party's favorite part of the Constitution."[20] Declaring that all powers not explicitly assigned in the Constitution to the federal government, or denied by the Constitution to the states, are reserved to the states and to the people, Tea Partiers invoked the amendment to challenge health care reform and critique what they saw as an expansion of the federal government under the Obama administration. During 2009 Tea Partiers in seven states passed "state sovereignty resolutions," and another twenty-eight voted down such resolutions, asserting their rights under the Tenth Amendment. In less than a couple of years the claim of "states' rights" became for many Tea Partiers synonymous with their claim that they "support the Constitution." All these themes could be found at the 2009 American Vision Worldview Conference, held when the Tea Party movement was just a few months old.

Herb Titus's back-to-back lectures at the conference were entitled "Restoring State Sovereignty: The 10th Amendment" and "Restoring the Sanctity of Human Life State by State." Titus explained that he had grown up as a Mormon, had been homeschooled, graduated from Harvard Law School, and was "saved" in the 1970s in an Orthodox Presbyterian Church. Titus has traveled in Reconstructionist circles for most of his adult life and has spearheaded the movement's efforts to use the legal system to return America to what he thinks are its Christian foundations.[21] He claims that while he was "influenced by Rushdoony" he is not a Reconstructionist. Yet, in addition to being one of the main speakers at this Reconstructionist conference, he articulates views in line with Christian Reconstruction, ranging from the proper role of civil government to presuppositionalism, he has served as legal counsel to several Reconstructionists, and he was allegedly let go from his position as dean of Pat Robertson's Regent University Law School because of his dominionist leanings. He supervised the master's thesis of Virginia Governor Bob McDonnell, which drew on Ray Sutton's volume in Gary North's *Biblical Blueprint Series, Who Owns the Family.* In 1996 Titus ran as a vice presidential candidate on the Christian Reconstructionist-oriented Constitution Party ticket with presidential candidate and Reconstructionist Howard Phillips. Titus has also served as legal counsel to the Gun Owners of America, a group with Reconstructionist ties.

In his lecture explaining the significance of the Tenth Amendment, Titus emphasized the importance of the notion of the covenant to the

Constitution to which we appeal to secure our rights. "Why should we care what the founders wrote?" he asked. "Why should we be bound by words written 200 years ago?" He answered: "We as Christians understand the nature of the covenant: there are certain principles that are fixed, they do not change over time; they are universal principles . . . Apart from biblical notion of covenant we have no way to explain why after 200 years we go back to the Constitution to decide what authority the government has."

Titus went on to articulate the view that American liberties are merely recognized by the Constitution but granted by God and secured by the biblical limits God has placed on delegated authority. Titus argued that the "separation of powers is based on the idea that there is no final authority but God . . . The very purpose of the Constitution is to tell us the authority that our government officials have in governing our lives," Referencing the Tenth Amendment, he said, "Powers not delegated are reserved to the states or to the people." He then proceeded to give several examples in which local and state officials had successfully used the Tenth Amendment to challenge what they saw as unconstitutional federal actions. In Titus's view, the "restoration of the Tenth Amendment" is a restoration of the Constitution as a biblical covenant, bringing the federal government into conformity with the limitations set by God and recognized by the founding fathers.

This is the view that the Tea Party has popularized. It is why they invoke the Declaration of Independence and the phrase "endowed by the Creator" as the context for the Constitution. Indeed, Titus opposed the nomination of Elena Kagan to the Supreme Court on grounds that might be obscure to some but were clear to those schooled in this perspective. Kagan was asked during her confirmation hearings, "Did the Second Amendment codify a preexisting right or was it a right created by the Constitution?" Kagan answered that she had never thought of the question. This was, to Titus, so damning that it was grounds to reject her: "Here's a woman who's being nominated to sit on the United States Supreme Court and she's never thought about the question whether rights are given by God or given by men . . . She's never even considered it!"[22] For Titus, rights come from God and, in the case of the American Constitution, they are recognized and protected by a covenant between the people and the government. The limits on the power of the federal government are articulated in the Tenth Amendment. The Second Amendment exists to permit godly resistance to tyranny. In

January 2010, Tea Party candidate for the US Senate Sharron Angle of Nevada echoed these themes:

> You know, our Founding Fathers, they put that Second Amendment in there for a good reason and that was for the people to protect themselves against a tyrannical government. And in fact Thomas Jefferson said it's good for a country to have a revolution every 20 years. I hope that's not where we're going, but, you know, if this Congress keeps going the way it is, people are really looking toward those Second Amendment remedies and saying, my goodness, what can we do to turn this country around?[23]

That previous summer, Titus had made just those points at the Christian Reconstructionist Worldview Conference, arguing that gun rights are not in the Constitution for hunters or self-defense against criminals but for citizens to protect themselves from "tyrannical" government. In an interview, he told journalist Sarah Posner: "If you have a people that has basically been disarmed by the civil government then there really isn't any effectual means available to the people to restore law and liberty and that's really the purpose of the right to keep and bear arms—is to defend yourself against a tyrant."

Reconstructionists claim that when the civil government overreaches its legitimate biblical authority, the right to resist it is rooted in the authority of God.[24] Titus's second lecture applied the argument that the Tenth Amendment is the constitutional remedy for what he perceives of as the overreach of the federal government in the form of a strategy to bring about an end to legal abortion through "Personhood Amendments." Titus's argument is that while the US Supreme Court did not find a "right to life" in the Fourteenth Amendment, this does not preclude states, under the Tenth Amendment, from establishing a higher standard of protection in their various state constitutions. In his view the federal Constitution does not give the federal government the power to decide when life begins so, based on the Tenth Amendment, states may do so.[25]

None of this is to say that these ideas originated solely with Christian Reconstructionists, only that within that tradition these ideas have been given philosophical and theological sanction and that Reconstructionists have been active in Tea Party groups from the beginning, creating opportunities for cross-fertilization. The Tea Party movement promotes positions Gary North and Gary DeMar have expounded for more than

twenty-five years, and the organizations with which they are now affiliated are deeply connected to the structure of the Tea Party.

At the 2010 Worldview Conference, "Sovereignty and Dominion,"
DeMar returned to a recurrent theme in Christian Reconstructionist literature: neither biblical dominion nor the solution to the problems faced
in the contemporary world is primarily political.[26] Reconstructionists
insist that those outside the movement do not understand this fact either
because they have not read Reconstructionist books or because they are
"humanists" who believe that the state (through politics) can bring salvation. DeMar began:

> Many people who come to a conference like this think that the solu-
> tions to our problems are political rather than governmental. I bring
> this up because there's usually one person that's in our audience
> who is a "ringer." Someone from the outside who pretends to be part
> of our worldview thinking, and they're really a reporter and about
> six days or so after the conference they'll write an article about the
> conference . . . We're not trying to take over the government through
> armed revolution; we don't believe that there's salvation through
> politics; we don't believe there's salvation through law . . .This par-
> ticular talk is designed to put things in perspective for us and maybe
> to help you articulate to others what we're all about.[27]

DeMar defines government as "regulation of power and force" and
argues that there is only one form of "government" that is political: civil
government. He critiques those who use the terms "government" and
"politics" as though they are synonyms, claiming that only a small part of
"dominion" is political and that the Reconstructionist goal is to use politics not to expand civil government but to limit it.

> We want to get involved in politics today not so we can lord it over
> other people but so that we can put civil government in its proper
> role. We want to limit its jurisdiction . . . we're not after power.
> We're after ministry. The civil magistrate is a minister of God
> and we want the civil magistrate to get back to being a minister
> of God.

In his view the only alternative to limited civil government is tyranny and
slavery: "Every time we give more power to the civil magistrate we have to

remember that that power is backed up by the power of the sword. Some people are comfortable with that. They like being slaves."

He reminds listeners that government is a good thing when kept within the limits of biblical jurisdiction: "Too much regulation [by] government will give you tyranny; too little regulation will give you anarchy. We have to find this balance." And, "What is the best way to set forth the parameters of good government?" he asks. He then asserts that the Bible and the Constitution are largely in agreement on the proper role of civil government. DeMar seems to suggest that if the opponents of Christian Reconstruction knew that they were not intent on establishing a theocracy by force, if people would just report on them accurately, that concerns would be alleviated. But he went on to say that since Christians have not been sufficiently involved in politics, now "we have homosexuals driving the legislation, the courts, and the educational establishment." The desire to keep "homosexuals" out of the legislatures, the courts, and the schools is just one example of how, put into practice, his version of limited government is not as limited as he claims.

What Does a "Right-Wing Echo Chamber" Look Like? Brandon Vallorani and Liberty Alliance LLC

In 2004 Brandon Vallorani became executive vice president of American Vision. He had been executive vice president of the creationist organization Answers in Genesis. At the same time he cofounded Tolle Lege Press with his father. In just a few years, while working at American Vision, Vallorani built a media empire at the nexus of the religious right, the Tea Party, patriot groups, gun groups, and others. Vallorani's network promotes far-right paranoia, claiming that President Obama, with his "missing" birth certificate, is a Muslim and a socialist looking for an excuse to completely disarm the American people to bring about a Marxist coup and put Christians in concentration camps.[28] By the end of 2012, Vallorani's name dropped off the staff listing on American Vision's website, though he apparently remains on the Board of Directors. More interesting is the interlocking web of Internet newsletters, blogs, and merchandising sites that are owned by Brandon, his brother Jared, or other associates, all which share an address with American Vision.

Like Joel McDurmon, Vallorani cultivates an image that is far from what one might expect for someone at the forefront of promoting a Christian world and life view. Vallorani enjoys fine wine, has his own vineyard, and heads Safari Cigars, a company he co-owns with Doug Giles, the owner of a Liberty Alliance partner website. Vallorani's webpage details his hobbies, which include not only cigars and wine, but guns, big-game hunting, and trophy collecting. Interestingly, however, he gives no hint as to his religious identification. His website promotes him as an aggressive and successful entrepreneur. He "quickly rose through the ranks at a large non-profit organization in the Heartland," it states, but there is no indication that the nonprofit in question is the creationist organization Answers in Genesis, with its now-famous Creation Museum. His move to American Vision (under less-than-ideal circumstances) becomes merely a move "to the South where, as Executive Vice President, he grew another non-profit organization by nearly 600% in less than 4 years," again without mention of that organization's name. About his work as CEO and co-founder of Tolle Lege Press, we learn of the "historic accomplishment" of its re-publication of the Geneva Bible, described as the "Bible the Puritans brought to America." When he discusses the founding of one of his most important current ventures, what became Patriot Depot, after the successful marketing of a bumper sticker following the 2008 election, there's no hint of the far-right and conspiracy-oriented character of the products Patriot Depot sells.

Vallorani founded Patriot Depot in 2007 and created several "news" websites with inflammatory blogs to drive traffic to his store. In a symbiotic relationship with the rise of conservative anger at President Obama (both facilitating it and benefiting from it), Vallorani built his network. In 2007, reporter Keith Thomson became interested in the relentless forwarding of e-mails that was seemingly a key part of the 2009 "conservative revolution" that was the Tea Party. He enlisted a systems analyst and traced many of them to Vallorani and his various interests. He found that "almost every day, Patriot Depot sent more than 100,000 individuals emails with original content," and he concluded that "a good deal of the 'conservative revolution' is produced by Patriot Depot™." At the time, Patriot Depot had nine employees and an estimated $3.5 million in annual revenues.[29] Vallorani's website reports in 2013 that "in less than 5 years, [his] Tolle Lege Press, Discount Book Distributors, Response Beacon, [and] Liberty Alliance conglomerate . . . employs more than 55 full-time staff members and anticipated gross revenue of over $9,000,000 in 2013."[30]

In 2013, Liberty Alliance's website claimed to generate "more than 1,000,000 page views each day." While Liberty Alliance is owned by

Vallorani,[31] its ties to American Vision remain strong, illustrating nicely the permeability of the boundaries between these groups. That is, what appear to be different groups are actually often owned and operated by the same individuals, and other groups, which are somewhat distinct, still share leaders. At least half of the Liberty Alliance's leadership was formerly associated with American Vision; this includes Vallorani, his brother Jared, James DeMar (who is Gary DeMar's son), Eric Rauch, and Stuart Adams.[32] The Advisory Board includes Gary DeMar, Michael O'Fallen, Kent Thelen (who is board chairman of American Vision Ministries and Creation Ministries International), and Jefferey Ventrella, whose work has been published by American Vision. Liberty Alliance also lists "Strategic Partners" including American Vision, American Vision News, Vision to America, and others that are owned by Liberty Alliance, Brandon Vallorani, or American Republic Media Group, which is also located at American Vision's address.

Of the thirty-seven member sites, almost all are owned either by Brandon Vallorani or his brother Jared. Among those not owned by one of these two, most of the remaining are owned by other people whose e-mail addresses are affiliated (either with Liberty Alliance itself or Patriot Depot). Several of the sites are targeted to Tea Party conservatives and do not make explicit reference to religion. These include Gary North's Tea Party Economist and also Conservative Byte, Girls Just Wanna Have Guns, Minutemen News, Patriot.tv, PolitiChicks, and many more. Zionica aggregates Christian news and mainstreams the far-right Christian Reconstructionist material by placing it alongside other articles about religion.

Of special note in the Liberty Alliance network are the "celebrity" websites of Rick Green, Kirk Cameron, and Victoria Jackson. Green is co-host of David Barton's Wallbuilders radio show, and while he affiliates with Liberty Alliance, the website is his own and predates the affiliation. So, too, with Cameron's website, though in both Green's and Cameron's cases there are significant ties to Christian Reconstruction. Victoria Jackson's website, however, is owned by Vallorani. Jackson became famous as part of the cast of *Saturday Night Live* but in recent years has become known more for her Tea Party activities, including a failed campaign for county commissioner. She has traveled on the study cruises where DeMar has lectured and has appeared on his radio show. Her affiliation with American Vision is no small contributor to her becoming the "Tea Party princess." Her 2012 autobiography *Is My Bow Too Big?* was published by Whitehall

Press (which is Liberty Alliance), and Vallorani conceived of and produces her radio show. When the *Village Voice* noted the tie between Jackson and Vallorani, they gave him credit for his part in her comeback among Tea Partiers but made no note of the far-right religious influence of Christian Reconstruction.[33] Also interesting, though, is the way the various affiliated websites circulate and recirculate content, giving the impression to an un-suspecting subscriber that the whole world is talking about the particular conspiracy of the day. Of course, they all link back to Vallorani's various sites that sell books, T-shirts, and bumper stickers.

Conclusion

American Vision has, since the 1980s, presented a popularized version of Rushdoony's work, a version that was accessible to churches and Chris-tian homeschools through Gary DeMar's *God and Government* series. It continues in this vein with a new generation of writers such as Joel Mc-Durmon. American Vision has been innovative and nimble in its ap-proach to engaging conservative Christians but has remained true to its foundational goals and principles. This can be no better illustrated than with the aggressive and entrepreneurial style of Brandon Vallorani and the media network he has built—Christian Reconstructionism packaged for the Tea Party.

9

David Barton, Rushdoony, and the Tea Party

EARLIER, I CLAIMED that the popular dissemination of Reconstructionist ideas is evident in the framing and language used by people in the religious right, if you have an ear for it.* I think of this as analogous to the way in which a New Englander can hear the difference between a Maine accent and a Boston one, or how a Southerner can tell if a speaker is from North Carolina or South Carolina; it is subtle, but it is undeniably there.

There is perhaps no better example of Christian Reconstructionist influence on the broader culture than the work of Tea Party "historian" David Barton.[1] Barton does not explicitly identify as a Christian Reconstructionist, and Christian Reconstructionists would not claim him as one of their own.[2] Barton does have ties to several Reconstructionist groups, including the Providence Foundation; he occasionally cites the work of Rushdoony and promotes views on race and slavery that are rooted in Rushdoony.[3] While Barton doesn't use the language of theonomy or postmillennialism, as we will see, he speaks of dominion, biblical law, the necessity of bringing every area of life under the lordship of Christ, and sphere sovereignty of biblically ordained institutions. He embraces the whole range of political views advocated by Reconstructionists from the right-to-life and creationism to more narrowly held positions on issues such as the history of slavery and opposition to the Federal Reserve System. As we shall see, the approach to history that has made Barton famous is rooted in Rushdoony's biblical philosophy of history.

Barton was born in 1954, raised in Aledo, Texas, and graduated from public high school in 1972, the same year his parents started a house church with Pentecostal leanings.[4] By 1974 the church had moved into facilities that now also house the Christian school they started in 1981, as well as Barton's organization, Wallbuilders. After high school, Barton attended Oral Roberts University, where he received a degree in religious education in 1976. Upon returning home, he became principal of Aledo Christian School until, a decade later, as he tells it in an interview, God led him to his first book by showing him the connection between the Supreme Court decisions on prayer and Bible reading and "plummeting" academic achievement scores and "soaring" student crime and immorality.[5]

> In July 1987, God impressed me to do two things. First, I was to search the library and find the date that prayer had been prohibited in public schools. Second, I was to obtain a record of national SAT scores . . . spanning several decades. I didn't know why, but I somehow knew that these two pieces of information would be very important.[6]

The result was his *America; to Pray or Not to Pray*, which is a statistical analysis of the "volume of prayers being offered" overlaid with data on a number of social problems, to compare the "prayer years with the post prayer years." According to Barton, the drop in prayer was so dramatic that its impact was felt not just in the schools but in every aspect of our national life.[7] Barton seemed unaware of the notion that correlation is not causation.

A self-styled historian with no real academic credentials, Barton went on to build an extensive collection of primary source documents from America's founding era and write several "Christian American history" books that argue that the founding fathers intended America to be a Christian nation and that argue for a Christian reading of the Constitution they wrote. This work has shaped a generation of Christian school and homeschool students.

Despite being roundly rejected by scholars, Barton claims to be a "recognized authority in American history and the role of religion in public life." For example, an *amicus* brief filed by Wallbuilders in *McCollum v. California Department of Corrections and Rehabilitation* claims Barton

> works as a consultant to national history textbook publishers. He has been appointed by the State Boards of Education in states such as California and Texas to help write the American history and government standards for students in those states. Mr. Barton also consults with Governors and State Boards of Education in several states, and he has testified in numerous state legislatures on American history.

Examples include a 1998 appointment as an advisor to the California Academic Standards Commission and a 2009 appointment as a reviewer in the Texas Board of Education's effort to revise the state's social science curriculum.[8] In each case, Barton was one of three conservative "outside experts" appointed to review the curriculum to ensure that children learn that America was founded on biblical principles. As "experts" they sought changes to the curriculum to ensure that Christianity was presented "as an overall force for good—and a key reason for American Exceptionalism, the notion that the country stands above and apart."[9] Indeed, when Barton invoked his position as a curriculum consultant on Jon Stewart's *Daily Show*, Stewart asked for whom he had done this work, and Barton refused to name anyone, saying "if they don't name names then I don't."

In 2005 Barton was included in *Time* magazine's list of the twenty-five most influential evangelicals, but it was his association with Fox News' Glenn Beck, who called him the most important man in America, that catapulted him into another level of influence. By 2011 Barton could boast that Republican primary presidential candidates Newt Gingrich and Michelle Bachmann consulted him. Bachmann even invited him to speak to her congressional Tea Party Caucus on the history of the Constitution. Mike Huckabee infamously said that "every American should be forced to listen to Barton at gunpoint." Barton's presentation style makes on-the-spot critical engagement difficult. He jumps, at lightning speed, from one piece of data to another, interpreted through his "biblical" framework; he creates a barrage of information, tied to small pieces of familiar truth and rooted in an apparently vast collection of primary documents. Barton is one of the very best examples of the way in which the Tea Party is about much more than taxes, and he's been at the center of its rise. In addition to being promoted by Glenn Beck, he travels the country presenting his Constitutional Seminars and selling materials promoting his views to churches, civic organizations, Christian schools, and Christian homeschoolers.

Barton's work has been the subject of extensive critique by bloggers, reporters, and other critics, some of whom are scholars publishing peer-reviewed critiques, but, for the most part, scholars have not devoted a lot of attention to debunking his claims.[10] Beginning in about 2011, two conservative Christian professors from Grove City College, Warren Throckmorton, professor of psychology, and Michael Coulter, professor of humanities and political science, published a critique of Barton's *The Jefferson Lies* entitled *Getting Jefferson Right: Fact Checking Claims about*

Our Third President.[11] The book was received well by scholars, and the authors' credentials as conservative Christians undermined Barton's defense that criticism of his work was ideological rather than factual. *The Jefferson Lies* was withdrawn by its publisher. One might expect under the weight of such resounding rejection, Barton would disappear into obscurity. Yet Barton's supporters remain as devoted as before. Criticism from scholars (whether Christian or not) is dismissed as liberal, socialist, and even pagan.[12] Discredited in the larger culture, Barton remains influential in the conservative Christian subculture.

Barton and the Philosophy of History

Although Barton is frequently lambasted for his historical revisionism, what is at stake is much bigger than a selective reading of history. Barton's concern—and Rushdoony's—is the meaning and purpose of history. Rushdoony called it a "Biblical Philosophy of History"; Barton often uses the term "Providential History." For them, the purpose of studying history is devotional; it is to discern God's hand in it and to come to understand God's plan. Barton's focus is on revealing the special relationship between God and the history and purpose of America. An episode of Barton's online radio show called "Why History Matters" offers a window into how close Barton's view of history is to Rushdoony's. Barton says, "If you do not see the divine hand working behind the scenes with what's going on in history, history will be an incomprehensible enigma." He then describes contemporary secular history as an intentional effort, by the likes of Robert Ingersoll and professional historians such as Charles and Mary Beard, to rewrite American history without God. For Rushdoony and Barton *history* is not the academic discipline most of us have in mind when we use the term: the effort to assemble evidence from the past to understand events, their context, and change over time. The history that Barton promotes is, indeed, theological. In this framing, history, like every other aspect of culture, becomes a conflict between two diametrically opposing worldviews, based in mutually exclusive presuppositions. Therefore, when historians—even Christian historians—criticize his work, Barton dismisses them as deluded by pagan professors.[13]

As Rushdoony writes, history always begins with an act of faith. For him there are two diametrically opposed versions. One is the humanistic faith that history can be understood in naturalistic terms. The other, for Christians, is that history is meaningful in every detail. Just as creation reveals the nature of God, history reveals God's plan for the human race. The reason to study history is not to understand past events, but to understand God and our place in his plan. It is exactly this sacralizing of history that has made organizations like Vision Forum so effective among homeschoolers. Rather than being lost in the mundane trials of everyday life, Christian homeschoolers, and believers who embrace this vision of history, find themselves at the center of the plans of almighty God, building "multigenerational faithfulness." It is undoubtedly a moving and heady experience.

Barton on the Bible

Barton, like the Reconstructionists, sees the Bible as a coherent whole, from Genesis through Revelation. The Old and New Testaments are integrated and still applicable today, though some requirements in the Old Testament are no longer required of "us." They are understood as "ceremonial law" and have been fulfilled in Christ. As an example, rituals associated with sacrifice in the Old Testament are understood to prefigure the "one true sacrifice." Now that Jesus has fulfilled this role, the rituals are no longer relevant. The unity of scripture means that all three members of the Trinity were present at creation and throughout the Old Testament period. This is a view distinctly different from that of most other contemporary Christians, who see a "God of wrath in the Old Testament and God of love in the new." In this view the God who commanded Moses to commit genocide in Deuteronomy 20:17 is the same God worshipped in the New Testament as Father, Son, and Holy Spirit.[14] That the God of Christianity resolves the problem of sin in the world with the brutal execution of his own son serves as both warning to the faithful to bring the nation into conformity with God's law and justification for the destruction of those outside the covenant. This is a view developed by John Calvin and, in some ways, influential in all of Protestantism; but it is today embraced in its full form in only a few of the more extreme branches of Protestantism, including Christian Reconstructionism, through which Barton likely encountered it.

Barton believes we must apply the Bible to specific policy questions, which brings us to another point where the influence of Rushdoony and the Reconstructionists is important: the framework Barton uses to discern the application of biblical texts to all areas of life developed in the post-Reformation period.[15] This framework provided the basis for

Rushdoony's biblical interpretation and undergirds most of his work. It was Rushdoony who framed it in a way in which it could be disseminated in popular theology.

Remember, in Rushdoony's version of sphere sovereignty, sometimes called jurisdictional authority, God ordained three distinct realms of authority—civil, ecclesiastical, and familial—over which he and he alone remains the ultimate authority. The institutions in each sphere are given authority over those aspects of life, and believers are obligated to submit to the leaders God places in charge of each, civil authorities (or magistrates, as they call them, following Calvin), pastors, and fathers. Families are the central institution for the exercise of dominion and are charged with raising children; churches are charged with teaching and preaching the Gospel, nurturing families in their responsibilities and warning against the tendency of civil government—in the hands of unbelievers—to become tyrannical; and civil government, rightly constrained, protects property and punishes evildoers. In both Rushdoony and Barton there is a strong emphasis on the claim that each sphere can do only that which is delegated to it by God and no more. Any activity outside the limits of the specifically delineated jurisdictional authority is condemned on two grounds: it is humanism, elevating human reason above God's authority, and socialism, allowing the civil government to move toward becoming all-encompassing.

So, like Rushdoony, Barton finds that public education is unbiblical on the basis that education is primarily a family responsibility and secondarily a church responsibility. Likewise, feeding the poor is the job of families and churches, not the state. Tax schemes designed to fund these illegitimate functions of government are unbiblical and considered legalized theft. By failing to stop illegal immigration, the government is failing in its biblical obligation to protect private property, and, in seeking to enact policies to limit global warming, the government is intruding on individual and familial obligations to exercise dominion.

Barton and the Constitution

In 2011, Barton's radio program *Wallbuilders Live* carried a three-part series on the Constitution and "the principles of limited government" that illustrated well how he draws the conclusions he does regarding what the Constitution meant to the founders.[16] The spectrum of activists calling themselves "constitutionalists"—including Barton but ranging from avowed Reconstructionists to Tea Partiers who claim their movement is solely about taxes and limited government—read the Constitution in the context of the Declaration of Independence to invoke the authority of the Creator in an otherwise godless document. The first of Barton's three-part series lays out exactly how this works.

Many look at the US Constitution and see little mention of religion and wonder how conservative Christians can insist that it is a template for a Christian nation. But Barton is careful to speak, instead, of our "original national founding documents." For Barton and his followers, the Declaration of Independence, though never ratified and carrying no legal authority, has the same status as the Constitution. Indeed, in their view, the Constitution can only be read in the context of the Declaration:

> Go back to our original national document, our original founding document, the Declaration of Independence. In the first forty-six words . . . they tell us the philosophy of government that has produced America's exceptionalism . . . two points immediately become clear in that opening statement of our first national government document. Number one, they say there is a divine creator, and number two, the divine creator gives guaranteed rights to men . . . there's a God and God gives specific rights to men.

Barton asserts that the founders believed there were a handful of unalienable rights, the most important of which are life, liberty, and property. He occasionally acknowledges that the language in the Declaration is slightly different (life, liberty, and the pursuit of happiness), but he argues that the pursuit of happiness is grounded in property, making the two terms interchangeable. He more often uses the term "property." These rights are understood to come directly from God, and the purpose of government (and therefore the Constitution the founders wrote) is limited to securing those rights. According to Barton, in language that became common Tea Party rhetoric, an inalienable right is "a right to which we are entitled by our all-wise and all-beneficent creator; a right that God gave you, not government."[17] Any other perceived rights, not understood as coming from God, cannot be legitimately protected by the civil government.

This is the very point of criticism made of Supreme Court nominee Elena Kagan by Herb Titus, described earlier. Rooted in the three-part division of authority popularized by Rushdoony and the Reconstructionists,

Barton argues that the Bible (which he believes the founders read in the same way he does and upon which he believes they based the Constitution) limits the jurisdiction of civil government. That life, liberty, and property are "among" the God-given rights that Barton finds in the Declaration left room for the articulation of more rights derived from God to be "incorporated" into the Constitution, most clearly in the Bill of Rights, which he calls "the capstone" to the Constitution. "They said, we're going to name some other inalienable rights just to make sure that government does not get into these rights . . . When you look at the ten amendments that are the Bill of Rights, those are God-granted rights that government is not to intrude into." He then offered some unique interpretations of the rights protected in the first ten amendments. The First Amendment religion clauses, for Barton, become "the right of public religious expression." The Second Amendment right to keep and bear arms is, according to Barton, "what they called the biblical right of self-defense." The Third Amendment prohibiting the coerced quartering of soldiers is the biblical and constitutional protection of the "the sanctity of the home." Finally, all the protections against unjust prosecution in the Fifth Amendment are reduced to the protection of "the right to private property."

While the "limited government" enshrined in the Constitution protects basic rights given by God and precludes government from doing anything not within the purview of its biblical mandate, it also, according to Barton, prohibits abortion. Barton says that, according to the founders, the first example of "God-given inalienable rights is the right to life." Barton claims that when the founders invoked the God-given right to life they intended to prohibit abortion. He claims that "abortion was a discussed item in the founding era." As evidence he says, "as a matter of fact we have books in our library of original documents—observations on abortion back in 1808," and that "early legislatures in the 1790s were dealing with legislation on the right to life on the abortion issue." But Barton gives no examples and provides no references to any evidence. After this slippery claim, he goes on at length with quotes from founders on the right to life, none of which mention abortion. "They understood back then that abortion was a bad deal and that your first guaranteed inalienable right is a right to life. Consider how many other founding fathers talked about the right to life." In another example of slipperiness, he quotes founder James Wilson: "Human life, from its commencement to its close, is protected by the common law. In the contemplations of law, life begins when the infant is first able to stir in the womb." Realizing that this won't do the work of banning abortion from conception, Barton redefines the question, moving the focus from the development of the fetus to what the mother "knows."

> Very simply, he [Wilson] says as soon as you know you're pregnant, as soon as you know there's life in the womb, that life is protected by law. That's where the technology difference is, we can know that there's life in the womb much earlier today than what they knew back then. But the point is the same there: as soon as you know there's a life there, it's protected.

But this is not what Wilson said, and Barton's argument gets worse. In his view this understanding of the right to life is a bellwether for a number of other issues that are at the top of the religious right's agenda: "Our philosophy of American exceptionalism is very simple: there is a God, he gives specific rights, [and] the purpose of government is to protect the rights he's given." If someone is "wrong" on "life issues," they're likely to be wrong on the right to self-defense (the right to own guns), the sanctity of the home (his interpretation of what it means to not have soldiers in your house), private property (his reading of the rights of the accused culminating in the protection against eminent domain), and "the traditional marriage issue" (for which he makes no connection to the founders or the Constitution). Barton's interpretation doesn't even resemble a close reading of the text with an eye toward the founders' intentions—or any coherent application of the value of limited government—yet he successfully frames it as such in populist discourse.

In 2011, the Ninth Circuit Court rejected an appeal challenging the policy of the California Department of Corrections and Rehabilitation that allows only leaders of "five faiths" (Protestant, Catholic, Muslim, Jewish, and Native American) to serve as paid chaplains (*McCollum v. CDCR*). The ruling had nothing to do with the legitimacy of the claim that the policy unconstitutionally favors some religions over others but rather whether McCollum (a Pagan minister) had standing to bring the case. An amicus brief filed by Wallbuilders in support of the CDCR to privilege the "five faiths" provides a glimpse into how Barton reads the Constitution.

For him the Constitution represents a consensus—as though there is a singular view that can be attributed to "the founders." Barton's style of reading the Constitution is modeled on his style of reading the Bible, which he also treats as a coherent document that can be read from start to finish to yield a clear, undisputed, objective meaning, instead of a collection of fragmented texts written over a very long period of time in different cultures, assembled into larger texts, then chosen from an even larger collection of texts in a political process, translated from ancient languages, and finally interpreted in different ways by different communities. Every stage of that process continues to be profoundly disputed by scholars, and there is always an interpretative framework (albeit all too often an unrecognized one) underlying any reading of it. While the US Constitution is a newer document, and it is therefore somewhat less difficult to discern its meaning(s), the fact remains that it is the product of hard-fought compromise among leaders, bound in time and culture, who profoundly disagreed with each other. There is no reason to believe they thought they were writing a sacred text to which all subsequent generations of Americans were bound by a process that amounts to divining a singular "intent."

The argument Barton made in the brief, moreover, illustrates a second important point. He is being disingenuous when he insists he just wants everyone to have the opportunity to practice his religion freely. In his appearance on the *Daily Show*, he defended the practice of Christian religious observance in otherwise secular contexts when the majority wants it by saying that a Muslim-majority community should be able to make "Sharia law" the law of the land. There was a significant outcry from his anti-Muslim supporters, and he backtracked on the point in a subsequent episode of *Wallbuilders Live*.[18]

In this brief, however, he argued that only those religions that fit with what he thinks the founders meant by "religion" should be protected. Protected religion is either Christianity alone or perhaps the larger category of monotheism—Barton asserts that rights of conscience don't extend to atheists either (and by implication also not to Buddhists and Hindus): "whether this Court agrees that 'religion' meant monotheism or believes that it meant Christianity . . . it is clear that atheism, heathenism, and paganism were not part of the definition of 'religion.'" Barton has argued against the free exercise of rights of Muslims, as have other religious right promoters of Islamophobia, claiming Islam is "not a religion."[19] Indeed, the term "religion" does have a complicated history, and it has often been used (or denied) to legitimize dominance of one group over another. Initially Africans were said to be "without religion," legitimizing their enslavement, and, in another example, Native Americans were considered "without religion" to justify taking their land. Barton's brief is important because it made explicit that which he often tries to deny: that only Christianity (and maybe Judaism) is protected under his reading of the Constitution.

Barton on the Free Market and Socialism

On another segment of *Wallbuilders Live*, Barton and co-host Rick Green discussed the effort by the Obama administration to prohibit Internet service providers from charging for service based on usage (known as Net Neutrality) because it violates biblical economics and is "socialist." It's easy to dismiss that charge as nothing more than demagoguery, but, in fact, the discussion illustrates what they mean by socialism and, ultimately, how they understand freedom. Both points trace directly back to Rushdoony. Most of us understand socialism as a system that limits private ownership of property and in which power (political and economic) is centralized in the state; Tea Party accusations that any policy they oppose is "socialist" seem, at best, like hyperbole. But in Barton's view, any move away from what he sees as an unfettered free market, any regulation or involvement on the part of government, is a move toward socialism—and of course he thinks that private ownership and free markets are biblically sanctioned. Net Neutrality prohibits ISPs from charging for Internet service based on usage. This seems straightforward to Barton and Green: "what they mean is we're not going to let you choose who you need to charge more to." Maybe more interesting, though, is the subsequent exchange between Rick Green and his "good friend" Texas congressman Joe Barton, who was sponsoring legislation to overturn the Obama administration's Net Neutrality regulation. Joe Barton tried to explain Net Neutrality and, in the process, revealed important aspects of how such people understand freedom in entirely economic terms. Joe Barton says that we

> cannot regulate the Internet, it should be open and free. Democrats' definition of Net Neutrality is we want to give FCC the authority to tell people who actually provide the Internet what they can and can't do with it. Now, what people like yourself and myself mean [by freedom] is no government interference; it's pretty straightforward. Republicans and conservatives have always tried to keep the Internet totally free.

But of course they have not tried to keep it totally free, except in one very narrow economic sense. They certainly do not mean "free" in a way that includes broadly available access, because that's socialism; "redistribution of wealth through the Internet . . . this is socialism on the Internet." Nor do they mean free regarding content, as David Barton made explicit when he returned to the conversation at the end of the show saying, "We're not suggesting moral license, we don't want to have obscenity, pornography, child pornography . . . You still have moral laws to follow." Economic freedom is nearly absolute, but it is still subordinate to moral law.[20]

At the height of the debate over the federal budget and the Tea Party demands that Congress not raise the debt ceiling during the summer of 2011, David Barton and company tackled the question posed by the "religious left" in the budget debate: What would Jesus cut? They devoted an entire episode of *Wallbuilders Live* to the question: "Why Do People Think Government's Role Is to Take Care of the Poor?"[21] The episode is promoted with the assertion that "The role of the government is not to exercise mercy, but to exercise justice. It is improper for government to take care of the poor. That is up to us, as individuals." With guest Michael Youseff, who had recently written on his blog about the application of the Bible to government spending and the poor, David Barton and Rick Green invoked the framework for limited biblical jurisdiction developed and promoted by Rushdoony.[22] They claimed that the Bible has "205 verses about taking care of the poor" and asserted that "only one is directed to government," which simply requires no more than the poor be "treated fairly in court." Barton and Green employ Rushdoony's framework of three God-ordained spheres of authority and the view that any action on issues outside those responsibilities is tyrannical and socialist. The responsibility to take care of the poor is limited to families and churches.

As we have seen, Rushdoony, Gary North, David Chilton, George Grant, and others have written on this topic. One of the more accessible places to find their view is in George Grant's volume in Gary North's *Biblical Blueprints Series*. Barton and Green borrow from them to assert that taking care of the poor is not the job of the government. Charity is up to individuals, families, and churches. Moreover, it should not be extended to everyone. The architects of the framework on which Barton bases his view are quite clear: biblical charity may extend to the four corners of the earth, but *only* to those who are in submission to biblical law as it is articulated by the Reconstructionists.

Barton on Race

David Barton is also the popularizer of a revisionist history of race in America that has become part of the Tea Party narrative. Drawn in part from the writings of Christian Reconstructionists, that narrative recasts modern-day Republicans as the racially inclusive party, and modern-day Democrats as the racists supportive of slavery and postemancipation racist policies. Barton's website has included a "Black History" section for some time.[23] Like Barton's larger revisionist effort to develop and perpetuate the narrative that America is a Christian nation, the "Republicans-are-really-the-party-of-racial-equality" narrative is not entirely fictive. Some historical points Barton makes are true; but he and his biggest promoter, Glenn Beck, manipulate those points, remove all historical context, and add patently false historical claims in order to promote their political agenda. Barton appeared regularly on Beck's show to disseminate his alternative reading of African American history, carrying with him, as he does, what he claims are original documents and artifacts that he flashes around for credibility.

In June of 2010 I traveled to central Florida to attend a Tea Party event sponsored by the Florida chapter of Beck's "9–12 Project" held at a Baptist church (with a Christian school that was established in the late 1970s). The church sanctuary was decked in patriotic trimmings, including eight big flags on the wall, bunting all over the altar area, and a collection of small flags on the altar itself. As I waited for the event to begin, I overheard people talking about homeschooling and David Barton's work on "America's Christian Heritage," all while Aaron Copland's "Fanfare for the Common Man" played over the sound system. For those unconvinced of the religious dimensions of at the Tea Party movement, the strain of it exhibited here was indistinguishable from the church-based political organizing efforts of the religious right dating back at least to the 1980s. As each local candidate spoke, it was clear how profoundly conservative, Republican, and Christian (in the religious right sense of Christian) this gathering was.

The event was promoted as a response to charges of racism in the Tea Party movement. The banner at the entrance to the event read: "9–12 Project: not racist, not violent, just not silent anymore." The pastor of the church introduced the meeting, the Tea Party–supported candidates for local office spoke, and all invoked "Christian American history" and the "religion of the founders." The "9–12 Project" refers both to post-9/11 America (when "divisions didn't matter") and to the "nine principles and twelve values" of the group, initiated and promoted by Beck. The "principles" are a distillation of those in *The Five Thousand Year Leap,* a 1981 book by Cleon Skousen, which was referenced repeatedly by speakers at the event. The book has long been a favorite for Christian schools and homeschoolers and among Reconstructionists despite the fact that Skousen is a Mormon (perhaps because he is also a strong advocate of the free-market Austrian School of economics). I was surprised to learn that Skousen's book was enjoying a resurgence in popularity as a result of Beck's promotion and is available in a new edition with a preface by Beck. The fight over the degree to which America was "founded as a Christian nation" is important in that it is a fight over our mythic understanding of ourselves. That is, it is a fight over the narratives through which Americans construct a sense of what it means to be American and perpetuate that sense through the culture and in successive generations.

Intended to counter the charges of racism made against the Tea Party movement, the main speaker was an African American, Franz Kebreau, from the National Association for the Advancement of Conservative People of all Colors (NAACPC). The event was in a more rural part of Florida than where I live, and I passed a number of Confederate flags on my way there. I expected an all-white crowd making arguments about "reverse discrimination," libertarian arguments against violations of state sovereignty (especially with the Civil Rights Act), and maybe even some of the "slavery wasn't as bad as people say" arguments. What I found surprised me. Kebreau gave a detailed lecture on the history of slavery and racism in America: a profoundly revisionist history. In Kebreau's narrative, racism is a legacy of slavery, but it was a socially constructed mechanism by which people in power divided, threatened, and manipulated both blacks and whites. Many of the pieces of historical data he marshals in favor of this thesis are not unfamiliar to those who have studied this aspect of American history, but they are probably not as well known among Americans in general: some slave owners were black, not all slaves were black, black Africans played a huge role in the slave trade, and very few Southerners actually owned slaves. While at least most of these points are undeniably true, they were presented with a specific subtext: with the goal of lending credence to the view that contemporary critics of racism make too much of America's history of slavery. In this view, it is Democrats who are primarily responsible for fostering racism to solidify power. Southern Democrats opposed civil rights laws, voting rights, integration, and so on. Northern Democrats fanned racial tensions by promoting social programs that made African Americans dependent on government. Race-baiting demagogues like Jesse Jackson and the Reverend Al Sharpton perpetuate the divisions today.

In August of 2010, Beck held his Restoring Honor Rally, bringing many Tea Party groups—Tea Party Patriots, Freedom Works, 9–12 Project, Special Operations Warrior Foundation, and others—together at the Lincoln Memorial. While Beck initially promoted the event as a nonpolitical effort to return to the values of the founders, he claims he only realized later that he scheduled it on the anniversary of Martin Luther King Jr.'s "I Have a Dream" speech. He suggested that while he did not realize the significance of the date, "God might have had a hand" in the coincidence. Beck was criticized for both his timing and his crediting the Almighty. Beck fancies himself a contemporary King, "reclaiming the civil rights movement," and while he was widely mocked for drawing this parallel, it was less recognized that he did it on a foundation laid by David Barton and his revisionist history, which relies in no small part on the work of Rushdoony.

In his essay "The Founding Fathers and Slavery," Barton quotes extensively from the writings of the founders and claims that many of them were abolitionists. He maintains that the overwhelming majority of the founders were "sincere Christians" who thought American slavery was "unbiblical," blamed England for imposing the institution on the colonies, and set in motion processes to end it. Scholars dispense with these claims. According to Diana Butler Bass, "It was nearly universally accepted by white Christian men that the Bible taught, supported, or promoted slavery and it was rare to find a leading American intellectual, Christian or otherwise, who questioned the practice on the basis that it was 'unbiblical.' Some intellectuals thought it was counter to the Enlightenment."[24] Historian Mark Noll argues that the reverse of Barton's view with regard to the British is correct: evangelicals in the Church of England, not in America, argued that slavery violated the Bible. Again, according to Bass, "the American biblical argument against slavery did not develop in any substantial way until the 1830s and 1840s. Even then, the anti-slavery argument was considered liberal and not quite in line with either scripture or tradition."

Another essay on Barton's website, "Democrats and Republicans in Their Own Words: National Party Platforms on Specific Biblical Issues," compares party platforms from 1840 to 1964—the period before Southern Democrats who blocked civil rights legislation began switching to the Republican Party. In Barton's narrative, the modern Republican Party is the party more favorable to African Americans because the Republicans led the fight against slavery and for civil rights from the formation of the

Republican Party as the "anti-slavery party" and the "election of Abraham Lincoln as the first Republican President," to the Emancipation Proclamation, the Thirteenth and Fourteenth Amendments, the passage of civil rights laws during Reconstruction, and the election of blacks to office. Barton writes that while the Democratic Party platform was defending slavery, "the original Republican platform in 1856 had only nine planks— six of which were dedicated to ending slavery and securing equal rights for African-Americans." Democrats, on the other hand, supported slavery, and they then sought to ban blacks from holding public office and to limit their right to vote via poll taxes, literacy tests, grandfather clauses, and general harassment and intimidation, and they established legal segregation under Jim Crow laws.

Barton takes issue with the claim that "Southerners" fought for racist policies, because "just one type of Southern whites were the cause of the problem: Southern racist whites." Rather, he argues (missing the logical inconsistency), we should lay the responsibility for racism at the feet of Democrats:

> Current writers and texts addressing the post-Civil War period often present an incomplete portrayal of that era . . . To make an accurate portrayal of black history, a distinction must be made between types of whites. Therefore, [it would be] much more historically correct— although more "politically incorrect"—were it to read: "Democratic legislatures in the South established whites-only voting in party primaries."[25]

Because he says very little about contemporary Democrats, it's clear that Barton's purpose is to connect them with racist Southern Democrats, while completely ignoring the relationship of modern-day Republicans with racism. Most glaringly, the Republican "Southern strategy" is entirely missing from Barton's account of the parties' political strategies with regard to race.[26] From the Johnson administration through the Nixon and Reagan campaigns, Republican strategists effectively used race as a "wedge issue." Southern Democrats would not support efforts by the national party to secure civil rights for African Americans. By focusing on specific racial issues (like segregation), Republicans split off voters who had traditionally voted for Democrats. The contemporary "states' rights" battle cry at the core of the conservative movement and Tea Party rhetoric is rooted in this very tactic. Barton and Beck want to rewrite American history on race and slavery in order to cleanse the founding fathers of responsibility for slavery and, more importantly, blame it and subsequent racism on Democrats.

But Barton's rewriting of the history of the founding era and the civil rights movement alone doesn't quite accomplish that. He has to lower the bar even more and make slavery itself seem like it wasn't quite as bad as we might think. And for that, he turns to Stephen McDowell of the Reconstructionist-oriented Providence Foundation. Wallbuilders' website promotes a collection of "resources on African American History." Much of the material is written by Barton himself, but one of the essays is McDowell's, drawn almost entirely from Rushdoony's work in the early 1960s. McDowell's discussion of slavery, written in 2003, comes directly from Rushdoony's *The Institutes of Biblical Law.* McDowell attributes his views to Rushdoony and uses precisely the language that Rushdoony used as early as the 1960s. Rushdoony's writings on slavery are often cited by his critics. Rushdoony did argue that slavery is biblically permitted. While criticizing American slavery as violating a number of biblical requirements, he also defended it in his writings. By promoting McDowell, and by extension Rushdoony, Barton promotes a biblical worldview in which slavery is in some circumstances acceptable. This worldview downplays the dehumanization of slavery by explicitly arguing that God condones it in certain circumstances.

McDowell writes that, while it was not part of "God's plan" from the beginning, "slavery, in one form or another (including spiritual, mental, and physical), is always the fruit of disobedience to God and His law/ word," meaning that the slave is justifiably being punished for his or her disobedience. McDowell argues that slavery is tightly regulated, though not forbidden, in the Bible, and that American Southern slavery was not "biblical" slavery because it was race-based. Following Rushdoony, he argues that there are two forms of biblically permissible slavery: indentured servitude, in which "servants were well treated and when released, given generous pay," and slavery, in which, in exchange for being taken care of, one might choose to remain a slave. Moreover, he maintains that the Bible permits two forms of involuntary slavery: criminals who could not make restitution for their crimes could be sold into slavery and "pagans, [who] could be made permanent slaves."[27] Of course, Rushdoony defines "pagans" as simply non-Christians. This means that slavery was/is voluntary only for Christians; non-Christians can be held in nonvoluntary perpetual slavery. Barton shares this understanding of the legal status of "pagans," at least in terms of their rights under the First Amendment. McDowell is explicit that race-based kidnapping and enforced slavery are unbiblical. In fact, they are punishable by death. All this comes directly from *The Institutes of Biblical Law*. McDowell argues, as did Rushdoony in the early 1960s, that while American slavery was not biblical slavery, neither was it the cause of the Civil War. The major point of dispute between North and South, they argue, was, not slavery but "centralism,"—that is, the increasing centralization of power in the federal government, an argument frequently echoed today by the states' rights agitators and Tenth Amendment Tea Partiers. Although in one essay Barton parts company with Rushdoony and McDowell over the significance of slavery as a cause of the Civil War (Barton argues instead that slavery was a cause, in service of his argument that the present-day Republican Party is more racially inclusive than the Democrats), he nonetheless continues to promote, on his website, their view that slavery is biblical.[28]

The historical revisionism with regard to race in America that gained a hearing in the Tea Party (thanks to Glenn Beck and activists such as Franz Kebreau) is rooted in Barton's and Wallbuilders' writings, which have been deeply influenced by Rushdoony.

Christian Reconstruction and the Constitution Party

While for the most part the Tea Party is aligned with the Republican Party, the alliance is tenuous, and many Tea Partiers are critical of both major parties; for them, the choice between the established parties is a false one. The Constitution Party, the third party of choice for Tea Partiers, was founded by the late Howard Phillips as the U.S. Taxpayers Alliance. Third parties in the American system rarely have a measurable impact on elections, but they do, as in this case, help create the climate in which a small, more extreme, faction can push the major party toward its direction. That Tea Partiers would consider leaving the Republican Party for the Constitution Party gives them more clout. And, in this case, the third party has deep ties to Christian Reconstruction.

Former US congressman and Republican presidential candidate Ron Paul is a prominent example. Leading Reconstructionist Gary North worked on Paul's congressional staff decades ago, and the ties between them remain strong.[29] North recently led a campaign that convinced Paul to develop and promote a homeschool curriculum.[30] Ron's son, Kentucky senator and presidential candidate Rand Paul, has identified himself closely with the views of his father. Both men are at the core of the Tea Party movement, especially the libertarian wing that is generally considered distinct from the religious right. Yet Ron Paul has spoken at Constitution Party events, and Howard Phillips spoke in favor of his candidacy as president.

The influence of Rushdoony is apparent in the mission of Phillips's Constitution Party, which seeks to reestablish America as a republic organized around biblical principles under the authority of Jesus Christ. While to many this will seem diametrically opposed to the requirements of the Constitution, their reading of the Constitution is the same as Barton's and Rushdoony's. It elevates the Declaration of Independence as an equal, and necessary, companion to the Constitution and relies on a pre-Fourteenth Amendment reading that secured the autonomy of states. This dovetails exactly with the beliefs of the Tea Partiers. In this view, the limits on the relationship between church and state did not apply to the states but only to Congress (to whom the First Amendment religion clauses were addressed). Moreover, an examination of the Constitution Party platform shows positions on numerous issues that have long been developed and promoted by Rushdoony and his followers.[31] It is not only Reconstructionists who hold these views (they come from the John Birch Society, the libertarian movement, the Moral Majority and various other places) but the list of positions, the way in which they are held together, and the ties to Phillips point to Reconstructionists' underlying influence.

So when the platform uses the phrase "civil government," it does so to emphasize the distinction between the three distinct biblical spheres of government, civil government being only one. Reconstructionists criticize the "conflation" of spheres of government. The Constitution Party platform calls the family one of three governing institutions established by God. Likewise, the platform articulates support for Christian schooling and homeschooling and does so on the basis of Reconstructionist framing: the family is understood as a form of government, given by God, with a specific sphere of authority that includes raising children without the interference of the civil government. Opposition to welfare, in the platform, is based on the argument that welfare is more properly understood as charity and is legitimately within the authority of the church, not the civil government.

The platform calls for economic reform, including a return to a hard money standard, elimination of the Federal Reserve, as well as fractional reserve banking (the requirement that banks hold only a small percentage of their deposits in reserve). In April 2009, Rand Paul spoke to the Campaign for Liberty rally to end the Federal Reserve, in front of the Federal Reserve building in Minnesota.[32] He cited libertarian icon Ayn Rand, but he drew on Gary North. He argued against centralized banking on the grounds that North lays out in *Honest Money*. North argued that the cause of the international debt crisis of the 1980s was the Federal Reserve System and the solution lay in eliminating that institution and moving to a hard money standard, all based on the biblical command to have "just weights and measures." Paul, in very similar language, attributed our current debt and economic crises to the Federal Reserve and fractional reserve banking. Behind Paul at the platform was a sign that read: "Honest Money." Rand Paul went on to serve as the keynote speaker at the Minnesotan Constitution Party event.[33]

How can the Constitution Party appeal to both theocrats and libertarians? In other words, how can they advocate limited government and, at the same time, application of biblical law? An understanding of the subtleties of Christian Reconstruction is really helpful here. Again, the answer to the seeming paradox lies in the way in which "legitimately delegated biblical authority" is framed in terms of the three distinct spheres. For Reconstructionists, the civil government's authority is limited to protecting citizens from criminals. Family authority and ecclesiastical authority are established to uphold (and enforce) other aspects of biblical law. That is not to say that any of these institutions is understood as functioning autonomously; all are under the authority of God and are to function according to biblical law. But each is independent of the others. So for libertarian Reconstructionists (as many of them are) limited government means limited civil government. Their form of libertarianism is distinct from the more libertine versions because no area of life is outside biblical authority, though much of it is outside civil authority.

There are those who dismiss efforts to trace these influences as "guilt by association," but I am not assessing guilt. My interest is in tracing the intellectual history and the sociology of knowledge. While the Tea Party is a confluence of a number of ideological strands in American politics the ties between them and the Christian Reconstructionists are more substantial than the fact that a particular leader has been invited to speak to groups with whom he agrees on one or two issues. The ties between Ron and Rand Paul, the Tea Party, the Constitution Party, and Reconstructionists are significantly revealed in the formulation of Ron and Rand Paul's views, not just in who they know.

David Barton Goes to Hollywood

In the spring of 2012, former teen star turned evangelical heartthrob Kirk Cameron released a new film he described as a personal journey to trace the steps of "the founders" and learn their recipe for success in building the freest, most prosperous nation the world has ever seen. *Monumental: In Search of America's National Treasure* was heavily promoted in churches, by Tea Party groups, on the Internet, and in a series of interviews ranging from mainstream media appearances on Piers Morgan and an interview in *Christianity Today*, to appearances in venues much further to the right, such as the Conservative Political Action Conference and the Christian Reconstructionist film festival sponsored by Doug Phillips. If *Monumental* had footnotes, they would have traced back directly to R. J. Rushdoony. The Christian Reconstruction biblical worldview and the interlocking theological notions of presuppositionalism, postmillennialism, and theonomy have been popularized over half a century in terms that are now very familiar. The critique of secular humanism as an alternative religion and the impossibility of neutrality; the dominion theology that calls for the transformation of all aspects of culture; and the application of biblical law to the reconstructed society are all widespread among the religious right.

Based on prerelease film clips and interviews, many people, myself included, pointed out the ties between the people Cameron was relying on as experts (especially David Barton and Herb Titus) and Christian Reconstruction. I went to see it at the theater, and I was stunned at how thoroughly the film was shaped by the worldview articulated by Rushdoony. I never expected to see "my folks" (as ethnographers often call the people we study) on the big screen in an overflow movie theater presenting R. J. Rushdoony's worldview to evangelicals, homeschoolers, and Tea Partiers, who never heard his name nor knew that he was the source for much of what was presented in Cameron's film. Not evident from prerelease promotional material was the central influence of Marshall Foster, as both co-producer and "guest" through much of the film. Foster, president of the Mayflower Institute (now the World History Institute), was the "David Barton" of Christian schooling and Christian homeschooling before David Barton. I wrote earlier that when I told Foster that I was writing about the influence of R. J. Rushdoony, he embraced Rushdoony's influence on all of his work, and indeed, it is Rushdoony's philosophy of history that Foster articulates throughout the film.

Cameron was once at the center of mainstream conservative evangelicalism with his starring role in the premillennialist *Left Behind* movies and his efforts to support creationism. In the past few years he had become involved in the Christian homeschooling movement, with Christian Reconstructionist Doug Phillips's Vision Forum and San Antonio Independent Christian Film Festival (SAICFF), and now his website is part of Brandon Vallorani's Liberty Alliance. In the weeks leading up to the release of the film, and his many public appearances to promote it, Cameron embraced popularized versions of the Reconstructionist framework. For example, on David Barton's *Wallbuilders Live*, Cameron embraced presuppositionalism, the myth of neutrality, and the inescapability of authority. The language of inescapability echoes Rushdoony.

> Faith is always involved in politics; even those who are secular humanists, they are importing their secular humanist faith and religion and morality and imposing it on everybody else through the laws that they make. So the idea of faith in government is inescapable; it's always going to be somebody's faith, even if it's faith in atheism.

At Doug Phillips's SAICFF in 2012, Cameron ridiculed premillennialism, sounding distinctly postmillennial in ways that echo both Foster and Phillips: "Their attitude [the Puritans] was not 'uh-oh, the beast and the Antichrist is [sic] here . . . let's just keep our heads down and wait for the end of the world.' Instead they said, 'Let's make a 500-year plan and go start a nation.'"[34] And in *Christianity Today* he connected American history to ancient Israel (which he called a republic) and biblical law in a narrative that follows the one presented by Doug Phillips at Reformation 500 in Boston.

> The true roots of America go all the way back to the ancient Hebrew republic. You can trace those roots at Jamestown back to Europe as well. This is the trail of freedom that leads us all the way back to the ancient Hebrews under Moses, where he first delivered those laws of liberty—when he told them to elect leaders, men of character that you willingly submit yourself to, to self-govern rather than have a king.[35]

Combining a postmillennial attitude with the same language Reconstructionists use to argue for a difference between a "top-down" theocracy and a "bottom-up" Reconstruction of society, he told Janet Mefferd that the Puritans "didn't believe change happens from the top down; you build it from the bottom up and from your heart and then it slowly works its way out to every other sphere of society." Invoking another Christian Reconstructionist trope, Cameron told the *Global Christian Post* "what people are actually doing is looking to the government to be their savior . . . and when you do that, you give all of the power to the savior that you are depending on."[36] The film puts forth a Reconstructionist worldview over and over. Nearly every "expert" Cameron cited had Reconstructionist ties, including Stephen McDowell, interviewed but not identified on screen. The film includes ongoing renunciation, and even ridicule, of premillennialism, in favor of an "optimistic vision." Cameron repeats the critique of secular humanism based in presuppositionalism; explores "God's hand in the founding of America" with Puritan New England as the model for the application of biblical law to society; challenges separation of church and state; and promotes Reconstructionist views on education, stopping just short of advocating elimination of public schools, which he does call "government schools," using Rushdoony's term.

The point is not that Kirk Cameron is secretly working toward the re-establishment of biblical law. But this illustrates nicely the gradual and subtle influence of Rushdoony's work in the broader culture, in places where his name is completely unknown. Cameron affiliates with Christian Reconstructionists, supports their organizations, and promotes their theological framework. And he does so in a rather unidentifiable way among mainstream evangelicals and Tea Partiers. When I attended the Tea Party–promoted screening in Jacksonville, the crowd filled one theater (which was sold out more than two hours before its start time) and more than half of an additional overflow theater. As I left the theater after the film, I stopped in the hallway to listen to a woman explain to a small group that had gathered all the work that Doug Phillips had done for the homeschooling community.

Conclusion

David Barton and Wallbuilders' reliance on Reconstructionist works is an excellent example of Rushdoony's meandering influence among the religious right. Rushdoony outlined an early version of Christian American history and an argument in favor of "Christian revisionism" as early as 1964. He argued for the use of the Bible as the only source of authority.

He developed a critique of federal "centralism" in favor of states' and counties' rights. He laid the philosophical basis for unraveling the public school system in favor of Christian schools and homeschools, and helped ensure the legal basis for those alternative forms of education. He developed "biblical" arguments against government "welfare," taxation beyond the 10 percent described in the Bible, and socialism and communism. Many of these positions are embraced by activists in today's Tea Party—thanks to David Barton, Glenn Beck, and others.

Little slivers of Rushdoony's work seem to be everywhere. The Tea Party is not Reconstructionist, nor is it entirely religious, but there are clusters within the Tea Party whose concerns are shaped by the work Rushdoony was doing as early as the 1960s. Rushdoony was crucial to the rise of the Christian school/homeschool movements, the creationist movement as we know it today, Christian American history, biblical economics, and the religious right. And while the contemporary Tea Party movement brought together a variety of diverse groups, at its center were God-and-country Republicans who were disgruntled with the status quo. Their notions of the appropriate functions of government, the relationship between government and religion, and the role of religion in public life were formed in Christian schools and homeschools, and in creationist, Bible-believing, dominion-oriented churches. By the middle of 2013, many claimed that the Tea Party was waning in influence. Yet from state to state we see efforts to privatize and/or defund public education and dismantle public social safety nets, to radically decentralize government, and to shore up white male privilege. It's not yet clear whether the Tea Party organizations will remain on the scene, but their agenda is very much alive.

10

Christian Reconstruction and Violence

RELIGIOUS TRADITIONS ARE neither "essentially peaceful" nor "essentially violent." They can promote peace, empowerment, reconciliation, and justice as well as violence, domination, and oppression; they aid groups in ascribing to themselves the role of the "good guys" while ascribing the role of "bad guys" to their rivals. In *Holy Terrors: Thinking about Religion after September 11,* Bruce Lincoln describes religion as a force that secures a culture's values and power arrangements in transcendent authority in a way that can lead to the use of violence in their defense.[1] Raising the stakes in this fashion—imagining what Mark Juergensmeyer calls a cosmic war—heightens the risk of the use of violence.[2] In this chapter we will explore a variety of examples of the relationship between Christian Reconstruction and violence.

Violence, the Nature of God, and the Imposition of Biblical Law

Recall that Reconstructionists understand the Bible to be a coherent whole, rejecting the idea that there is an inherent incompatibility between a violent God and a loving God, or between the God described in the Old Testament and the message of Jesus. God loves, but this in no way negates or undermines his violence. Calvinism shapes this understanding of God as both a wrathful judge and a loving savior. God's justice requires judgment and humans, being utterly depraved, deserve judgment. Yet some of those fallen human beings are rescued from their depravity and elected to salvation in an act of undeserved grace. That is proof of God's love. Or as Rushdoony graphically writes, regarding the claim that God loves everyone equally, "God's law is never spoken of as promiscuous in Scripture. God definitely indicates his hatred of many people. His love and His sovereign grace, His predestinating council, His demands of righteousness, His requirement of obedience, are closely linked."[3]

Reconstructionists contend that contemporary reinterpretations of Old Testament violence are humanistic rejections of what God called justice. The New Testament is not a replacement for the Old; there is no "God of Love" replacing a "God of Wrath." God is loving and forgiving, and just and vengeful as revealed in the three persons of the Trinity and present at creation. Old Testament biblical law, with its numerous capital offenses, must be the model for Christian life, and civil law today.

Reconstructionists thus support the imposition of violent punishments (stoning and death) for all manner of behaviors that they consider sin (or, in their terms, that God considers sin). They insist that such punishments would only be exacted after society has been transformed by the Holy Spirit such that the overwhelming majority of citizens would be believers who would submit willingly to biblical law. How this would play out in practice, though, is less clear, and they do not usually address this in the context of their protestations that their vision is "not political" and not "imposed from the top."

Reconstructionist pastor Brian Schwertley's essay, "Political Polytheism," builds on the argument made by Gary North in his book by the same name to explore exactly this point.[4] Schwertley is a graduate of Reformed Episcopal Seminary, pastor of Covenanted Reformed Presbyterian Church, and founder of a new denomination called the Westminster Presbyterian Church United States of America. He has published essays in several Reconstructionist venues. Schwertley's church website hosts numerous essays based on Rushdoony, North, and Greg Bahnsen. He challenges contemporary evangelicals who think they can live according to the Bible and build a Christian nation while embracing a political culture of pluralism: "The Bible teaches that God hates all false religions and that the nations which permit idolatry and paganism to flourish will receive judgement."[5] Christians in leadership positions are bound by the authority of God to enforce the biblical prohibition on idolatry: "A nation that becomes an explicitly Christian nation that covenants with God and adopts His law-order cannot permit the open, systematic subversion of that law order. It cannot permit treason toward Jehovah." Of course, he believes (as do all those who argue that America was founded as a Christian nation) that the Puritans covenanted with God on behalf of our nation in just this manner, such that tolerating religious pluralism is nothing short of treason toward God. Moreover, the penalty for such treason is dictated by the Old Testament: death. As Schwertley writes, leaders in a Christian nation who "apostatize . . . must remain silent or perish." While some Reconstructionists argue that their political goal is merely decentralization, Schwertley articulates the violent logical conclusion of the entirety of Rushdoony's teaching: "If a city is given over to a false religion or a cult (e.g., Mormonism) that city should be proceeded against according to the law. The . . . open practice of idolatry is forbidden. It is a capital offense (Dt. 17:2–7)."[6] Reconstructed leaders in positions of authority are obligated to "proceed against" cities that permit religious pluralism. Schwertley not only asserts this but also makes it clear that this is required by the Reconstructionist framework. Schwertley cites the example of biblical kings who pleased God with their intolerance toward religious diversity:

> In accordance with the law and Romans 13:16 the righteous kings wield the sword against the wicked and praise the righteous. They execute and banish those who openly practice false religions; they obliterate all idols and the remnants of idolatry; and they completely destroy all idolatrous temples. These kings recognized that a Christian nation that permits the open violation of the first commandment has committed spiritual adultery and has violated the covenant.[7]

Christians elected to serve in civil government are thus obligated to do what they can to establish and enforce biblical law, including the use of force. Schwertley, like Rushdoony and North, denounces Christians who argue that the civil government is accountable to God for enforcing only part of the law contained in the Bible:

> Those who want to dismiss the civil magistrate's responsibility to uphold the first table of the law must also explain how laws that are moral, that are based on God's nature and character, can be set aside by God. Idolatry, theft, false witness, adultery, and so on are always wrong because they are ethical absolutes. They are inconsistent with God's nature. Can God forbid murder and child sacrifice in one era and then allow them in another? Absolutely not, for they are not ceremonial or positive laws. Therefore, God can no more countenance the practice of idolatry than he can approve of bestiality, homosexuality or murder.[8]

Moreover, he defends the employment of violence by civil authorities to enforce the entirety of biblical law. The civil magistrate is to praise good behavior and punish evildoers.

"Rulers are not a terror to good works, but to evil" (vs. 3) . . . How is a civil magistrate supposed to determine what is an evil act punishable only by a church court and what is an evil act that also is a crime punishable by the state? Clearly, the only standard by which a civil magistrate can rule justly is the Bible, the stand-alone infallible Word of God. Whenever the state makes laws that contradict the law of God, or ignores some of the laws in God's word such as laws against the open practice of idolatry, or makes laws that contradict God's limited role for the state (e.g., welfare programs, public schools, food stamps, etc.) then that state is in rebellion against God in those specific areas.[9]

Reconstructionists, from Rushdoony himself to the father of his great-grandchildren Joel McDurmon, insist that these penalties would only come into play in a Reconstructed society in which almost everyone is a Christian. They insist that their concerns are not primarily political and that they reject any notion that society can be transformed through politics. While this may be true in theory, in actuality it merely avoids the logic that would require them to exercise the use of force (politically legitimated violence) to punish those who violate biblical law should they ever be in a position to do so, whether they represented the overwhelming majority of citizens or not. And Reconstructionists all advocate Christian involvement in politics. McDurmon is involved in the Georgia Republican Party, and he certainly is not alone. Most Reconstructionists do follow Calvin in the argument that legitimate force by the civil government must be exercised in the context of duly delegated authority (i.e., they oppose vigilantism). They call such biblically legitimate leaders "magistrates," so, for example, any legitimate political revolution has to occur under the authority and leadership of a "lesser magistrate." Translated into contemporary terms: a county sheriff (a low-level legitimate authority or lesser magistrate) can lead citizens in a legitimate rebellion against, say, a governor or a president.

Despite their disagreement over the fact, the view that Christian leaders must work for—and where possible implement—biblical law, with violence if necessary, is consistent with their biblical worldview. One of the most notorious sanctions is the death penalty for homosexuality; even the rhetoric on homosexuality in general is characterized by a disturbing level of vitriol. Ray Sutton, for example, argued that the AIDS epidemic was judgment from God and that any Christian who doesn't believe so is "wimpy and liberal."[10] Referring to such a "wimpy" evangelist he saw on a talk show, he writes:

> The interviewer . . . came right out and asked the evangelist if he thought that AIDS is a judgment sent by God. The evangelist said, "No, God wouldn't do such a thing." Odd, isn't it? This evangelist believes that God will send millions and perhaps even billions of people to hell for all eternity, to be forced to tolerate screaming intolerable agony and loneliness forever, without hope forever. But God wouldn't send a few thousand homosexual perverts the plague of AIDS . . . Compared to hell, AIDS is nickel-and-dime sort of judgment.[11]

While Reconstructionist advocacy of violence, in terms of support for the death penalty, against those in the LGBT community is well documented, they do not advocate or condone other literal acts of violence by individuals (i.e., what we would call hate crimes). But their rhetoric is inflammatory, and they support policies that make prosecution for acts of violence more difficult (for example, they oppose hate crime legislation).

Reconstructionists and Anti-Semitism

Among the accusations frequently lobbed at Christian Reconstructionists is the charge that they are anti-Semitic. As postmillennialists who see no unique tie between the Kingdom of God and Jews or the nation of Israel, and having developed in the context of the conspiratorial view of history popularized by the John Birch Society, it seems inevitable that Christian Reconstructionist views on Jews, Judaism, and the State of Israel will be complex and controversial. Clearly they are a Christian group that believes (like a great many Christian groups) that the only path to salvation is through Jesus. Reconstructionists hold that Judaism, like all other religions, is a false religion. For many in contemporary culture, evangelizing Jews is an act of anti-Semitism. But there are more explicit and more pernicious forms of anti-Semitism; it is important to differentiate them from these generic forms.

Some of Rushdoony's comments on Jews betray biases and stereotypes that strike us as profoundly anti-Semitic. In a discussion of crime in his *The Institutes of Biblical Law*, for example, he says there are usually few Jews in prisons because "Jews are normally law abiding; their trouble with the law usually involves money,"[12] invoking common stereotypes about Jews and money. In other contexts Rushdoony argues that Jews have been persecuted historically because of their faithfulness to biblical law and because that faithfulness has made them successful and influential.[13] "Towns and cities were products of merchantmen and their communities, and these were largely Jewish. Commercial law and urban law thus had their origins in the Jewish communities and their intense devotion to Biblical law."[14] Writing of the relations between Saxons and Jews under Charlemagne, Rushdoony continues: the Saxons' "level of accomplishment was clearly below that of the Jews for some centuries. People hate few things in others more than superiority."[15]

While such statements may have been common among midcentury Americans, in other places Rushdoony draws on deeply anti-Semitic sources. The most inflammatory charge that Rushdoony was anti-Semitic is the claim that he was a Holocaust denier. In *The Institutes of Biblical Law*, Rushdoony discusses the way in which evil perpetuates evil and the relative evil of the Holocaust compared to the murders by communists and the genocide in his own homeland, Armenia.[16] In a commentary on the eighth commandment's prohibition on bearing false witness Rushdoony uses, as one example, what he claims are exaggerations about the number of Jews killed in the Holocaust. His otherwise uncontroversial point is that real evil, made worse by false witness, leads to even more evil. He does not deny the Holocaust occurred and, in fact, he calls it evil. He does draw on the work of anti-Semite Vicomte Leon de Poncins, but he labels him anti-Semitic and uses him as an example of those who are desensitized to evil: "Poncins, bitterly anti-Jewish, is ready to report errors in the accounts of Nazi murders of Jews; but he is not ready to be distressed that *any* were murdered."[17] Rushdoony explicitly says that his goal is not to minimize the evil of the Holocaust but to illustrate another point about growing insensitivity to evil and how it breeds increasing evil. Rushdoony did imply that the numbers of Jews killed has been exaggerated, and he draws on what he admits are anti-Semitic sources as evidence. That he chose this as an example indicates that it is a view that he held, though it was not central to his work (as, for example, is his advocacy of the death penalty for homosexuality).

More problematic, in my view, is his characterization of the sect of Judaism that many Christians revile, the Pharisees, the identification of modern-day Jews with the Pharisees, and the assertion that goes with it: the Jews killed Jesus. Rushdoony suggests, for example in his critique of the manipulation of guilt for political ends, that it is "paradoxical" that "we are assured by the same theologians that the Jews are innocent of Christ's blood, even as Christians are declared guilty of the deaths of Jews who died centuries ago!"[18] Or, in another example:

> For the Christian, Phariseeism, Sadduceeism, and Essenism were departures from biblical faith, and all the nation [Israel] was in heresy and apostasy when it crucified Christ . . . The term "Judeo-Christian" is most commonly used by adherents of the religion of humanity who are insistent on reading their religion into both Judaism and Christianity.[19]

This line of anti-Semitism is even more explicit in Gary North's *The Judeo-Christian Tradition*, in which North argues that there is no such thing as a Judeo-Christian tradition (a position Rushdoony had taken in 1965). According to North, Judaism, in all but its Orthodox form, has been co-opted by Enlightenment humanism, and Orthodoxy is itself the religion Jesus rejected.[20] North's book was promoted in a most unusual style, which has conspiratorial, anti-Semitic undertones. I have, with my copy, a letter sent in advance of the release of the book. The goal of the letter is to sell copies, "sight unseen," to raise money to send free copies to every major college and university. In an ominous style that is quite typical of Gary North, it begins:

> There is no return address on this sheet. You know where it came from.
> I have a book at the printers that is potentially so explosive that I'm not going to advertise it . . . I call this book "the little black book." I write in as low key as anything I've ever written. Nevertheless until it's actually in my warehouse—not my regular warehouse—I'm not even going to hint at its topic. I don't want pressure brought against the printer, which I think could happen. Sorry about the vagueness of all this, but when you read the book, you'll understand why. If times were normal, there would be no problem, but times are surely not normal. It's wise for me to maintain a low profile on this project.
> Not just low . . . invisible.

Supporters may have purchased copies without knowing the topic of the book, but now that we do know, the coded language implicating danger-ous, sneaky, and manipulative characters who can pull behind-the-scenes strings to pressure a printer to pull a book becomes clear as a not-so-veiled reference to a conspiratorial worldview in which Jews have inordinate power and are a serious threat to a Christian world order. It strikes one as either paranoia or shrewd marketing (or both).

North's intended audience is conservative Christians who believe either that all Jews remain in the covenant God made with Abraham or, that Orthodox Jews are really just "Christians without Jesus." In North's view, contemporary Judaism is divided into two parts: the Enlightenment hu-manism of mainstream Judaism and modern-day Pharisees. The notion of a Judeo-Christian tradition, he says, is a myth invented by Enlighten-ment humanists to promote pluralistic social values. North says that most Christians (by whom he means conservative Protestants) think of Ortho-dox Jews as sharing their values and a worldview derived from their shared sacred text: the Old Testament. But, he writes, "There is no way to recon-cile the following rival principles of biblical interpretation in Judaism and Christianity . . . Jesus as the sole fulfillment of Old Testament messianic prophesies vs. Jesus as a false prophet and blasphemer for which he was lawfully executed." According to North, Christians who take Jesus' words literally, "for had you believed in Moses you would believe in me," must conclude that Jews are at war with the Old Testament.[21] According to North, Orthodox Jews belong to a "rival religion," rejected by Jesus, in which the Talmud supersedes the Old Testament and the followers of which crucified Jesus.

Reconstructionists and Racism

In our culture, the term "racist" is ill defined and, in fact, contested. In its most basic form, the term is used to describe a person who makes judgments about or discriminates against an individual on the basis of his or her race. This is often the meaning of the term employed by con-servatives. But when people discuss racism, many are talking about more than individual attitudes and actions. They mean also the institutional structures in American society that serve to reinforce racial divisions and ideological structures that perpetuate the power and privilege of whites— especially, but not only, white Protestant males. They mean cultural sen-sitivities and assumptions that shape the way we see the world, as well as institutional structures that perpetuate those assumptions and sensitivities, and which function to preserve a social structure in which white males are the "unmarked" category—the standard—and where whites in general are afforded privileges denied others.

Christian Reconstruction certainly seeks to preserve and even restore a patriarchal social structure in which whites are the dominant group, and their values and cultural preferences are infused with the authority of the transcendent. Reconstructionists would deny that white privilege is real, though they continue to benefit from it. Rushdoony, in *The Politics of Guilt and Pity*, argues that civil government denies the freedom from guilt wrought by the resurrection and, ultimately, demeans and dehumanizes those it claims to help. In that volume he essentially outlines a defense of social inequality and, before the term "white privilege" was even used in this way, he critiqued the concept as nothing more than the "cultivation of guilt" as a means to power.[22]

> The political cultivation of guilt is a central means to power, for guilty men are slaves; their conscience is in bondage, and hence they are easily made objects of control. Guilt is thus systematically taught for purposes of control. Several instances can be cited readily. For example, the white man is being systematically indoctrinated into believing he is guilty of enslaving and abusing the Negro.[23]

And, in language that could come from a conservative Christian website today, he wrote that humanism uses indoctrination to create a situation in which "the Christian has no right to his identity; he must recognize all others and their 'rights,' but he himself has none. The principles of the atheist must govern the state and school; the wishes of all others have status before law, and his have none."[24] Defending social inequality, Rushdoony asserts the superiority of Christian culture, specifically over "savage" Africa:

> The Christian can agree that the savage is not a primitive; he's like all men a child of Adam. His problem is not primitivism but degeneracy. To equate the Christian cultures with those in Africa, and to demand appreciation of Africa's past and present, as many textbooks . . . do, is to ask us to endorse and accept degeneracy. Such an approach converts Africa from a mission field desperately in need

of God's saving grace into a sister culture of equal dignity and character. To accept this premise is to reject Christianity.[25]

In a maneuver that is common on today's political Right, Rushdoony
argues that those opposing racism are the real racists: "Indeed, the liberal,
religion of humanity . . . is simply a form of racism."[26]

Stephen McDowell drew on Rushdoony's discussion of slavery, arguing that it is biblical and voluntary (except for when it isn't) in *The Institutes of Biblical Law*. We find a more elaborate discussion of it in *Politics of
Guilt and Pity*. Rushdoony believed that slavery takes three forms. The
first is the one most commonly recognized, the "private ownership" of the
labor of one human being by another, which he contends "has usually
been the minor aspect of human slavery."[27] The second form of slavery,
for Rushdoony, is the claim of ownership to the lives of citizens by a humanist state. Slavery to the state, in his view, is the most common form of
slavery and characterizes all who look to civil government for help: "A true
slave always seeks a master and the security of a slave master. The slave
mind wants security, a trouble-free, cradle to grave or womb to tomb security, and it demands a master to provide it." The third form Rushdoony
identifies is a traditional Christian notion of spiritual bondage to sin.

Rushdoony's comments about African Americans are often made in
the larger context of his criticism of the overreaching civil government,
with humans in idolatrous relationship to it. This phenomenon is not limited to African Americans, but Rushdoony most readily identifies it with
them. It's this division into three forms that gives us the contemporary
conservative rhetoric that minimizes literal slavery and at the same time
exaggerates the onerousness of our communal obligations such that taxes
become slavery.

> In virtually all the world today, the citizenry is moving into slavery
> to the state. The obligations of citizenship are being replaced by the
> obligations of slavery. Since involuntary servitude is defined by the
> Constitution as equivalent to slavery, every employer who is com-
> pelled to keep books and withhold taxes for the Federal Govern-
> ment is thus required to perform involuntary servitude or slave
> labor.[28]

And again, "from a very limited system of privately owned slaves, the
entire United States has, from the Civil War era, gone into debt-money

slavery."[29] So while "slavery" to the government (i.e., paying taxes) is intolerable, the severity of "private ownership" of human beings is minimized for those who "choose" it:

> Slavery offers certain penalties as well as certain advantages. Objectively, the penalty is the surrender of liberty. Subjectively, the slave does not see the surrender of freedom as a penalty, since he desires escape from freedom. Even as a timid and fearful child dreads the dark, so does the slave mind fear liberty.[30]

Rushdoony asserts that American slavery was unbiblical, yet he nonetheless defends it in terms of its impact on African Americans.

> The private ownership of slave labor in the American South has been the subject of extensive distortion. The Negroes were slaves to their tribal heads in Africa, or prisoner-slaves of other tribes . . . The Negro moved from an especially harsh slavery, which included cannibalism, to a milder form . . . [Many of the slave ships] were very bad, but it is important to remember that slaves were valuable cargo and hence property normally handled with consideration.[31]

In fact, echoing paternalistic, antebellum proslavery arguments, he asserts that slavery for African Americans was a positive good.

> Granted that some Negroes were mistreated as slaves, the fact still remains that nowhere in all history or in the world today has the Negro been better off. The life expectancy of the Negro increased when he was transported to America. He was *not* taken from freedom into slavery, but from a vicious slavery to degenerate chiefs to a generally benevolent slavery in the United States. There is not the slightest evidence that any American Negro had ever lived in a "free society" in Africa; even the idea did not exist in Africa. The move from Africa to America was a vast increase of freedom for the Negro, materially and spiritually as well as personally.[32]

Rushdoony also compares the lot of African Americans brought here as slaves to Irish immigrants, whom he claims were in "semi slavery in Ireland." By doing so, he seeks to elide the differences in experience, absolve America of any responsibility, and lay the blame for current problems squarely on the shoulders of African Americans. According to Rushdoony, the conditions of the Irish transport were as bad or worse than what we know of slave ships, and the condition of Irish immigrants on arrival was "far worse than that of slaves: they had no master to feed and clothe them or to provide shelter." Yet the Irish succeeded where the Africans failed: "after a century and a quarter, or less, the Irish are a leading power in the United States, and the Negroes remain on the lowest strata. The basic difference between the Irish and the Negro has not been color: it has been character."[33] This difference in "character" is rooted, for Rushdoony, not in the first form of slavery, but in the second and third; a slave mentality that is ultimately a spiritual failing leading to dependency.

> After the Civil War and emancipation many Negroes continued to demand that their former masters continue their care of them. One Southern family moved to New Jersey, only to be followed there by their former slaves. [For generations they] continued to depend on that family . . . They needed a master. Today, millions of Negroes, joined by millions of slave whites, are demanding that the Federal government become their slave-master and provide them with security and care.[34]

I've quoted Rushdoony at length because I think it is important that rather than characterize his views for the reader, especially on issues as sensitive as these, I let him speak for himself. But when reading his words, it becomes clear that, long after Rushdoony's death, the language and framing he used half a century ago echoes in our current political discourse. We heard it in David Barton, in Kebreau's Tea Party presentation, and in the confrontation involving Nevada rancher Cliven Bundy. We also hear it in the conservative hyperbole about tyrannical government making slaves of its citizens. In 2010 at American Vision's Worldview Conference, Gary DeMar brought much of the preceding discussion of Rushdoony's writings to bear when he said:

> You read about slavery in the Bible, and it's very difficult to be a slave in the Bible. You had to jump through a whole lot of hoops to be a slave in the Bible. They made it embarrassing for you to be a slave in the Bible. So much so that you had to go up to someone and they'd take an awl and jam it through like having your ears pierced to show everybody you wanted to be a slave. It was voluntary. Our

government today makes it easy for people to become slaves . . . You can go back and look at Katrina. You had people literally ware-housed in government buildings. You had Katrina come in, and you saw that you had three generations of people living as slaves; worse than slaves.[35]

These examples come firmly from within the Reconstructionist camp. But the movement is broad-based and loosely tied, so while there are those who embrace Christian Reconstruction, others who are more generally influenced by it, there are also those who use Reconstructionist argu-ments in ways that other Reconstructionists oppose. The neoconfederate movement is a good example.

The Institute on the Constitution has ties to the League of the South and both have ties to Reconstructionists.[36] There is cross-fertilization among Reconstructionist groups, militia groups, so-called patriot groups, the Constitution Party, extreme gun rights advocates like Gun Owners of America, and others. These groups retain enough autonomy to be able to deny association with one another, yet they speak at each other's meetings and conventions, publish in each other's newsletters and websites, and rarely denounce the controversial things said and done by their friends. Steve Wilkins and Doug Wilson, authors of the 1996 book *Southern Slav-ery as It Was*, fit in this category. As we have seen, Rushdoony was an im-portant force in the reinvigoration of the influence of Southern Presbyterian and slavery apologist Robert L. Dabney, an effort that, until recently, Doug Phillips continued. Whether one puts Wilkins and Wilson in the Recon-structionist camp or assumes that they, like Rushdoony, developed their defense of the South from Dabney, their work shows the continued sali-ence of this line of thinking.

Wilkins and Wilson parallel Rushdoony on nearly every point. In their view that the North had "apostatized," being captured by the Unitarians and becoming "radical," while the "intellectual leadership of the South was conservative, orthodox, Christian."[37] The "war between the states" was not a war over slavery, but a war over the "biblical meaning of consti-tutional government."[38] It is important to note that they are not merely joining the debate over whether the war was about slavery or states' rights (though they are doing that), but doing so in Reconstructionist terms, especially the notion of biblical government. They argue both that slavery is biblical and that in a culture in which slavery is legal Christians may own slaves.[39] While it would have been unbiblical to capture Africans and force them into slavery, because the Africans enslaved in America had allegedly already been enslaved by other Africans, Christians were biblically permitted to own them and, in fact, according to Wilkins and Wilson, may have had a moral duty to do so. They then move to their main point that American slavery was not as horrific as it has been characterized, that "there were specific roles for blacks and whites and each 'knew their place.'"[40] They argue that slavery in America actually constituted an improvement in the lives of Africans. Finally, they assert that the problem with slavery is that it created a "slave mentality" and an opportunity to "increase the size and power of federal Government [creating a] messianic state which seeks to bring salvation by law." They conclude that criticism of what they consider a benign form of slavery "was used to provoke a revolution in 1861 . . . and the much worse form of slavery [i.e., slavery to the government] has *increased* in our land as a result."[41]

Rushdoony was also an opponent of interracial marriage, which he saw as related to the Bible's prohibition on hybridization, a "violation of kinds."[42] He cites for support prohibitions on literal unequal yoking of an ox and an ass in Deuteronomy (22:10) and the metaphorical meaning of this in II Corinthians (6:14), having to do with believers and unbelievers being bonded together whether in marriage or "generally." He concludes that since the Bible describes a woman's role in marriage as that of "helpmeet," she cannot be distinctly different from the man she marries. "'Helpmeet' means a reflection or a mirror, an image of a man . . . a woman must have something religiously and culturally in common with her husband [and therefore] the burden of the law is thus against inter-religious, inter-racial, and intercultural marriages."[43] Moreover, he implies a prohibition on integration (religious, racial, and cultural) when he notes that the biblical notion of unequal yoking includes more than marriage: "In society at large [unequal yoking] means the enforced integration of various elements which are not congenial. Unequal yoking is in no realm productive of harmony."[44]

Here we see ties between Christian Reconstructionists and groups even further to the right. "Kinists," for example, argue that Greg Bahnsen's defense of theonomy (that all Old Testament law not specifically abrogated in the New Testament is still applicable) dictates that the Old Testament prohibitions on race mixing (and therefore any form of integration, multiculturalism, or cultural pluralism) are binding on Christians today.[45] Moreover, they cite Rushdoony's work and conclude that he is "with them."[46] In the context of his writing about the split between

Rushdoony and himself, Gary North argues that Rushdoony's designation of the family as the central institution to which God delegated authority (with the church and the civil government being secondary) was effectively racist.[47] While Mark Rushdoony has asserted that his father did not oppose interracial marriage, neither he nor his father renounced these statements that seem to imply that he did.[48] The younger Rushdoony's desire to distance himself, and the movement, from Kinist views suggests some change over time. Nonetheless, groups that virulently oppose race mixing find in Rushdoony (and other Reconstructionists) biblical support for their views.

Christian Reconstruction and Abortion-Related Violence

Christian Reconstructionist Mike Bray was one of the subjects of Mark Juergensmeyer's study of religiously motivated violence in *Terror in the Mind of God.*[49] Both Bray and Paul Hill, who was executed in 2003 for shooting an abortion provider and his bodyguard, identified with Christian Reconstruction and saw their support for the use of violence to stop abortion as derived from Rushdoony and others. As we shall see, their view is contested within the tradition.

The all-or-nothing character of the abortion debate, including the belief held by some that Christians can legitimately use violence to stop abortion, begins with the assertion that abortion is the violent taking of a human life that is in no salient way different from the killing of any other innocent person. It is this first principle that makes the pro-life arguments comparing abortion to the Holocaust and slavery more than rhetorical hype. Legalized abortion is understood as part of a larger cultural transformation, a "culture of death," in which increasing opportunities and life choices for women have changed notions of childbearing. In the 1970s and 1980s opponents of abortion who also opposed the use of contraception were mostly found within the Catholic wing of the movement. In the late 1980s this began to change, with growing numbers of Protestants coming to see contraception as part of a "Planned Parenthood mentality" in which children are to be planned rather than welcomed as blessings from God. Those Protestants, many of whom were steeped in Christian Reconstruction, became what we now call the Quiverfull, or biblical patriarchy, movement.[50] Quiverfull families endorse a marriage model that requires the complete submission of women, whose primary calling is to produce as many children as possible.

While Christian Reconstructionists are unanimous in their opposition to abortion, there is disagreement over the legitimacy of the use of violence to stop it. Yet the most consistent and systematic defense of those who have engaged in antiabortion violence has come from Christian Reconstructionists. Lutheran pastor Mike Bray is author of *A Time to Kill*, a historical, theological, and philosophical defense of the use of violence to stop abortions. Bray is also widely believed to be the author of the radical antiabortion Army of God's underground tactical manual. Bray identifies with the Army of God, though he refuses to confirm or deny authorship of the manual. His position is that he supports the Army of God and is in "solidarity with one who is being maligned for writing such a book."[51] Bray's argument is not explicitly Reconstructionist and has been rejected by Gary North.[52] But it fits within that larger theological system.

I met Bray in the early 1980s. I knew him and his family for several years; worked on an election campaign in which his brother Dan ran for the County Board of Supervisors; and engaged with him in many lengthy theological discussions about Christian Reconstruction, feminism, and the biblical roles of women. Eventually, Bray was convicted of setting fire to seven abortion clinics. (Widely referred to as "abortion clinic bombers," Bray and his accomplice did not employ bombs.) I was not in contact with Bray at the time, though I have since received sporadic e-mail communications that he sends to a distribution list, and I encountered him at the vigil/protest outside the Florida State Prison when Paul Hill was executed.[53] As we shall see, Bray's support for the use of violence to stop abortion is rooted in the argument that the tactic is not a political strategy but a defensive act. His stated intent was to cause damage to the clinics sufficient to halt their operation. While he articulates a theoretical justification for the assassination of abortion providers (and there have been those who have acted specifically on his encouragement), he insists that to be biblical the motivation must be to stop subsequent abortions. The punishment of abortion providers for murder (which he supports) must be handled by duly constituted civil authorities and not individuals. He claims that while only civil authorities may lawfully "punish evildoers, the moral requirement to defend the innocent falls to anyone who is present and capable."[54] The violence for which he was convicted took place at night when the clinics were empty, and no one was injured or killed. His 1994 book, *A Time to Kill*, explores examples from the Bible and from history in which "the righteous" have violated civil law, even to the point of using force, to, as he understands it, protect the innocent.[55]

Drawing on such figures as Reinhold Niebuhr, Dietrich Bonhoeffer, and Martin Luther King Jr., Bray argues that the Christian tradition permits the use of violence to defend the defenseless and argues that unborn fetuses are the most defenseless of human beings. But his argument is essentially biblical in character. Like other Reconstructionists, Bray invokes an understanding of God's nature rooted in the unity of scripture in which the New Testament is read in the context of the Old. Referencing Leviticus, he writes:

> Force, even lethal force, is not only commanded by God and performed by Him on innumerable occasions in the older Scriptures, it is also prescribed in the Law for citizens' participation. When a man sacrificed his own children to a false God, the whole community was obligated in an execution by stoning . . . Use of lethal force is not only commanded as a judicial act, but granted to the individual in cases of self-defense and defense of others.[56]

Bray challenges the contemporary readings of the Bible that neglect the Old Testament "God of War," a "God who slays His apostate people" and who "commands the slaughter of idol worship[pers]." For Bray and other Reconstructionists, the sanitized "New-Testament-only" reflection on the nature of the Godhead abandons the revelation of the "preincarnate" Christ. He argues that contemporary Christians have a one-dimensional understanding of the character of Jesus. While some would argue for pacifism based on Jesus' Sermon on the Mount, according to Bray, "Neither the life of Christ, nor His teachings, abolish the Law regarding godly force. Jesus of Nazareth came in humiliation to die. Yet even in that role, He had occasion to act forcefully."[57] Citing examples in which Jesus encouraged his disciples to take up swords and to fight injustice, Bray contends that the key to what might otherwise seem contradictory characteristics is to understand that Jesus functioned in a number of different roles and that different roles require different actions: "There is a time to kill to protect oneself and others, and there is a time to suffer and die voluntarily. In another passage, the account of Jesus commanding His disciples to take swords with them illumines both the continuity of the biblical teaching on legitimate force and the principle of role distinction."[58] Bray contends that pro-lifers who call abortion murder and then stand by while it occurs are guilty of gross inconsistency.[59] Moreover, he calls America to account for its failure to stop abortion, citing the Deuteronomic principle of bloodguilt in which unpunished evildoers bring down God's wrath upon the whole community. But there is disagreement within the ranks of Reconstructionists, and it is most evident in an exchange of letters between Paul Hill and Gary North while Hill was awaiting execution in a Florida prison for abortion-related violence.

In September of 2003 I drove just over an hour from Jacksonville to the Florida State Prison in Starke to observe the vigil, as part of the fieldwork for this project, awaiting the execution of Paul Hill for the 1994 murder of abortion doctor John Britton and his bodyguard James Barrett. The substantial crowd was tense, and the police had marked off areas for each of three separate groups: death penalty opponents who were protesting the execution; supporters of abortion rights who were awaiting justice (there were just a handful of these); and the largest of the groups, supporters of Hill who believed his execution was unjust and who considered him a martyr. Among those supporters were Mike Bray and several people to whom he introduced me, and who identified themselves as members of the Army of God. Many held signs depicting either a smiling Paul Hill or gruesome images of abortions. As the hour of Hill's execution drew near, a menacing Florida thunderstorm approached. Thunder boomed and the darkened sky split apart as terrifying bolts of lightning reached from above the clouds all the way to the ground. To Hill's supporters this display was understood as a signal of God's wrath over the killing of the innocent: Hill and the unborn they all sought to protect.

In the view of his supporters, Hill was not a murderer but a defender of the unborn; a martyr who made himself a willing sacrifice to stop Dr. Britton from performing abortions. Though Hill's arrest, trial, and execution received extensive media coverage, very little attention was paid to his ties to Christian Reconstruction or the degree to which he saw his justification for his actions as rooted in that tradition. Hill had been trained at Reformed Theological Seminary under Reconstructionist apologetics professor Greg Bahnsen. He had been a pastor in both the Orthodox Presbyterian Church and the Presbyterian Church in America (PCA). These are two of the most Calvinist of America's Protestant denominations and have often been home to Reconstructionists (both denominations had excommunicated him). Hill had written extensively and given several interviews, some while in prison awaiting execution.

Hill argued that the responsibility for individual Christians to protect the unborn includes biblical sanction to do so by whatever means necessary. For Christians asserting that life begins at conception and that abortion is murder, Hill insists that the sixth commandment obligates them to intervene on behalf of a baby in the womb with exactly the same measures they would take to protect a child that had already been born. While Hill was a member of the PCA, the denomination adopted a resolution in favor of nonviolent civil disobedience practiced by groups such as Operation Rescue. In a position paper, Hill critiqued the resolution as inconsistent.[60] He asserted that the PCA-recognized moral obligation to protect the unborn, even when such action violated human law, must extend to the use of violence when necessary.

> It is sinful to neglect the " . . . necessary means . . . " for defending the innocent. And since the PCA asserts that the unborn have a right to the " . . . full protection of the Sixth Commandment . . . " it necessarily follows that it is sinful to neglect the means necessary for defending the unborn. (Ellipses in original)

He argued that with regard to the requirement that Christians obey civil authorities, nonviolent civil disobedience is in no way different from the employment of violence in a defensive action. If the denomination can countenance nonviolent civil disobedience then it has no biblical justification to oppose "necessary" use of force. In response to a Southern Baptist Commission statement on the matter, and quoting the commission's report, Hill wrote:

> Under the current circumstances, it is hardly surprising that only a " . . . small number of Americans . . . " relatively speaking, understand the practical implications of defending born and unborn people similarly. In time, no doubt, these things will become clear to the masses, but as yet, most people's eyes have not adjusted to the darkness that descends when the government so radically departs from the light of the Moral Law. This radical reversal in the law must necessarily result in a similar reversal in the Christian's relation to the law, and the government that enforces it.[61]

Hill's writings exhibit the legal/judicial style of reading the Bible and an emphasis on both the Old and New Testaments common to Reconstructionists.

Perhaps most indicative of his identification with that tradition, though, was his correspondence with Gary North, in which he cited Rushdoony and sought North's support for his actions. After Michael Griffin's assassination of Dr. David Gunn, Hill wrote essays in support of Griffin. North replied to Hill, engaging his arguments, though not until after Hill had killed Dr. Britton. North later published his responses in *Lone Gunners for Jesus: Letters to Paul Hill.*[62]

The first point at which North challenges Hill is not related to the use of violence, per se. Hill, as noted, had been excommunicated. In Reconstructionism, indeed in the broader Reformed tradition, ecclesiastical authority is taken every bit as seriously as the authority of the civil government and the authority of the father in the family. In fact, North's response to Hill came at about the same time that North was writing denunciations of his father-in-law (Rushdoony) over what he claimed was a rejection of Calvinism in the form of a rejection of ecclesiastical authority.[63] Hill's church had required that he cease speaking publicly in defense of the use of violence to stop abortion, and he failed to submit to their ecclesiastical authority. Compounding his rebellion, rather than taking the excommunication as an impetus to repentance and submission to legitimate biblical authority, according to North, Hill began his own house church and administered sacraments in flagrant rebellion. North's central critique of Hill's position is on the issue of covenantal authority. Legitimate biblical killing, says North, is misconstrued as self-defense when it is more properly understood as defense of covenantal authority.

> A man can defend his household against an unauthorized criminal invader (Ex. 22:2–3). He is the head of his household: a covenantal office. This is not self-defense as such; it is the defense of a legitimate sphere of authority, the home, by one charged by God through the civil government to take defensive action. But this right is never said to be universal in the Bible; it is limited to the protection of one's family.[64]

Invoking the concept of jurisdictional authority, North asserts that the "distinguishing mark of the right to execute an enemy of God was the holding of a covenantal office."[65] He charges Hill with "the classic mistake of the revolutionary," which is the abandonment of covenantalism in favor of "radical individualism" and anarchism.[66] So, of course, while Hill identifies with Christian Reconstructionism, and I have classified him as such, North rejects his argument as a legitimate application of Christian Reconstruction and, on the basis of Hill's excommunication and his lack of repentance for his rebellion from legitimate biblical authority, would argue that Hill was not even a Christian.

In Bray's terms, the goal of legitimate violence is not to protest abortions but to prevent them from taking place, and he has argued that there is a difference between killing a retired abortion doctor and one who continues to practice.[67] Bray holds that the employment of violence to stop abortions is legitimate if not always required. In anticipation of the execution of a man he called his friend, Bray, in characteristic style, wrote, "Paul Hill was called to abort the abortionist, and his wife and children were called to suffer the loss of husband and father for righteousness sake. Most of us have other callings, theoretically."[68] Situating the execution in the context of the concept of God consistent across Christian Reconstruction, Bray wrote:

> We are reminded that the hand of God sometimes falls hard upon us; He is, indeed, both good and severe (Rom. 11:22). How good He was to the innocents Paul defended and to us who have been encouraged by his courage and obedience. And yet, how severe He is in depriving children and wife. Yes, we are reminded that God doesn't mess around. He is serious; he is severe. And these truths about our God are not happily recalled. It is a fearful thing to fall into the hands of an awesome and holy and everliving God.[69]

Even Operation Rescue, the antiabortion movement sometimes lauded by the opponents of abortion-related violence, skirts the edges of the endorsement of violence. Randall Terry, the founder of Operation Rescue, converted to Catholicism in 2006 but prior to that was influenced by Christian Reconstruction. [70] Like Bray and Hill, Terry challenged Christians who claimed that abortion is murder to act as though they really believed that. [71] Operation Rescue held sit-ins to block clinic doors; "rescuers" chained themselves to clinic doors and abortion equipment and sought to overwhelm police and jails to slow the clearing away of protesters. Intended to both prevent specific abortions and create social tension that Terry believed could bring about an end to legalized abortion, the protests were preceded by rallies and church services in which would-be rescuers were taught Martin Luther King Jr.'s principles of nonviolence and passive resistance. In the 1980s I participated in some of these protests and attended these rallies. We were required to sign pledges, which read, in part:

> I understand the critical importance of Operation Rescue being unified, peaceful and free of any actions or words that would appear violent or hateful . . . I understand for the *children's sake* each Rescue must be orderly and above reproach . . . I commit to be peaceful and non-violent in both word and deed. Should I be arrested, I will not struggle with police in any way (whether deed or tongue), but remain polite and passively limp, remembering that mercy triumphs over judgment.[72]

In keeping with King's views on civil disobedience, rescuers often pled guilty and sometimes chose jail time over fines to further "clog the system." All the while, in ways I did not see at the time, Terry and Operation Rescue were setting the stage for a move away from nonviolence:

> Pro-lifers were saying that abortion was murder, and yet all we were doing about it was writing a letter now and then. If my little girl was about to be murdered, I certainly would not write a letter to the editor! I would dive in with both hands and feet to do whatever was necessary to save her life.[73]

The assent to nonviolence creates, for Terry, a deniability of responsibility for violence. Yet he argues that the United States is in a state of war and that "we need to 'declare war' on the child killing industry."[74]

> The most critical need in the war against abortion is for *front-line soldiers* who are willing to place their bodies where the battle rages. Rescuers who have been motivated by Higher Laws and a burning desire to save the children scheduled to die *today* are answering the call to the trenches.[75]

In 2010 when Scott Roeder was tried for killing Dr. George Tiller, Terry issued a statement that perpetuated the ambiguity with regard to the use of violence. Defending Roeder, Terry claimed that Roeder had not been given a fair trial and that Tiller was a mass murderer and had deserved to die.[76] Despite his assertions that he is committed to nonviolence, calling for war, casting those with whom you disagree as cosmic enemies, and recruiting soldiers, even if intended metaphorically, lend support to those who want to build a case for the use of violence. Like Bray and Hill, Terry's view of God and his emphasis on bloodguilt (the view that God punishes the whole community for sin tolerated by that community) lend themselves to justification of violence. Terry ridicules Christians for whom God is a "jolly old perennial gift giver," a "semi-senile heavenly grandfather," or a "Cosmic Watchmaker." Instead, "God is the awesome, fearful, dread sovereign Lord of the universe to whom all men will give an account. It matters not to Him whether we acknowledge Him . . . He is our judge."[77] And, according to Bray, Hill, and Terry, God will hold us all to account for our failure to stop abortion. Christians were urged to participate in Operation Rescue because

> the question is *not,* will America be judged? Judgment is inevitable because the blood of the children already killed must be avenged. Even if abortion were outlawed today, our nation will still pay for the blood of the past. The real question is, will we be judged and then restored, or will we be wiped out never to be restored? What form will God's judgment take? Will the judgment stop at AIDS and perhaps an economic collapse, drought and famine; or will we become an ash heap beneath the fallout of Russian or Chinese missiles?[78]

Terry's rhetorical violence, in the hands of Bray and Hill, becomes literal violence.

Conclusion

AROUND 1960 R. J. RUSHDOONY began articulating what would become Christian Reconstruction, a version of Christianity built on presuppositionalism, postmillennialism, and theonomy. Presuppositionalism posits two mutually exclusive worldviews, each fundamentally and inevitably at war with the other over authority, giving Reconstruction its uncompromising character. Christian Reconstruction, applied consistently, is irreconcilable with any other way of seeing the world: neutrality, pluralism, tolerance, and compromise are impossible. Postmillennialism gives Reconstruction both the confidence that it will ultimately win out and an extraordinary time horizon (thousands of years or more) that allows it to incorporate seeming setbacks as nothing more than short-term losses in an overarching trajectory of victory secured by the promises of an all-powerful God. Theonomy asserts that the Bible speaks to every area of life and is operationalized in sphere sovereignty or jurisdictional authority, allowing Reconstructionists to assess any action or policy in terms of its compliance with what they see as biblical law.

Reconstructionists seek to build an America that is distinctly different from the one we live in now. They want to organize every aspect of culture and society to conform to what they understand to be biblical law. They would create a world in which anyone who is not a Christian as they define the term—gays and lesbians, divorced people, women not in submission to male authority—would have severe, explicit limitations on how they live their lives, if they are allowed to live at all. Racial and ethnic minorities would likely face more subtle limitations (i.e., women as a class of people would face *de jure* restrictions; African Americans and Latinos, on the other hand, would face *de facto* restrictions). Some Reconstructionists argue that women should not be allowed to vote; they do not *argue* that African Americans should not be allowed to vote, but they support policies that inhibit their voting on other grounds. The Reconstructionists' world would have a very limited, decentralized civil government whose authority would extend only to providing protection from invaders and punishing people who commit crimes described in the Bible. The death penalty would likely be invoked for a wide array of behaviors that are currently legal (though, as we've seen, there is debate about this). Since many violations of criminal law would be punishable by death and noncapital crimes would be punished by restitution, the prison system would be eliminated. Public education, Social Security, Medicare, Medicaid, and other aid to the poor would also be eliminated. People deemed deserving of charity could seek help from churches. Community assets like roads and bridges would be privately owned. Much of the work that civil courts do would be done by ecclesiastical courts, with churches backing up their rulings such that excommunication would carry real consequences. Patriarchy is not only an apt description but a term Reconstructionists also enthusiastically embrace. Patriarchal families, seeking to maximize the father's dominion with as many children as possible, would control every aspect of raising children, who would also be schooled at home. Women would be subservient to their husbands' vision for dominion, and girls would be schooled primarily to serve this role in their future husbands' families. Economic activity would also fall exclusively within family authority, and any outside regulation beyond ensuring honesty would be a usurpation of that authority.

Put in these stark terms, Reconstructionism seems so extreme, so far from the everyday reality in which most of us live, that it would be tempting to categorize it as yet another utopian (or dystopian) vision of the future. But because they hope to usher in this transformed world incrementally, we do not need to share their belief that this world will ultimately and inevitably come to pass in order to think that we should pay attention to their strategies and goals. Many aspects of their vision are at the center of our current culture wars, albeit usually without a thoroughgoing commitment to the underlying philosophical and theological underpinnings on the part of the culture warriors.

Throughout this book I have pointed to the influence of Rushdoony and the Reconstructionists in places where that influence is not always obvious. I am not claiming *causality* but arguing for *influence*, based largely on the themes, language, and personal contacts among the actors. You need to know quite a bit about Christian Reconstruction to see the contours of that influence. During the summer of 2010, the *Washington Post* ran a story about the contentious race for the US Senate in Nevada. Incumbent Senator Harry Reid's campaign had given the *Post* a 27-page dossier that alleged ties between Reid's opponent, Sharron Angle, and

Christian Reconstructionists.[1] The dossier said that "Christian Reconstructionism is a dangerous secret society intent on turning the United
States into a theocracy," which reporter Amy Gardner dismissed as "something of a stretch." She wrote: "at its peak in the 1990s, the Christian Reconstructionist movement was small and mostly ignored. The group's
founder, R. J. Rushdoony, tried to start a political party, but it went no-
where. When Rushdoony died nine years ago, the movement dried up."

The reporter's observations show a real lack of understanding of the
movement and its significance. Rushdoony never tried to start a political
party. And if you look to electoral politics for his influence you won't see
it. He (and the Reconstructionist writers who came after him) insisted
that the primary goals of the movement were not political. He did advocate theocracy, by which he meant that God's authority extends over all of
society, including civil rulers who, taking their authority from God, are
obligated to follow biblical law; and he meant this in very specific and literal ways. Rushdoony's view is in direct contradiction to the notion that
government derives its authority from the consent of the governed. Support for Christian Reconstruction has hardly "dried up." Reconstructionists have helped shape generations of homeschooled and Christian-schooled
leaders and are nothing if not invigorated in the current political climate,
especially within the network built by Brandon Vallorani. They post on
blogs and discussion boards daily and sponsor conferences around the
country. It's not clear whether "secret society" is Gardner's term or is
taken from the dossier, but it's certainly not accurate. Christian Reconstruction is more a school of thought than an organization (or society).
Though there are organizations that ascribe to this school of thought and
though they can be secretive, they are anything but secret societies: they
publish more books outlining not only their goals but also their strategies
than anyone—even a full-time academic—can read. I once heard Gary
North say that his life's goal was to leave a shelf of culture-changing
books. He has certainly done that, and many of the titles are available for
free online, as are the daily updates from the interlocking network of Reconstructionist websites and organizations.

On Theocracies

As I have explained throughout, Reconstructionists insist that the cultural transformation they seek cannot be imposed on a non-reconstructed
society; that what is required is a "bottom-up" transformation that begins

in the regenerated souls of "men." The vision they put forth is, in their telling of it, not political, though we see that this means that the aspects pertaining to civil government are merely part of a wholesale revolution. Whether they call it political or not, they do seek a complete transformation of every aspect of life, bringing it entirely under biblical law. They seek to accomplish this through efforts that are much bigger (and potentially more effective) than engaging the political process, most importantly building a separate and distinct subculture in which they can raise their large families without the influence of "humanism."

Their emphasis on smaller and decentralized civil government is consistent with this commitment, in theory. Yet when we think through the practical outworking of their views the result is inevitably coercive, despite their protestations to the contrary. For Reconstructionists, accepting the "myth of neutrality" is tantamount to joining the other side. Indeed, the willingness of American evangelicals in general and the religious right in particular to seek compromise and to work within a secular constitutional order is seen as irrational and unbiblical. Reconstructionists see this as the reason the religious right has not succeeded. The vision of a social order governed by biblical law is inherently incompatible with any other form of government, so decentralization does not really mean, for them, that they would set up a self-contained community that affected no one outside it (if such a thing were possible). Reconstructionists are explicit that religious pluralism—indeed, every form of pluralism—is nothing more than idolatry, the elevation of human reason above the authority of God. And while they argue that the transformation cannot come through political change, they persist in being actively engaged in politics. It would be completely inconsistent (something they abhor) for them to be in positions of authority and not seek to enforce biblical sanctions for what they see as violations of biblical law. In our contemporary cultural context infused with a dominant style of religion shaped by a combination of the Enlightenment and pietistic Protestantism, where religion is a private, personal affair, or what Bruce Lincoln calls minimalism, we can easily mistake the Reconstructionist claim that they are not political to imply that their goals are private and they don't seek to impact the lives of the rest of us. But Reconstructionists are maximalist; they seek to bring every aspect of life under the authority of biblical law. The claim to not be political in no way indicates that their goals are more limited than they would be if they were political. On the contrary, their goals are all-encompassing.

I've traced ties between public figures that point to the subtle dissemination of Reconstructionist thinking and shown how their worldview has filtered into the broader conservative Christian subculture, especially in Christian schooling and homeschooling circles but also more recently in the Tea Party. According to Lincoln, culture is the "prime instrument through which groups mobilize themselves, construct their collective identity, and effect their solidarity by excluding those whom they identify as outsiders, while establishing their own internal hierarchy."[2] Christian Reconstruction is a distinct subculture that performs each of the tasks by virtue of Rushdoony's insistence that the Bible speaks to every area of life, his relentless devotion to explain how that is so, and the consistent efforts to continue that work among those who have followed him. This has resulted in a worldview so systematic that it can serve as an interconnected web that reinforces the strength of the rest of the web at every point. You can see this in the way the various organizations and institutions relate to each other and in the lives of the interconnected individuals involved in those organizations. A web of meaning is always appealing, but it becomes even more so in times of turmoil. And if Joshua Cooper Ramo, author of *The Age of the Unthinkable,* is right, our current lack of stability, our constant state of change, makes systems of meaning such as this one appealing to many.[3]

On Conspiracies

Reconstructionists often argue in favor of bringing about these changes in ways that won't be recognized by the rest of us for what they are. They call it "being wise as serpents," often neglecting the second half of this biblical admonition to be as "harmless as doves." In an essay in *The Failure of American Baptist Culture,* North writes about the Christian school movement and advocates stealth tactics. And we should remember that the Christian school movement itself is a stealth tactic.

> As a *tactic* for a short-run defense of the independent Christian school movement, the appeal to religious liberty is legitimate . . . The major churches of any society are all maneuvering for power, so that their idea of lawful legislation will become predominant. They are all perfectly willing to use the ideal of religious liberty as a device to gain power, until the day comes that abortion is legalized

(denying the right of life to infants) or prohibited (denying the "right of control over her own body," after conception, to each woman). Everyone talks about religious liberty, but no one believes it . . . So let us be blunt about it: we must use the doctrine of religious liberty to gain independence for Christian schools until we train up a generation of people who know that there is no religious neutrality, no neutral law, no neutral education, and no neutral civil government. Then they will get busy in constructing a Bible-based social, political, and religious order which finally denies the religious liberty of the enemies of God.[4]

Many bloggers, activists, and organizations who study Christian Reconstructionists and other Christian nationalists do so from within the political conflict with the religious right. I appreciate their work, and draw on it myself, but some of them write in inflammatory language so they are dismissed as alarmists and shrill conspiracy theorists, even when they are making a strong point about Reconstructionist influence. I do not claim objectivity and even agree that it is ultimately impossible to attain. But there is a division we draw between scholars of religion and religious people; that of researcher and data. We struggle not to become the data. There is a difference between trying to understand a worldview and trying to build a case against it (which is, methodologically speaking, the same as trying to build a case for it). I'm not necessarily opposed to case-building, but I think case-building and understanding are different tasks and, frankly, effective case-building starts with real understanding. Thus I reject the idea that people I don't understand must be "crazy" or "brainwashed," and I try to avoid "warfare" language and even the tendency to assume that someone I don't yet understand is being deceptive (that's not to say I preclude that possibility). So, while I attempt to tone down the rhetoric about Christian Reconstruction, the religious right, and religious nationalism, I don't dismiss their detractors as conspiracy theorists.

Rushdoony was explicit that he believed conspiracies exist. Both he and Gary North come from a long line of conspiracy theorists (the Birchers and other anticommunist groups of the 1950s). In fact, for Rushdoony, to some degree, history is the outworking of Satan's conspiracy against the authority of the sovereign God of the universe.[5] To suggest that some groups of people "conspire" to bring about certain events is not crazy.

On the Future

There is disagreement among observers whether America's culture wars still rage; some argue that liberalism has won the day. They point to real gains in equality for women, broadly held views that racism is unacceptable, and the sea change in popular attitudes and LGBT legal rights as evidence that the Right has failed, that America remains a nation of moderates (and even liberals) moving toward pluralism and tolerance instead of away from it. Yet conservatives (Christian and secular) have not disappeared; they have doubled down, building on a framework developed and disseminated by a core group of conservatives whose views are rooted in religion—in some measure Reconstructionist dominionism. That core has contributed to the all-or-nothing character of contemporary American conservatism and much of its emphasis on decentralization, which has invigorated the gun culture and fostered a war against women, minorities, public employees, and public education. Its core is regional, and it follows roughly the boundaries of the Confederacy, but it spills over from there. We used to imagine the American electorate as made up of a left wing and a right wing with the vast majority of Americans in the middle. I suggest that we are seeing the loss of the middle, with the majority of Americans just left of what used to be center but with the Right remaining entrenched and gaining some support from the crumbling middle. So while the national culture may, indeed, be moderate to liberal, conservative strongholds remain where the Right—even the Far Right—dominates the culture.

My goal has been to trace Reconstructionist influence on the larger conservative Christian subculture, most especially in the ways in which Reconstructionist language and thinking have made their way into the public discourse and shaped that discourse. Much of that language is very typically "American." The patriot, or Tea Party, movement's adoption of the eighteenth-century Gadsden flag (Don't Tread on Me) and the term "Tea Party" prove this point. There is secessionist and limited-government language, defense of the Second Amendment in terms of the need to protect oneself from government tyranny, and the occasional defense of the use of force. The anti–gun-control arguments rooted in self-defense against the government were prevalent in the 1980s as homeschoolers and unlicensed Christian schools clashed with the government. Christian Reconstructionism has contributed to the persistence of those tropes as one of the sources of the preservation of the values and worldview of the

Old South. I have not argued that the Tea Party movement or the Christian Right are "really" Reconstructionist. Reconstructionists are not the only source of the current popularity of these views. But in circles where these concerns serve to mobilize, build group identity, and foster group solidarity (in part by making some people outsiders and setting up a social hierarchy within the group), Reconstructionists have played an important role, and I expect they will continue to do so. On the other hand, the claim by Reconstructionists that their movement is not essentially political is important and, in ignoring it, observers have often missed the real source of its potential for enduring influence. Christian Reconstructionists have their sights set much higher than elections and legislation. They have political goals (even in their very narrow way of using the term), but what they seek is a complete transformation of every aspect of life and culture. I do not expect that they will achieve that transformation. But in working toward it, they may well influence the direction of the culture in ways that matter very much to the rest of us.

Notes

PREFACE

1. For examples of work that shaped my views on this aspect see Russell T. McCutcheon, *Critics Not Caretakers* (Albany: SUNY Press, 2001), and Bruce Lincoln, *Discourse and the Construction of Society* (Oxford: Oxford University Press, 1989).

2. See, for example, Ingersoll, "Religion and Politics," and Julie J. Ingersoll, "Mobilizing Evangelicals: Christian Reconstructionism and the Roots of the Religious Right," in *Evangelicals and Democracy in America*, ed. Steven Brint and Jean Reith Schroedel (New York: Russell Sage Foundation, 2009).

3. For a comparison between the conservatism rooted in New England puritanism with that rooted in Southern plantation aristocracy see Michael Lind, *Made In Texas: George W. Bush and the Southern Takeover of American Politics* (New York: Basic Books, 2006), and Sarah Robinson, "Conservative Southern Values Revived: How a Brutal Strain of American Aristocrats Have Come to Rule America," AlterNet, June 28, 2012, http://www.alternet.org/story/156071/conservative_southern_values_revived%3A_how_a_brutal_strain_of_american_aristocrats_have_come_to_rule_america_?page=entire.

4. My elementary school classmates will attest to this as they remind me that in the mid-1960s, in sixth grade, I led a protest of the rule that required girls to wear dresses to school.

5. Julie J. Ingersoll, "Train up a Child: A Study of Evangelical Views on Education" (master's thesis, George Washington University, 1990). While this thesis remains unpublished, parts of it appear in chapter 4 of this volume.

6. Leo Ribuffo, *The Old Christian Right* (Philadelphia: Temple University Press, 1988).

7. Balmer, *Thy Kingdom Come*, xxvii.

8. For example, Gary North has made many of the works he owns available here: http://www.garynorth.com/freebooks/sidefrm2.htm.

INTRODUCTION

1. This comment was made at a birthday celebration for Rushdoony's 80th. The text of Phillips's speech was on the web at http://www.ustaxpayers.org/hp-rushdoony-bday.htm (site no longer valid, accessed Feb. 2, 1998).

2. Gary North, "R. J. Rushdoony, R.I.P.," Feb. 10, 2001, http://lewrockwell.com/north/north33.html.

3. Bruce Bartlett, "The Industrial Revolution: Pro and Con," *Journal of Christian Reconstruction* 3, no. 2 (Winter 1976–1977): 157–165.

4. James B. Jordan and Gary North, eds. *Christianity and Civilization: The Failure of American Baptist Culture* no. 1 (Spring 1982), Geneva Divinity School.

5. Phone interview with author. 7/31/2007.

6. See Kathryn Joyce, *Quiverfull: Inside the Biblical Patriarchy Movement* (Boston: Beacon Press, 2009).

7. Frederick Clarkson, *Eternal Hostility: The Struggle Between Theocracy and Democracy* (Monroe, ME: Common Courage Press, 1997), 107.

8. Earlier versions of the historiographical narrative traced throughout this introduction appeared in Ingersoll, "Religion and Politics"; idem; and "Mobilizing Evangelicals: Christian Reconstructionism and the Roots of the Religious Right," in *Evangelicals and Democracy in America*, ed. Steven Brint and Jean Reith Schroedel (New York: Russell Sage Foundation, 2009), 179–208.

9. Balmer, *Thy Kingdom Come*, xvi.

10. Ibid., xvii.

11. My thanks to Oxford University Press' anonymous reviewer of this manuscript for encouraging me to update this historiographical section.

12. Darren Dochuk's *From Bible Belt to Sunbelt: Plain Folk Religion, Grassroots Political, and the Rise of Evangelical Conservatism* (New York: W.W. Norton, 2011); Donald T. Critchlow, *Phyllis Schlafly and Grassroots Conservatism: A Woman's Crusade* (Princeton, NJ: Princeton University Press, 2005); Daniel K. Williams, *God's Own Party: The Making of the Christian Right* (Oxford: Oxford University Press, 2010).

13. There has also been some excellent nonacademic work on Christian Reconstruction; for example, see Chip Berlet, ed., *Eyes Right! Challenging the Right Wing Backlash* (Boston: South End Press, 1995); Clarkson, *Eternal Hostility*; James C. Sanford, *Blueprint for Theocracy: The Christian Right's Vision for America* (Providence, RI: Metacomet Books, 2014); and numerous articles by Sarah Posner.

14. Ingersoll, "Religion and Politics."

15. Sharlet, *The Family*; Juergensmeyer, *Terror in the Mind of God*; Diamond, *Not By Politics Alone*, and *Roads to Dominion*; Goldberg, *Kingdom Coming*; Balmer, *Thy Kingdom Come*; and Shupe, "Christian Reconstruction and the Angry Rhetoric of Neo-Postmillennialism." While each of these scholars points to the influence of the Reconstructionists, none develops an analysis of them at length. In fact, it has been Juergensmeyer's constant encouragement that led me to work on the larger project of which this chapter is a part. Two more thorough treatments of this movement do appear in Barron, *Heaven on Earth?*; and English, "Christian Reconstruction after Y2k."

16. An important exception to this characterization of the scholarship is Molly Worthen, "The Chalcedon Problem: Rousas John Rushdoony and the Origins of Christian Reconstructionism," *Church History* 77, no. 2 (June 2008): 399.

17. See for example, Ingersoll, *Evangelical Christian Women*. Other scholars have also made this point. For examples see Marsden, "Preachers of Paradox"; Woodberry and Smith, "Fundamentalism," 25–56.

18. Ingersoll, "Religion and Politics."

19. For scholarship on the influence of Schaeffer see Barry Hankins, *Francis Schaeffer and the Shaping of Evangelical America* (Grand Rapids: Eerdmans, 2008); and Schaeffer's son's work, especially Frank Schaeffer, *Crazy for God*. For work on the influence of the anticommunist movement see Donald T. Critchlow, *Phyllis Schlafly and Grassroots Conservativism* (Princeton, NJ: Princeton University Press, 2006); Kevin Kruse, "Beyond the Southern Cross: The National Origins of the Religious Right," in *The Myth of Southern Exceptionalism*, ed. Matthew Lassiter and Joseph Crespino (New York: Oxford University Press, 2010); as well as Markku Ruotsila, *The Origins of Christian Anti-Internationalism: Conservative Evangelicals and the League of Nations* (Washington, DC: Georgetown University Press, 2008).

20. Rushdoony, *By What Standard?*

21. The labeling here can be confusing. The global denomination is called the Anglican Communion. In the Colonial period, Americans affiliated with the Church of England were called Anglican (like everyone else affiliated with the church), but since the Revolutionary Era they have been referred to exclusively as Episcopalians. The Episcopal Church is the American branch of the Church of England or the Anglican Communion. Recent members of the American church, dissenting from its current direction, have adopted the label "Anglican" to differentiate themselves from the larger American church.

22. Lincoln and McCutcheon draw on classic theorists like Michel Foucault and Pierre Bordieu.

23. Unlike many religious groups, Reconstructionists have self-consciously worked out (and largely shared their processes of working out) what Foucault would call their "discursive formation."

CHAPTER I

1. This chapter is focused on the intellectual heritage that produced Christian Reconstruction. For a parallel discussion that traces these ideas from Calvin though Kuyper to Rushdoony and situates these thinkers in their historical context, see James C. Sanford, *Blueprint for Theocracy: The Christian Right's Vision for America* (Providence, RI: Metacomet Books, 2014), 59ff.

2. For those involved in theological debate within the Reformed tradition, the differences among these thinkers are supremely important. For our purposes, though, the commonalities among them, and the way in which Rushdoony developed the ideas of each, is most important. Contemporary followers of each of these theologians reject the trajectory in which Rushdoony took their work. I'm grateful to historian Diana Butler Bass for helping me sort this out.

3. David Biema, "Ten Ideas Changing the World Right Now," *Time*, March 12, 2009.http://content.time.com/time/specials/packages/article/0,28804,1884779_1884782_1884760,00.html .

4. Collin Hansen, *Young, Restless, Reformed: A Journalist's Journey with the New Calvinists* (Wheaton, IL: Crossway Books, 2008).

5. "Truth, Trust, and Testimony in a Time of Tension," *SBC Life: A Journal of the Southern Baptist Convention*, June–Aug. 2013, http://www.sbclife.org/Articles/2013/06/sla5.asp.

6. The five points are often referred to by the acronym TULIP.

7. I'm grateful to Sarah Posner, whose essay "Neo-Confederates and the Revival of 'Theological War' for the 'Christian Nation'" at http://www.religiondispatches.org/dispatches/sarahposner/4858/neo_confederates_and_the_revival_of__theological_war__for_the__christian_nation_, alerted me to some excellent scholarship on this question: Edward Sebesta and Euan Hague, *Neo-Confederacy: A Critical Introduction* (Austin: University of Texas Press, 2008); Sebesta, *The Confederate and Neo-Confederate Reader: The "Great Truth" About the "Lost Cause"* (Columbia: University Press of Mississippi 2010); and Sebesta and Hague, "The US Civil War as a Theological War: Confederate Christian Nationalism and the League of the South," *Canadian Review of American Studies* 32, no. 3 (2002): 253–284.

8. Phillips's own distillation of Dabney's work is subtitled The Prophet Speaks. (San Antonio: Vision Forum, 1998).

9. North, http://www.garynorth.com/freebooks/docs/a_pdfs/newslet/position/8407.pdf.

10. Sebesta and Hague, "The US Civil War as a Theological War," 263.

11. Rushdoony, *Nature of the American System*, 48ff.

12. Ibid., 2.

13. Ibid., 4.

14. Ibid., 8–10.

15. Rushdoony, *Institutes of Biblical Law*, 60.

16. Rushdoony, *Nature of the American System*, 45.

17. Sebesta and Hague, "The US Civil War as a Theological War."

18. Ibid., 256. Citing Michael Hill, "Treason and the Elites," League of the South, http://dixienet.org/rights/the_treason_of_the_elites.php.

19. See *The God Who Is There* and *How Should We Then Live* for examples of this work.

20. For more on Schaeffer and Rushdoony in conversation and as complementary to each other see Sanford, *Blueprint for Theocracy*, 20–53.

21. William Edgar, "The Passing of R. J. Rushdoony," August 2001, http://www.firstthings.com/article/2001/08/the-passing-of-r-j-rushdoony.

22. http://www.chalcedon.edu/blog/2008/01/did-francis-schaeffer-believe-rushdoony.php. Bruce Bartlett, "The Industrial Revolution: Pro and Con," *Journal of Christian Reconstruction* 3, no. 2 (Winter 1976–1977): 157–165.

23. John Whitehead became well known later as the attorney for Paula Jones in her legal dealings with President Bill Clinton.

24. There is disagreement among Reconstructionists as to whether the founding fathers sought to establish a Christian nation, shaped in part by the fluid invoking of the founding era. There is agreement as to the Puritans' goals as founders, but, by the era in which the Constitution was written, Reconstructionists acknowledge more divergence of opinion. Regardless of whether they center the argument for a Christian nation in the Bible and the founders or the Bible alone, they agree that a nation under biblical law is the goal. The inside debates about the founders are lost in the more popular discourse.

25. Greg Bahnsen, *No Other Standard* (Tyler, TX: Institute for Christian Economics, 1991), 3–4.

26. This basic argument appears in my essay "Religiously Motivated Violence in the Abortion Debate," in *Oxford Handbook of Religion and Violence*, ed. Mark Juergensmeyer, Margot S. Kitts and Michael Jerryson (New York: Oxford University Press, 2013).

27. Bahnsen, *By This Standard* (Tyler, TX: Institute for Christian Economics, 1985), 50–1.

28. Bahnsen, *By This Standard*, and *Theonomy and Christian Ethics* (Phillipsburg, NJ: Presbyterian and Reformed Publishing, 1977).

29. Bahnsen, *By This Standard*, 3–4.

30. Ibid., 16.

31. Joel McDurmon, "To Rachel Held Evans, RE: 'If my son or daughter were gay . . .'" July 3, 2013, http://americanvision.org/8628/rachel-held-evans-if-my-son-or-daughter-were-gay/.

32. North, *Millennialism and Social Theory*, 21.

33. Michael McVicar, *Christian Reconstruction: R. J. Rushdoony and American Religious Conservatism* (Chapel Hill: University of North Carolina Press, 2015), 59–64.

34. North, *Millennialism and Social Theory*, 239.

35. Ibid., 22.
36. Matthew 27:16–20, Genesis 1:28.
37. Chilton, *Paradise Restored*, 11.
38. Ibid., 15.
39. Ibid. The use of the first person in this quote (we, our, etc.) is Chilton's, not mine.
40. Ibid., 5.
41. Chilton claims that according to Christopher Columbus's journals, "unfulfilled prophecy" led the explorer to seek a route to the Indies for the purpose of bringing them the Gospel. Chilton does not give a us a source for this information though it is likely that he got it from the work of Peter Marshall and David Manuel, whose book, *The Light and the Glory* (Old Tappan, NJ: Fleming H. Revell, 1977), 30, which promoted the idea that America is a Christian nation, was widely read in churches and used as a textbook for American history courses in Christian schools. Marshall and Manuel cite Columbus's journals as support for this view but then tell us in their notes that the original journals were lost, and they traced the story to Bishop Bartolome de Las Casas, to whom Columbus allegedly told the story on a later voyage.
42. Chilton, *Paradise Restored*, 7.
43. There is an ongoing debate between full preterists and partial preterists, with Reconstructionists being technically partial preterists. The debate is not relevant to this discussion.
44. Chilton, *Paradise Restored*, 15.
45. Ibid., 16.
46. Ibid., 17.
47. Matthew 24:34, New American Standard Translation, cited by Chilton, *Paradise Restored*, 86.
48. Chilton, *Paradise Restored*, 85–86.
49. Ibid., 93.
50. Ibid., 21.
51. *None Dare Call it Witchcraft* is a play on the anticommunist book entitled *None Dare Call it Conspiracy*.
52. Jeff Sharlet, "Through a Glass, Darkly," *Harper's*, December 2006.
53. http://www.christianitytoday.com/books/features/rumorsofglory/070212.html.
54. This is classic Reformed theology, and there are interesting variations of this that have become justifications for alternative views on the environment in what is sometimes called the "evangelical Left."
55. *Last Train Out; Government by Emergency; Fighting Chance; Conspiracy: A Biblical View;* and *The Pirate Economy,* all by North.
56. North, *Conspiracy*, 126.

57. North, *Moses and Pharaoh*; and *Dominion and Common Grace*. Cornelius Van Til, *Common Grace and the Gospel* (Philadelphia: Presbyterian and Reformed Publishing, 1972).

58. For more on this see Matt Moen, *The Christian Right and Congress* (Tuscaloosa: University of Alabama Press, 1989), and Randall Balmer, *God in the White House* (San Francisco: HarperCollins, 2008).

59. For an example of this, Gary Demar, "Old Calvinism Is Now the New Calvinism," American Vision, http://www.americanvision.org/article/old-calvinism-is-now-the-new-calvinism/ (website no longer available). DeMar responds to *Time* magazine's list of "10 Ideas Changing the World Right Now," in which New Calvinism is number three. DeMar's point is that until the new Calvinists become consistent and jettison their nontheonomic, and sometimes dispensationalist, theological systems, they will be impotent.

60. North, *Conspiracy*, 141.

61. Ibid., 143.

62. North, *Marx's Religion of Revolution*, xxiv. Mine is a newer edition of his first book originally published by Craig Press in 1968. Most of the early Reconstructionists had ties to the John Birch Society; thus I have argued that they can be seen as a bridge between the Old Christian Right and the New Christian Right. See my article "Religion and Politics."

63. North, *Millennialism and Social Theory*, 308.

64. Ibid., 309.

65. George Marsden, *Fundamentalism and American Culture* (Oxford: Oxford University Press, 2006), 68–9.

66. North, *Millennialism and Social Theory*, 298–9.

67. *Conspiracy*, 135–59.

68. Tim LaHaye, *The Battle for the Mind* (1980), *The Battle for the Family* (1982), and *The Battle for the Public Schools* (1983).

69. Tim LaHaye and Jerry Jenkins, *The Remnant: On the Brink of Armageddon* (Wheaton, IL: Tyndale House, 2002), 401.

70. Ibid., 403.

71. George Marsden, "Preachers of Paradox," in *Understanding Fundamentalism and Evangelicalism* (Grand Rapids: Wm. B. Eerdmans, 1991).

72. Gary North, "Intellectual Schizophrenia," in *Christianity and Civilization: The Failure of the American Baptist Culture* (Tyler, TX: Geneva Divinity School, Spring 1982), 11.

73. Leo Ribuffo, *The Old Christian Right: The Protestant Far Right from the Depression to the Cold War* (Philadelphia: Temple University Press, 1988).

74. Phillip E. Hammond, *The Protestant Presence in Twentieth Century America* (Albany: State University of New York Press, 1992); and James Davison Hunter, *Evangelicalism: The Coming Generation* (Chicago: University of Chicago Press, 1991).

CHAPTER 2

1. It's a quaint bit of Reconstructionist lore that Rushdoony, to the end of his life, wrote in longhand. In the preface he thanks his wife for typing the manuscript.
2. Rushdoony, *Institutes of Biblical Law*, 2.
3. Ibid., 12.
4. Ibid., 218. This is, of course, a reference to the second part of the fifth commandment: "honor thy father and mother that thy days shall be long upon the land."
5. This point is in dispute among Reconstructionists. While Rushdoony saw the family as the preeminent institution ordained by God, others have argued that the church, with its ecclesiastical authority, is most central. See, for example, James B. Jordan, *The Sociology of the Church*.
6. Rushdoony, *Institutes of Biblical Law*, 164.
7. Lakoff, *Moral Politics*.
8. Lakoff is, himself, a progressive and sees his work as a blueprint for the reinvigoration of the Left. In fact, his critics have charged that his solution is far too simple and that "we" cannot overhaul American political culture by simply changing the "frame" of the debate. I have no such agenda, and the limitations of his work as a political strategy are not my concern. I am interested in his work as a theoretical model that helps explain how our political culture works. What is required, however, is a more complete portrait of conservatism, made possible by his model despite the fact that Lakoff's application of his own model to conservatism leads to something of a caricature.
9. Rushdoony, *Institutes of Biblical Law*, 194–5.
10. Ibid., 159.
11. Ibid., 163.
12. Ibid., 200.
13. Ibid., 201.
14. Ibid.
15. Ibid., 203.
16. Ibid., 182.
17. Ibid.
18. Ibid., 185.
19. Ibid., 184.
20. Christina Hoff Sommers, *The War Against Boys: How Misguided Feminism Is Harming Our Young Men* (New York: Simon and Schuster, 1990). Rushdoony, *Institutes of Biblical Law*, 2.
21. Rushdoony, *Institutes of Biblical Law*, 192.
22. Ibid., 166.
23. Ibid., 175.
24. Ibid., 166.

25. Ibid., 167.
26. Ibid., 186.
27. Ibid., 190.
28. North, *Millennialism and Social Theory*, 132.
29. Ibid., 134–5.
30. This five-point model is explored in chapter 3 of this volume.
31. *Law and Liberty*, 3.
32. North and Demar, *Christian Reconstruction: What It Is, What It Isn't* (Tyler, TX: Institute for Christian Economics, 1991), 35.
33. Ibid., 36.
34. Ibid., 92.
35. Bruce Lincoln, *Holy Terrors: Thinking about Religion after September 11* (Chicago: University of Chicago Press, 2003), 5.
36. North, *Millennialism and Social Theory*, 3.
37. Ibid., xv.
38. Ibid., 7–10.
39. Ibid., 33.
40. North and DeMar, *Christian Reconstruction*, 160–1.
41. North, *Millennialism and Social Theory*, 68.
42. This division arose from the work of Ray Sutton in which he argued that the Bible contains a five-point covenantal structure that can serve as a model for biblical theology. That model became central to Gary North's Christian Reconstruction in that he came to see the covenantal theology making the church hierarchy much more central than did Rushdoony and others. North described this as a Tyler–Vallecito split (i.e., the Tyler, Texas, faction of which he is part and the Vallecito faction; Vallecito, California, is where the Chalcedon Foundation is located) and it is considered the point of contention in a dispute that resulted in the estrangement between Rushdoony and North. The debate is described by Gary North at http://www.entrewave.com/freebooks/docs/html/gnbd/appendix_k.htm.accessed July 7, 2011.
43. North, *Millennialism and Social Theory*, 135.
44. Ibid., 133.
45. Ibid.
46. Ibid., 283.

CHAPTER 3

1. This essay appears at the end of every volume. See for example, Sutton, *Who Owns the Family*, 187–8.
2. Ibid., vol. 3, 188.
3. *Liberating Planet Earth: An Introduction to Biblical Blueprints* (vol. 1, 1987); *Honest Money: Biblical Principles of Money and Banking* (vol. 5, 1986); *Inherit the*

Earth: Biblical Principles for Economics (vol. 7, 1987); and *Healer of Nations: Biblical Principles for International Relations* (vol. 9, 1987).

4. He sees them as inconsistent in that they necessarily presuppose an order to the universe that by denying biblical revelation they simultaneously undermine.

5. The degree and longevity of his participation is evident in the archives of the website lewrockwell.com, where he regularly posts.

6. This view is apparent in most of North's work. See, for additional examples, *An Introduction To Christian Economics* (1973); *Boundaries and Dominion* (1994); *Marx's Religion of Revolution* (1989); *Moses and Pharaoh* (1985); *Political Polytheism* (1989).

7. North, *Liberating Planet Earth*, 3–5. North takes Marx's text from "Contribution to the Critique of Hegel's Philosophy of Right," in *Karl Marx: Early Writings*, ed. T. B. Bottomore ed. (New York: McGraw-Hill, 1964), 52.

8. North, *Honest Money*, 88.

9. Ibid., 118.

10. North, *Inherit the Earth*, 140–1.

11. Ibid., 119

12. Ibid., 164.

13. Ibid., 77–8.

14. Ibid., 137.

15. Perhaps ironically, while conservatives opposed to social welfare policies often invoke this phrase to legitimate their understanding of American exceptionalism in the way that Ronald Reagan did, Winthrop actually warns of God's wrath should the Puritans fail to care for one another and fail to put the needs of the community above their own in a ringing endorsement of communitarianism that North would label socialism.

16. Ibid., 53.

17. Ibid., 34–6.

18. Ibid., 166.

19. Gary DeMar, *Ruler of Nations: Biblical Blueprints of Government* (Ft. Worth, TX: Dominion Press, 1987) and George Grant, *The Changing of the Guard: Biblical Principles for Political Action* (Ft. Worth, TX: Dominion Press, 1987).

20. DeMar, *Ruler of Nations* 16, 33.

21. Ibid., 33.

22. Ibid., 142.

23. Ibid., 142.

24. Ibid., 128.

25. Grant, *Changing of the Guard*, 33.

26. Ibid., 13.

27. Ibid., 13.

28. Ibid., 14.

29. Ibid., 40.

30. Gary North, editor's introduction to Grant, *Changing of the Guard*, xxv.

31. Grant, *Changing of the Guard*, 11.

32. Ibid., 50–1.

33. Bob McDonnell, "The Republican Party's Vision for the Family: The Compelling Issue for the Decade," Regent University thesis, http://www.scribd.com/doc/19247833/Regent-University-Thesis-Of-Bob-McDonnell.

34. Author and blogger Diana Butler Bass sent me a query about McDonnell since she was writing about him and saw the subtle influence of Reconstructionists in his views. She sent me the link to the thesis, and I was able to give her some explicit examples, including the references to Sutton. See Diana Butler Bass, "Bob McDonnell's Thesis: Christian Reconstruction and the Virginia Governor's Race," http://blog.beliefnet.com/progressiverevival/2009/10/bob-mcdonnells-thesis-christia.html.

35. For example, see McDonnell, "The Republican Party's Vision for the Family," 61.

36. Sutton, *Who Owns the Family*, vol. 3, xv.

37. Ibid., vol. 3, xxi. To clarify the manner in which the family has authority to resolve this problem I include the full quote here. "The head of the household of the daughter who becomes pregnant is to decide whether to compel the marriage between the sinning daughter and her sinning male consort. If the parent decides against the marriage, he or she can demand that the male (or his family) pay a sufficient amount of money to pay for the birth of the baby—not its execution, but its birth. The civil government does not have any independent authority in this regard; it simply supports the decision of the legally sovereign parent (Deuteronomy 22:28–29). Finally, if the unmarried daughter decides to have an adopting family pay for the expenses, she can keep the money paid by her consort—what in some societies might be called a dowry. It gives her some protective capital before she enters a marriage—something that is hers that she takes into the marriage."

38. Sutton, *Who Owns the Family*, 18.

39. Ibid., 169.

40. Ibid., 129.

41. Matthew 1:19 cited in Sutton, *Second Chance*, vol. 5, 74.

42. Ibid., 169.

43. Ibid., 169–70.

44. Grant, *In the Shadow of Plenty*, 19.

45. Max Weber, *The Protestant Ethic and the Spirit of Capitalism*, Talcott Parsons, Anthony Giddens, trans. (Boston: Unwin Hyman, 1930).

46. Grant, *In the Shadow of Plenty*, 9–10.

47. Ibid., 52.

48. Ibid., 95.

49. Ibid., 96.

50. Ibid., 123.

51. Ibid., 124.
52. Ibid., 127.
53. Ibid., 129.
54. Gary North, editor's introduction to ibid., xii–xiii.

CHAPTER 4

1. Some of this research was initially collected as part of my MA thesis: "Train Up a Child: A Study of Evangelical Views on Education" (George Washington University, 1990). It has never been published and has been updated and revised for this chapter.
2. Notable exceptions include two important influences on Christian Reconstruction: Robert L. Dabney and J. Gresham Machen.
3. For an excellent account of the historical development of this process see Stephen Prothero, *Religious Literacy* (New York: Harper One, 2007).
4. Though he doesn't mention the Volker Fund in the acknowledgements of this book he thanks specifically Volker Fund staff Ivan Bierly and David Hoggan in the 1963 preface.
5. Rushdoony, *Philosophy of the Christian Curriculum*, 3.
6. Ibid., 17.
7. Ibid., 23.
8. Ibid., 25.
9. Ibid., 37.
10. US Department of Education, National Center for Education Statistics, *The Condition of Education 2006* (NCES 2006–071), http://nces.ed.gov/fastfacts/display.asp?id=6; and US Department of Education, National Center for Education Statistics, *The Condition of Education 2009* (NCES 2009–081), http://nces.ed.gov/fastfacts/display.asp?id=6.
11. As I indicated in the introduction, I was married to one of those sons for ten years. Mark, my spouse, was one of the children who founded such a school during the time we were married.
12. Robert L. Thoburn, *How to Establish and Operate a Successful Christian School* (Fairfax, VA: Self-published, 1971), i.
13. Ibid., 8.
14. Ibid., 6.
15. This is a number put forth by the Thoburns that I have no way to verify. It was interesting that, in the course of updating this research on Christian schools, I stumbled upon the school that serves as the next case study: a school that lists the Thoburns as the resource that helped them start in the 1970s.
16. http://www.fairfaxchristianschool.com/.
17. Since I visited the campus in 2009 Lawson has been replaced as superintendent by Dr. Michael Mosley.

18. Thoburn, *How to Establish and Operate a Successful Christian School*.

19. Evolution, as an issue, has the force that it does, in part, because it is the symbolic representation of presuppositionalism, the centerpiece of this worldview.

20. Donald Lawson, interview with author, Feb. 19, 2009; digital recording in author's possession.

21. School website http://www.rbcs.org/aboutus_history.html.

22. Donald Lawson, interview with author, Feb. 19, 2009; digital recording in author's possession.

23. The Joneses work in the library at RBCS, and Archie writes occasionally for Gary DeMar's American Vision (where their daughter Jennie works). Archie has written for numerous Reconstructionist publications over the years including Rushdoony's *Journal for Christian Reconstruction*. Both Jordan and Bahnsen must be seen (with David Chilton) as in the second tier of influential Reconstructionist writers behind only Rushdoony and North.

24. Donald Lawson, interview with author, Feb. 19, 2009; digital recording in author's possession.

25. JoAnne Young, "Testing Proposed for Home Schoolers," *Lincoln Journal Star*, Jan. 27, 2008, http://www.journalstar.com/articles/2008/01/27/news/politics/doc479bbcefed877749489165.txt.

26. Julie Ingersoll, "Worldviews in Conflict: The State of Nebraska v. Faith Baptist Church" (paper presented to the American Academy of Religion Western Region, March 1993).

27. Neal Devins, "Nebraska and the Future of State Regulation of Christian Schools," in *Government Intervention in Religious Affairs*, vol. 2, ed. Dean M. Kelley (New York: Pilgrim Press, 1986), 107.

28. John Whitesides, "Lawmen Are Posted After School Backers Are Carried from Building," *Omaha World-Herald*, Oct. 18, 1982, 1.

29. The number of people who were at Faith Baptist varies widely from one account to another and is as high as one thousand. H. Edward Rowe, *The Day They Padlocked the Church: Pastor Sileven and 1,000 Christians Who Defied Nebraska Tyranny in America's Crisis of Freedom* (Shreveport, LA: Huntington House Press, 1983).

30. Everett Sileven, *Dear Legislator: A Plea for Liberty in Christian Education* (Orlando, FL: Daniels, 1983).

31. Ibid., 11.

32. Ibid., 22.

33. Ibid., 23.

34. Ibid., 25.

35. Ibid., 23.

36. Ibid., 31–2.

37. Gary North, "Why Churches Should Not Incorporate," Institute for Christian Economics, Position Paper No. 1 (July 1984).

38. Devins, "Nebraska and the Future of State Regulation of Christian Schools," 117.
39. For an excellent treatment of how "the sacred" is essentially contested see David Chidester and Edward T. Linenthal, ed., *American Sacred Space* (Bloomington: Indiana University Press, 1993).
40. Whitesides, "Sileven Says He Won't Go Willingly to Jail."
41. Rowe, *The Day They Padlocked the Church*, 12.
42. Ibid., 4.
43. Ibid., 3.
44. Dick Ulmer, "Sileven: State Education Parallels Nazi Germany," *Omaha World-Herald*, October 26, 1983, 1.
45. Sileven was born Everett Ramsey but was raised by a family member married to a Sileven. He now uses his birth name, Everett Ramsey. Information on him and his ministry is from his website, http://www.everettramseydd.com/ourministry.html.
46. See, for example, Rushdoony, *Messianic Character of American Education*.

CHAPTER 5

1. US Department of Education, Issue Brief, National Center for Education Statistics, December 2008.
2. See for example blogs http://www.patheos.com/blogs/lovejoyfeminism/; http://hsinvisiblechildren.org/; and http://homeschoolersanonymous.wordpress.com/; as well the *Daily Beast's* Michelle Goldberg, "Homeschooled Kids, Now Grown, Blog Against the Past," April 11, 2013, http://www.thedailybeast.com/witw/articles/2013/04/11/homeschooled-kids-now-grown-blog-against-the-past.html. And New Hampshire Public Radio's Virginia Prescott, "Home Schoolers Anonymous," April 29, 2013, http://www.nhpr.org/post/homeschoolers-anonymous.
3. For excellent work on Patrick Henry College and its ties to "dominion theology," see Hannah Rosin, *God's Harvard: A Christian College on a Mission to Save America* (Orlando, FL: Harcourt, 2007).
4. These are the numbers from the 2007 survey.
5. Greg Harris, *The Christian Home School* (Brentwood, TN: Wolgemuth and Hyatt, 1988), 86.
6. The HSLDA *Court Report* published a timeline for this case. "Homeschool Freedom & the California Case Timeline," *Home School Court Report*, http://www.hslda.org/courtreport/V24N6/V24N603.asp. Interestingly, HSLDA was asked to join USJF in the case when Michael Farris met USJF executive Director Gary Kreep at a meeting of the Council on National Policy (CNP). Much has been written about the CNP as a secretive clearinghouse for elite conservative leaders. Several Reconstructionists have reportedly been members: Rushdoony, Thoburn, North, Phillips, and others. For more on the CNP see Goldberg, *Kingdom Coming*.

7. "How Safe Is the Homeschool Horizon? Social Workers: Constitution! What Constitution?" *Home School Court Report*, http://www.hslda.org/courtreport/V23N3/V23N301.asp.

8. Chris Klicka, "No Fear: Social Workers Restrained!" Practical Homeschooling #65, 2005. http://www.home-school.com/Articles/no-fear-social-workers-restrained.php.

9. Michael Farris, *Anonymous Tip* (Nashville: Broadman and Holman, 1996).

10. Christopher Klicka, *The Right Choice: Home Schooling* (Gresham, OR: Noble, 1995).

11. The Johnsons' name has been changed. These interviews were conducted as part of the research for my unpublished master's thesis. Julie Ingersoll, "Train Up a Child: A Study of Evangelical Views on Education" (George Washington University, 1997). Klicka interview conducted July 11, 1989, at the HSLDA headquarters, then in Leesburg, Virginia. Tracy and Kathy Johnson, interview July 11, 1989, in their home in Fairfax, Virginia.

12. Ephesians 6:4 and Proverbs 6:20, respectively.

13. Robert Thoburn, *The Children Trap: the Biblical Blueprint for Education* (*Biblical Blueprint Series* vol. 6), Gary North, ed. (Tyler, TX: Dominion Press, 1986).

14. There is some inconsistency in terms of how they deal with higher education. Patrick Henry College specifically sells itself as a Christian college for homeschooled students. College Plus is an organization that aids students in getting college credit for work they do at home and then supplementing that work with online courses from Christian colleges and universities to complete degrees. Much of the rhetoric argues that higher education is unnecessary, especially for young women, yet they often recite lists of prestigious schools homeschoolers have attended, both public and private.

15. "Homeschooling Spells Success for 2007 Scripps Howard National Spelling Bee Winner Evan O'Dorney, a California Homeschooler," and "Keeping Homeschooling on the Map: The 2007 National Geographic Bee Winner, Homeschooler Caitlin Snaring, Receives a $25,000 scholarship," http://www.hslda.org/courtreport/V24N4/V24N401.asp.

16. The quotes are taken from the CLASS website, http://www.homeschools.org/index.html.

17. This is a reference to the first question in the Westminster Catechism: What is the chief end of man?

18. Gary North, "Tentmakers: Interdenominational Service," *Institute for Christian Economics* 7, no. 4 (July–Aug. 1984).

19. The seven principles are **Design:** Understanding the specific purposes for which God created each person, object, and relationship in my life and living in harmony with them. **Authority:** Honoring the responsibilities of parents, church leaders, government, and other authorities and learning how God works through them to provide direction and protection. **Responsibility:** Realizing

I am accountable to God for every thought, word, action, and motive. **Suffering:** Allowing the hurts from offenders to reveal "blind spots" in my own life, and then seeing how I can benefit their lives. **Ownership:** Understanding that everything I have has been entrusted to me by God, and wisely using it for His purposes. Yielding my rights to God brings *True Security*. **Freedom:** Enjoying the desire and power to do what is right, rather than claiming the privilege to do what I want. **Success:** Discovering God's purpose for my life by engrafting Scripture in my heart and mind, and using it to "think God's thoughts" and make wise decisions.

20. http://spiritualsoundingboard.com/category/organizations-movements/bill-gothard/

21. http://www.washingtonpost.com/national/religion/conservative-leader-bill-gothard-resigns-following-abuse-allegations/2014/03/07/0381aa94-a624-11e3-b865-38b254d92063_story.html

22. Kunzman, *Write These Laws on Your Children.*

23. In 2008 John Holzmann, co-owner of Sonlight Curriculum Ltd. engaged in a lengthy exchange with Kevin Swanson, Christian Reconstructionist and president of Christian Home Educators of Colorado (CHEC). CHEC had, after many years of co-partnering with Sonlight, banned them from exhibiting at their convention. Holzmann articulated thoroughgoing theological agreement with Swanson and CHEC. The dispute seems rooted in a disagreement about the extent to which curriculum should present viewpoints that are deemed incorrect (in this case alternatives to young earth creationism). http://johnscorner.blogspot.com/2009/01/change-of-interpretation-on-chec.html. I thank blogger Julie Anne Smith for pointing me to this controversy when I interviewed her on May 5, 2013, by phone.

24. Kunzman, *Write These Laws on Your Children*, 181.

25. Ibid., 68.

26. Rushdoony, *Messianic Character of American Education*, 123.

27. Kunzman, *Write These Laws on Your Children*, 103.

28. Vic Lockman, "Biblical Economics in Cartoons," http://www.viclockman.com/law.htm, referenced by Kunzman, *Write These Laws on Your Children*, 89.

29. See Ray Sutton, *That You May Prosper: Dominion by Covenant* (Tyler, TX: Institute for Christian Economics, 1986); Gary North, *The Sinai Strategy: Economics and the Ten Commandments* (Tyler, TX: Institute for Christian Economics, 1986); and David Chilton, *Days of Vengeance* (Tyler, TX: Dominion Press, 1987).

30. Kunzman, *Write These Laws on Your Children*, 62, 76.

31. Ibid., 135.

32. My thanks to the bloggers who first made me aware of this conference, two of whom aided me in acquiring no-longer-available recordings of twelve of the lectures (John Holzmann and Karen Campbell). Additionally, the writings of Holzmann and Campbell as well as bloggers Libby Anne and R. A. Stollar were

extraordinarily helpful. Stollar recovered archived versions of websites no longer available and provided links to them on his blog. I listened to and transcribed parts of the following lectures: "For Such a Time as This," Kevin Swanson; "Homeschooling: Capturing the Vision," Kevin Swanson; "Closing Remarks," Kevin Swanson; "A Father as Priest," Scott Brown; "A Father as Prophet," Scott Brown; "A Father as King," Scott Brown; "A Battle for the Family," Voddie Baucham; "Harvard or Heaven," Voddie Baucham; "A Vision for the Family," Doug Phillips; "Visionary Fathers," Doug Phillips; "The Homeschooling Movement in America," Brian Ray; and "Leading and Bleeding," Mike Cheney.

33. Quoted from the post by R. S. Stollar, "End Child Protection: Doug Phillips, HSLDA, and the 2009 Men's Leadership Summit," May 14, 2013, http:// homeschoolersanonymous.wordpress.com/2013/05/14/end-child-protection-doug-phillips-hslda-and-the-2009-mens-leadership-summit/. Stoller cited the archived website http://web.archive.org/web/20090213172933/http://2009 leadershipsummit.com/About.aspx.

34. Swanson recording, "For Such a Time as This."

35. I was not able to confirm the authenticity of the document Holzmann provided, but I believe it real because (1) everything in it is consistent with the perspective of the leaders involved; and (2) the lectures, which I was able to listen to for myself, amounted to an exposition of these basic points.

36. "HSLDA and Child Abuse: An Introduction," http://www.patheos.com/blogs/ lovejoyfeminism/2013/04/hslda-child-abuse-and-educational-neglect-an-introduction.html.

37. "HSLDA: Man Who Kept Children in Cages 'A Hero,'" May 6, 2013, http:// www.patheos.com/blogs/lovejoyfeminism/2013/05/hslda-man-who-kept-children-in-cages-a-her.html.

38. Lincoln, *Holy Terrors.*

39. Sociologist Sara Diamond has argued that it is this concern with every aspect of life that leads the religious right to develop a broad-based network of institutions and organizations, reaching far beyond politics, that accounts for its persistent vitality in American life. See also Erving Goffman, *Asylums: Essays on the Social Situation of Mental Patients and Other Inmates* (New York: Anchor Books, 1961) and Michel Foucault, *Discipline and Punish* (New York: Knopf Doubleday, 1995).

40. http://spiritualsoundingboard.com.

CHAPTER 6

*. I wish to express my gratitude to the Florida Blue Center for Ethics at the University of North Florida for their generous support in the form of a Summer Research Grant and the University of North Florida for a Sabbatical Grant, allowing me to write this chapter.

1. My perspective on this is shaped by the work of several scholars of religion. See, for example, Russell McCutcheon, "Myth," in *Guide to the Study of Religion*, ed. McCutcheon and Willi Braun (London and New York: Cassell, 2000), and *Critics Not Caretakers* (Albany: State University of New York Press, 2001); Bruce Lincoln, *Myth, Cosmos and Society* (Cambridge, MA: Harvard University Press, 1986), *Discourse and the Construction of Society* (New York: Oxford University Press, 1992), and *Authority: Construction and Corrosion* (Chicago: University of Chicago Press, 1994).

2. Frank Newport, "Four in Ten Americans Believe in Strict Creationism," Dec. 17, 2010, http://www.gallup.com/poll/145286/four-americans-believe-strict-creationism.aspx.

3. Rushdoony, *Mythology of Science*, 47.

4. Ronald Numbers, *The Creationists: The Evolution of Scientific Creationism* (New York: Alfred A. Knopf, 1992), 39.

5. David Livingston, *Darwin's Forgotten Defenders* (Grand Rapids, MI: William B. Eerdmans, 1987), 29.

6. Ibid., 44.

7. Ibid., 100–144.

8. Numbers, xi.

9. Ibid., 158

10. Ibid., xi.

11. Randall J. Stephens and Karl W. Giberson, *Anointed: Evangelical Truth in a Secular Age* (Cambridge: Belknap Press, 2011), 29.

12. Ibid., 30.

13. Cited in Numbers, xi, from Henry M. Morris, *Scientific Creationism* (El Cajon, CA: Master Books, 1974), 252.

14. Morris, *Scientific Creationism*, iii.

15. "FBC-Jax Honors Councilmen Who Vote Against Civil Rights Protections for Gays," http://www.youtube.com/watch?v=bJxOoD4d9Fo (website no longer available, accessed 5/19/2013).

16. All quotes taken from author's notes at ICF conference, Demand the Evidence, Jacksonville, FL, October 9–12, 2009.

17. Of course it is only this version of Christianity that would crumble without such a reading of Genesis. Most readings of the Christian tradition do not combine the Old and New Testaments in this way.

18. See for example, American Vision's Worldview Forum, a discussion board that divides topics into appropriate categories. Discussions of evolution are placed in the larger category of apologetics.

19. http://www.answersingenesis.org/home/area/bios/j_bergman.asp.

20. Bergman, *Slaughter of the Dissidents: The Shocking Truth About Killing the Careers of Darwin Doubters* (Southworth, WA: Leafcutter Press, 2008).

21. All quotes taken from author's notes at ICF conference, Demand the Evidence, Jacksonville, FL, October 9–12, 2009.
22. Wayne State University Catalog, http://tbf.coe.wayne.edu/eer/broch.htm.
23. http://www.cpuniv.us/faqs.htm (website no longer available, accessed 12/29/2010).
24. I did not, for example, enroll in any of ICR's online programs because they are open only to Christians and their application form requires that applicants make claims about their faith I could not honestly make.
25. These are pseudonyms.
26. Vision Forum Press Release, http://www.themysteriousislands.com/press/releases/index.aspx (website no longer available, accessed 12/29/2010).
27. Vision Forum Year End Report, *Ten Lessons from 2010, Ten Visions for 2011*, http://viewer.zmags.com/publication/ccfecb79#/ccfecb79/1 (website no longer available, accessed 12/29/2010).
28. Rushdoony, *Systematic Theology*.

CHAPTER 7

1. While most of the research for this chapter predated the scandal, my media work on it led to a request from the plaintiffs to serve as an expert witness in this case. I helped with the drafting of the complaint and expect to continue in that role through any litigation. Some of the material in this chapter has appeared in other versions in the *Religion Dispatches* and *Huffington Post*.
2. According to Guidestar, a nonprofit that collects and makes available data on charities in the interest of transparency. http://www.guidestar.org/organizations/74-2984736/vision-forum-ministries.aspx#recommendations.
3. Vision Forum Catalog, 2009, http://www.visionforum.com/search/productdetail.aspx?search=entrepreneur&productid=45,936 (site no longer available, accessed June 6, 2010).
4. Vision Forum Catalog, 2007, 58.
5. This appeared in a blog post as part of a controversy between Phillips and former members of his church. Ortiz posted a letter on Chalcedon's blog "In Defense of Doug Phillips." The letter was removed from Chalcedon's blog but can be read in a response to the controversy at "Chalcedon Ministry Sets 'Record Straight' about Relationship with Doug Phillips," Nov. 21, 2013, http://jensgems.wordpress.com/category/chalcedon/. I cite it here only as confirmation of the relationship.
6. For an excellent discussion of the Quiverfull movement, see Kathryn Joyce, *Quiverfull: Inside the Christian Patriarchy Movement* (Boston: Beacon Press, 2009).
7. Rushdoony, *The Biblical Philosophy of History*, 8.

8. Ibid., 61.

9. Ibid., 100.

10. I say "apparent" because there are no direct quotations and there are no references, only paraphrases attributed to some part of Dabney's body of work. While the statements seem to be in keeping with the character of Dabney's work, there is no way, from this volume, to check them. Doug Phillips, ed., *Robert Lewis Dabney: The Prophet Speaks* (San Antonio: Vision Forum, 1998).

11. Quotes from ibid., xv; xi; xiv.

12. As an aside, in an example of the way he sees certain biases of historians shaping their work, Rushdoony discusses the example of John Witherspoon and the limited attention he has been given. Vision Forum has named its School of Law and Public Policy for Witherspoon. This is an occasional four-day seminar at which former Alabama Chief Justice Roy Moore has presented and which is open only to men.

13. I was in Boston during this conference for an NEH summer seminar at Boston College, led by Alan Wolfe. This gave me the opportunity to attend most of the Reformation 500 Celebration. This section is drawn from that field research.

14. Quotes included in this section are from my field notes. For several of the sessions, I was able to sit in the audience with my laptop and write much of what was said in the presentation. These quotes are presented as accurately as possible in this setting but may not be recorded exactly as they were said. I believe they are accurate and convey the meaning as it was intended. The lectures could at one time be purchased from Vision Forum, which is now defunct.

15. This was taken from Phillips's opening remarks. I believe the reference to "the Ebenezers" is equivalent to "our elders." Hazzah! is a cheer, a term of great excitement.

16. The Geneva Bible preceded the King James Bible and was used by many of the Reformers. It has been reprinted and is also called the Patriot Bible. The reprint includes founding texts from early America and is published by White Hall Press and Tolle Lege Press (event sponsors).

17. Bruce Lincoln, *Authority: Construction and Corrosion* (Chicago: University of Chicago Press, 1994).

18. For discussions of this movement and its impact see Ingersoll, *Evangelical Christian Women*; and Pamela D. H. Cochran, *Evangelical Feminism: A History* (New York: New York University Press, 2005).

19. Doug Phillips, "The Tenets of Biblical Patriarchy," http://www.visionforumministries.org/home/about/Biblical_patriarchy.aspx (webpage no longer available, accessed June 16, 2010).

20. This recording was available on CD from Vision Forum and as a downloaded MP3 at its sister site www.Behemoth.com, both of which are now defunct. MP3 in author's possesion.

21. Joyce, *Quiverfull*.

22. As historian Colleen McDannell has argued, material culture is crucial to the production and reproduction of social groups in ways that are both subtle and powerful.

23. Vision Forum Catalog, 2009, 92.

24. Rushdoony, *Revolt Against Maturity*, 11; quoting Psalm 127:5.

25. It is not clear whether, in a Reconstructed society, violations of moral law such as abortion, adultery, and homosexuality would be punished by civil courts or ecclesiastical courts.

26. http://www.visionforumministries.org/events/wslpp/ (webpage no longer available, accessed June 20, 2010).

27. Alexandra Alter, "Banned from Church: Reviving an Ancient Practice, Churches Are Exposing Sinners and Shunning Those Who Won't Repent," *Wall Street Journal*, Jan. 18, 2008, /http://online.wsj.com/article/SB120061470848399079. html.

28. Ibid.

29. Rushdoony, *Institutes of Biblical Law*, vol. 2, *Law and Society*, 344.

30. Ibid., 344–5.

31. Ibid., 345.

32. Joyce, *Quiverfull*, 124.

33. For an example of a report quoting the original blog post by Driscoll, http://www. huffingtonpost.com/david-goldstein/whos-to-blame-for-pastor-_b_33,279.html. Links to Driscoll's post have been removed from the web as of June 6, 2010.

34. A timeline of events is posted at http://spiritualsoundingboard.com/2014/03/29/ attempting-to-set-the-doug-phillips-record-straight-part-3-the-timeline/. I cite it here to demonstrate what was being said, not as evidence of the accuracy of any specific claim.

35. Phillips public comments are available on the now-defunct Vision Forum website. http://www.visionforumministries.org/home/about/the_board_of_vision_forum_mini.aspx.

36. The text of the complaint can be seen here http://www.wnd.com/files/2014/04/ TorresComplaintFinalwithCoverSheet.pdf.

37. He made this admission in the resignation post at http://www.visionforum-ministries.org/home/about/the_board_of_vision_forum_mini.aspx.

38. Again, in the text of his resignation post at http://www.visionforumministries. org/home/about/the_board_of_vision_forum_mini.aspx.

39. While the complete video of Phillips's April 15, 2009, speech before the San Antonio Tea Party Rally is no longer available, a clip of it can be found at https:// www.youtube.com/watch?v=QO95zmotEaw.

40. Doug's blog, http://www.visionforum.com/hottopics/blogs/dwp/2008/08/4273. aspx (webpage no longer available, accessed June 11, 2010).

41. Vaughn Ohlman, "Unfair Fatherhood," *Presevero News*, June 22, 2013, http:// www.perseveronews.com/unfair-fatherhood/.

CHAPTER 8

1. My thanks to Anthea Butler for helping me structure the material in this chapter.

2. It should be noted that there are divisions within the identifiable Christian Reconstructionist world and some, including John Lofton (of Michael Peroutka's Institute on the Constitution and the American View), criticize DeMar for compromising with establishment conservatives who are insufficiently Christian. Such criticism reached a fevered pitch surrounding the decision over whether conservatives should support Republican candidate for president Mitt Romney against Barack Obama in the 2012 election.

3. North is notoriously secretive and rarely willing to talk to scholars or reporters. I only learned he had moved to the Atlanta area from his son-in-law McDurmon. DeMar described North's role at American Vision in his introduction to North's presentation at the 2009 Worldview Conference I attended.

4. Greg Bahnsen, foreward to DeMar and Leithart, *The Debate over Christian Reconstruction* (Ft. Worth, TX: Dominion Press, 1988), x.

5. Ibid., x.

6. Powder Springs, GA: Tolle Lege Press, 2011.

7. http://americanvision.org/countyrights.

8. Peroutka's appointment to the board is announced, along with his commitment to use the resources of his Institute on the Constitution to support the work of the League, in this Youtube video of the League's 2013 national convention https://www.youtube.com/watch?v=JC0AR5kyDFA&feature=youtu. be&t=39m10s. My thanks to Warren Throckmorton who cited this video in his block post "Michael Peroutka Pledges Resources of Institute on the Constitution to League of the South" http://www.patheos.com/blogs/warrenthrockmorton/ 2013/07/15/michael-peroutka-pledges-resources-of-institute-on-the-constitution-to-league-of-the-south/#ixzz3RAuBQ600 http://www.patheos.com/ blogs/warrenthrockmorton/2013/07/15/michael-peroutka-pledges-resources-of-institute-on-the-constitution-to-league-of-the-south.

9. http://www.perseveronews.com/9th-hour-attacks-on-caucus-resolution-play-semantical-ploys/.

10. http://www.perseveronews.com/the-georgia-tea-party-has-darnell-speak-on-switching-to-a-caucus/.

11. http://www.perseveronews.com/audio-of-georgia-tea-party-panel-discussion-on-caucus-vs-primary/. http://gacaucus.org/Audio/GA-T_Party8.8.13.mp3.

12. http://www.patriotcruise.com/av/.

13. The name of this group points to its Reformed heritage, a key aspect of which is the emphasis on the sovereignty of God.

14. American Vision produced and sold a video of this debate and a written transcript is available at http://mp3.aomin.org/805Transcript.pdf, Jan. 21, 2009.

15. Those themes have included Creation to Revelation: Worldview Super Conference I (2006), Preparing This Generation to Recapture the Future: Worldview

Super Conference II (2007), The Great Reversal: How Christians Will Change the Future: Worldview Super Conference III (2009), Biblical Blueprints for Victory: Worldview Super Conference IV (2010), and The National Prophecy Conference (2011).

16. I struggled with how to respond. This interchange raised issues about which many ethnographers have written. I later learned that his interpretation of the interchange was that I had lied to him.

17. For an excellent treatment of the origins of the movement, see Ben McGrath, "The Movement: The Rise of Tea Party Activism," *New Yorker*, Feb. 1, 2010, http://www.newyorker.com/reporting/2010/02/01/100201fa_fact_mcgrath#ixzz1RXaKt7zT.

18. http://www.entrewave.com/freebooks/docs/html/gnbd/appendix_k.htm.

19. He concludes with an interesting aside to those who have puzzled over the odd bedfellows of the theocrats and the humanist/atheist Austrian School of economists, whom he calls "right-wing Darwinists." He says their "view of money is" merely orthodox Christianity rewritten to make humans autonomous: "Von Mises and Rothbard were both humanists but [otherwise] consistent with a Christian worldview." They advocated the "non-autonomy of the messianic state: they didn't trust the state." For that reason, "their shared suspicion of the state" has made Reconstructionists able to cooperate with them.

20. Adam Liptak, "A 10th Amendment Drama Fit for Daytime TV Heads to the Supreme Court," *New York Times*, October 18, 2010, http://www.nytimes.com/2010/10/19/us/19bar.html.

21. James C. Sanford, *Blueprint for Theocracy: The Christian Right's Vision for America* (Providence, RI: Metacomet Books, 2014), 130.

22. Sarah Posner and Julie J. Ingersoll, "Gun Ownership: 'An Obligation to God,'" Religion Dispatches, July 6, 2010, http://www.religiondispatches.org/archive/politics/2910/gun_ownership:_%E2%80%98an_obligation_to_god%E2%80%99.

23. Greg Sargent, "Sharron Angle Floated Possibility of Armed Insurrection," *Washington Post*, June 15, 2010, http://voices.washingtonpost.com/plum-line/2010/06/sharron_angle_floated_possibil.html.

24. Posner and Ingersoll, "Gun Ownership."

25. Titus gave an interview for the Gary DeMar show prior to the Worldview Conference in which he outlines both arguments made in his conference presentations. The podcasts for those interviews are available at http://vimeo.com/5614504.

26. DeMar's talk at this conference is entitled, "Why Government CAN Save You (It All Depends on Your Definition of Government)."

27. I suspect that this was actually a reference to me as I had been at the conference a year earlier and later written an article with Sarah Posner at Religion Dispatches where we examined ties among Reconstructionists, the Tea Party, the

militia movement, and the gun rights movement. Posner and Ingersoll, "Gun Ownership." They had been unhappy with the article.

28. These are actual accusations I have read in e-mails from Vallorani's affiliated various groups over the last few years.

29. Keith Thompson, "The FWDing of the Conservative Revolution," Oct. 23, 2009, http://www.huffingtonpost.com/keith-thomson/the-fwding-of-the-conserv_b_278848.html.

30. http://thebrandonvallorani.com/.

31. I researched the ownership of these various sites on Aug. 17, 2013, at the website www.whois.com.

32. http://libertyalliance.com/about-us/.

33. Gus Garcia-Roberts, "Tea Party Princess," *Village Voice*, http://www.villagevoice.com/2012-01-25/news/tea-party-princess-Victoria-Jackson/.

CHAPTER 9

*. Various parts of this chapter appear in different forms in the online magazine Religion Dispatches, the editors of which (Sarah Posner, Evan Derkacz, and Lisa Webster) provided invaluable feedback and suggestions.

1. For a discussion of Barton's rise as a conservative Christian celebrity, see Randall J. Stephens and Karl W. Giberson, *The Anointed: Evangelical Truth in a Secular Age* (Cambridge, MA: Belknap Press, 2011), 61–98.

2. Reconstructionists will disagree with me about their influence because we are using different measures. They believe that their project will fail as long as Christians remain epistemologically inconsistent. I am not attempting to gauge whether they will succeed but rather pointing to the places in the broader subculture in which their influence can be seen.

3. Stephen McDowell "The Bible, Slavery, and America's Founders," http://www.wallbuilders.com/libissuesarticles.asp?id=120.

4. Aledo Christian Center, http://www.aledocc.org/historyvision.htm.

5. "A Converstion with David Barton," Pentecostal Evangel, http://www.ag.org/pentecostal-evangel/Conversations2007/4850_Barton.cfm.

6. David Barton, *To Pray or Not to Pray* (Aledo, TX: Wallbuilders Press, 1988).

7. I am not misusing the word "amount" here. He really is talking in terms of quantification and with the term "volume" he means quantity rather than amplitude.

8. Rob Boston, "Religious Right Cowboy David Barton's Fixin' to Rewrite the Social Studies Textbooks in the Lone Star State (And Maybe Your State Too)," Americans United for Separation of Church and State, July–Aug. 2009, http://au.org/media/church-and-state/archives/2009/07/texas-tall-tale.html.

9. Stephanie Simon, "The Culture Wars' New Front: U.S. History Classes in Texas," *Wall Street Journal*, July 15, 2009, http://online.wsj.com/article/SB124753078523935615.html.

10. One of the earliest critics to take on the details of Barton's work was Chris Rodda, senior research director for the Military Religious Freedom Foundation (MRFF) and author of *Liars For Jesus: The Religious Right's Alternate Version of American History* (self-published in 2006). For a scholarly critique see, for example, Randall J. Stephens and Karl W. Giberson, *The Anointed Evangelical Truth in a Secular Age* (Cambridge, MA: Harvard University Press, 2011).

11. Warren Throckmorton and Michael Coulter, *Getting Jefferson Right: Fact Checking Claims about Our Third President* (Grove City, PA: Salem Grove Press, 2012).

12. Barton made this charge on a podcast of the Steve Deace radio show, http://stevedeace.com/headline/deace-show-podcast-07-19-13/, cited in Warren Throckmorton, "David Barton Says 4 Professors Criticized the Jefferson Lies; He Forgot Some," July 23, 2013, http://wthrockmorton.com/2013/07/david-barton-says-4-professors-criticized-the-jefferson-lies-he-forgot-some/.

13. Warren Throckmorton, "David Barton: Christian Professors Were Trained By Pagan Professors Who Hate God," July 25, 2013, http://wthrockmorton.com/2013/07/david-barton-christian-professors-were-trained-by-pagan-professors-who-hate-god/.

14. "You must utterly destroy the Hittites, Amorites, Canaanites, Perizzites, Hivites, and Jebusites, just as the LORD your God has commanded you."

15. In the work of theologian Abraham Kuyper, reinterpreted by Herman Dooyeweerd.

16. http://www.wallbuilderslive.com/listen.asp?cs=high&mf=wma&fileName=WBLive2011-01-25.

17. Of course, this term refers to a right that cannot be transferred. It indicates nothing about its source.

18. http://www.wallbuilderslive.com/listen.asp?cs=high&mf=wma&fileName=WBLive2011-05-16.

19. http://www.rightwingwatch.org/category/individuals/david-barton.

20. These quotes are from a transcript of David Barton's online radio show from Tuesday, April 19, 2011. The show can be heard in its entirety in the archives at http://wallbuilderslive.com/listen.asp?cs=high&mf=wma&fileName=WBLive2011-04-19.

21. "Why Do People Think Government's Role Is to Take Care of the Poor?" July 7, 2011, http://wallbuilderslive.com/listen.asp?cs=high&mf=wma&fileName=WBLive2011-07-07.

22. Michael Youseff, "Keep Jesus Out of Your Socialism," June 7, 2011, http://www.michaelyoussef.com/michaels-blogs/keep-jesus-out-of-your-socialism.html.

23. http://www.wallbuilders.com/LIBdefault.asp.

24. Phone interview with author, August 23, 2010.

25. David Barton, "Democrats and Republicans in Their Own Words: National Party Platforms on Specific Biblical Issues," http://www.wallbuilders.com/resources/misc/Platforms.pdf.

26. For more on the way this developed see Alexander P. Lamis, *The Two Party South* (New York: Oxford University Press, 1990).

27. Stephen McDowell, "The Bible, Slavery, and America's Founders," http://www.wallbuilders.com/libissuesarticles.asp?id=120.

28. David Barton, "Confronting Civil War Revisionism: Why the South Went to War," http://www.wallbuilders.com/LIBissuesArticles.asp?id=92.

29. See for example Gary North, "Gary North on Auditing the Fed," http://www.ronpaul.com/2010-05-04/gary-north-on-auditing-the-fed/.

30. Gary North, "Ron Paul's Home School High School Curriculum—By Far the Best Curriculum, at the Right Price: Free!," http://www.garynorth.com/public/6442.cfm.

31. Constitution Party Platform, http://www.cpmn.org/platform/top.php.

32. http://www.youtube.com/watch?v=kQPnjJSAih8&feature.

33. https://www.youtube.com/watch?v=_4Z1rEPPx4s.

34. The video clip from which this quote was drawn is no longer available. I accessed it at http://vimeo.com/37775949, March 20, 2012.

35. Field notes in author's possession from Reformation 500, Boston, MA, July 1, 2009.

36. Katherine Weber, *Kirk Cameron Tells of God's 'Monumental' Role in America's Founding: Actor and Evangelist Insists in Documentary that Hope for Nation's Future Can Be Found in Its Past*, Christian Post, March 26, 2012. http://www.christianpost.com/news/kirk-cameron-tells-of-gods-monumental-role-in-americas-founding-72012/.

CHAPTER 10

1. Bruce Lincoln, *Holy Terrors: Thinking about Religion after 9/11* (Chicago: University of Chicago Press, 2010).

2. Juergensmeyer, *Terror in the Mind of God*; and Mark Juergensmeyer and Margot Kitts, *Princeton Readings in Religion and Violence* (Princeton, NJ: Princeton University Press, 2011).

3. Rushdoony, *Politics of Guilt and Pity*, 71.

4. Brian Schwertley, "Political Polytheism," 2003, http://www.reformedonline.com/uploads/1/5/0/3/15030584/webpolitical_polytheism.pdf.

5. Ibid., 69.

6. Ibid., 44.

7. Ibid., 53.

8. Ibid., 55.

9. Ibid., 60.

10. Sutton, *Who Owns the Family*, 145.

11. Ibid.

12. Rushdoony, *Institutes of Biblical Law*, 382.

13. Ibid., 792.

14. Ibid., 788.

15. Ibid., 792.

16. The charge that Rushdoony "denied" the Holocaust was first relayed to me by Crawford Gribben from the University of Manchester at a conference on millennialism sponsored by the Center for Millennial Studies at Hope University, Liverpool. The charge is repeated on the website of the Southern Poverty Law Center, and I thank Heidi Beirich at the Southern Poverty Law Center for the exact citation from Rushdoony's work.

17. Vicomte Leon de Poncins, *Judaism and the Vatican* (London: Britons, 1967), 178, cited in Rushdoony, *Institutes of Biblical Law*, 586–8.

18. Rushdoony, *Politics of Guilt and Pity*, 20.

19. Rushdoony, *Nature of the American System*, 69–70.

20. Gary North, *The Judeo Christian Tradition* (Tyler, TX: Institute for Christian Economics, 1990).

21. Ibid., 49, 53.

22. Rushdoony, *Politics of Guilt and Pity*, 19.

23. Ibid., 19.

24. Ibid., 20.

25. Rushdoony, *Philosophy of the Christian Curriculum*, 41–2.

26. Rushdoony, *Nature of the American System*, 127.

27. Rushdoony, *Politics of Guilt and Pity*.

28. Ibid., 27.

29. Rushdoony, *Nature of the American System*, 44.

30. Rushdoony, *Politics of Guilt and Pity*, 29–30.

31. Ibid., 25.

32. Ibid., 19.

33. Ibid., 26.

34. Ibid., 28.

35. Gary DeMar, American Vision's Worldview Conference, August 11, 2010, from field notes in author's possession.

36. To note just a few of the ties: Michael Peroutka, founder of the Institute of the Constitution, served on the Board of the League of the South. His appointment to the Board and his commitment to use the Institutes's resources to support the work of the League were announced at the 2013 Annual meeting of the League. https://www.youtube.com/watch?v=vze4fPPkgxY Peroutka has served as the Presidential candidate for Reconstructionist Howard Phillips' Constitution Party as noted on its own webpage. http://www.constitutionparty.com/?s=peroutka.

37. Steve Wilkins and Douglas Wilson, *Southern Slavery as It Was* (Moscow, ID: Canon Press, 1996), 5.

38. Ibid., 4.

39. Ibid., 7–8.

40. Ibid., 10.

41. Ibid., 1–8.

42. Rushdoony, *Institutes of Biblical Law*, 256.

43. Ibid., 257.

44. Ibid., 256–257.

45. William Borah, "The Siege Perilous," February 22, 2008, https://ehudwould. wordpress.com/2008/02/22/the-siege-perilous/.

46. Nil Desperandum, "The Futility of the Alienist's Claim of Rushdoony," July 2, 2012, http://faithandheritage.com/2012/07/the-futility-of-the-alienists-claim-of-rushdoony/ and William Borah, "I Affirm the Traditional Christian Doctrine of the Trustee Family," June 18, 2008, https://ehudwould.wordpress.com/2008/06/18/i-affirm-the-traditional-christian-doctrine-of-the-trustee-family/.

47. Gary North, *Baptized Patriarchalism* (Tyler, TX: Institute for Christian Economics, 1994), 13–7.

48. Mark Rushdoony, "Mark Rushdoony Says That His Father, R. J. Rushdoony, Was Not a Kinist," August 12, 2010, http://theonomyresources.blogspot.com/2010/08/mark-rushdoony-says-that-his-father-r-j.html.

49. Juergensmeyer, *Terror in the Mind of God*. Juergensmeyer was working on this project when I was a student at the University of California, Santa Barbara. I put him in touch with Bray and shared with him my collection of Bray's writings. Moreover, some of the material in this section appeared in my essay "Religiously Motivated Violence in the Abortion Debate," chap. 20 in *Oxford Handbook of Religion and Violence*, ed. Mark Juergensmeyer, Margot S. Kitts and Michael Jerryson, 2013 (Oxford: Oxford Univerity Press, 2013).

50. Joyce, *Quiverfull*.

51. Juergensmeyer, *Terror in the Mind of God*, 21.

52. Gary North, *Lone Gunners for Jesus* (Tyler, TX: Institute for Christian Economics, 1994).

53. As indicated in the introduction, during the years when I was involved in the Christian Reconstructionist world, I was also involved in several aspects of the right-to-life movement, including but not limited to various protest groups. I wish to be clear here, however, that my involvement was always nonviolent.

54. Michael Bray, *A Time to Kill: A Study Concerning the Use of Force and Abortion* (Portland, OR: Advocates for Life Publications, 1994), 46.

55. Ibid., 34.

56. Ibid., 41.

57. Ibid., 153; 42.

58. Ibid., 43.

59. Ibid., 78.

60. Paul Hill, "Does the PCA Endorse Anti-Abortion Force?" http://www.armyofgod.com/PHillBookAppendixCdoestjePCAendorseAnti-abortionForce.html, accessed Aug. 6, 2013.

61. Paul Jennings Hill, *Mix My Blood with the Blood of the Unborn*, Appendix B, 2003, http://www.armyofgod.com/PHillBookAppendixBWhySouthernBaptistsAre-Wrong.html.

62. North, *Lone Gunners For Jesus*.

63. Gary North, *Baptized Patriarchalism, and Tithing and the Church* (Tyler, TX: Institute for Christian Economics, 1994).

64. North, *Lone Gunners For Jesus*, 5.

65. Ibid., 6.

66. Ibid., 12.

67. Juergensmeyer, *Terror in the Mind of God*, 24.

68. Michael Bray, "The Impending Execution of Paul Hill," http://www.christiangallery.com/hill.html.

69. Ibid.

70. Gary North also published a defense of Operation Rescue and nonviolent civil disobedience entitled *Trespassing for Dear Life*, with a foreword by George Grant (Tyler, TX: Dominion Press, 1989).

71. Randall Terry, *Operation Rescue* (self-published, 1988, and New York: Reformer Library, 1995). Citations refer to the 1988 version.

72. Terry, *Operation Rescue*, 228.

73. Ibid., 22–3.

74. Ibid., 182–4.

75. Ibid., 184.

76. Terry's press release, "Dr. Tiller's Death: Randall Terry Releases Video for Pro-life Leaders Concerning Dr. Tiller's Killing," http://www.christiannewswire.com/news/7392310537.html.

77. Terry, *The Judgement of God, Windsor*, 3–4.

78. Terry, *Operation Rescue*, 161.

CONCLUSION

1. Amy Gardner, *Nevada Sen. Reid's campaign batters image of GOP challenger*, August 14, 2010, http://www.washingtonpost.com/wp-dyn/content/article/2010/08/13/AR2010081306224.html?wprss=rss_religion.

2. Lincoln, *Holy Terrors*, 52.

3. Joshua Cooper Ramo, *The Age of the Unthinkable* (New York: Little, Brown, 2010).

4. North, "The Intellectual Schizophrenia of the New Christian Right," *The Failure of the American Baptist Culture* in *Christianity and Civilization*, vol. 1, Spring 1982 (Tyler, TX: Geneva Divinity School), 24–5.

5. Rushdoony on conspiracies: Rushdoony, *Nature of the American System*, 134ff.

Selected Bibliography

Bahnsen, Greg. *By This Standard: The Authority of God's Word Today.* Tyler, TX: Institute for Christian Economics, 1985.

Bahnsen, Greg. *Theonomy and Christian Ethics.* Vallecito, CA: Craig Press, 1973.

Balmer, Randall. *The Making of Evangelicalism.* Waco, TX: Baylor University Press, 2010.

Balmer, Randall. *Mine Eyes Have Seen the Glory.* Oxford: Oxford University Press, 1989.

Balmer, Randall. *Thy Kingdom Come: How the Religious Right Distorts Faith and Threatens America.* New York: Basic Books, 2006.

Barron, Bruce. *Heaven on Earth?* Grand Rapids, MI: Zondervan, 1992.

Bartlett, Thomas. "Give Me Liberty or I Quit." *Chronicle of Higher Education*, May 19, 2006, A10.

Berlet, Chip, ed. *Eyes Right! Challenging the Right Wing Backlash.* Boston: South End Press, 1995.

Blumenthal, Max. *Republican Gomorrah: Inside the Movement that Shattered the Party.* New York: Nation Books, 2009.

Braun, Willi, and Russell T. McCutcheon, eds. *Guide to the Study of Religion.* London and New York: Cassell, 2000.

Chilton, David. *Days of Vengeance.* Ft. Worth, TX: Dominion Press, 1987.

Chilton, David. *Paradise Restored.* Tyler, TX: Reconstruction Press, 1985.

Clarkson, Frederick. *Eternal Hostility: The Struggle Between Theocracy and Democracy.* Monroe, ME: Common Courage Press, 1997.

Courtwright, David. *No Right Turn: Conservative Politics in a Liberal America.* Cambridge, MA: Harvard University Press, 2010.

Critchlow, Donald T. *Phyllis Schlafly and Grassroots Conservatism: A Woman's Crusade.* Princeton, NJ: Princeton University Press, 2005.

DeMar, Gary. *God and Government.* 3 vols. Atlanta: American Vision, 1982; and Brentwood TN: Wolgemuth and Hyatt, 1986.

DeMar, Gary. *Ruler of Nations: Biblical Blueprints of Government.* Vol. 2 of *Biblical Blueprint Series.* Gary North, ed. Tyler, TX: Dominion Press, 1987.

Diamond, Sara. *Not By Politics Alone*. New York: Guilford Press, 1998.

Diamond, Sara. *Roads to Dominion*. New York: Guilford Press, 1995.

Doan, Ruth Alden. *The Miller Heresy, Millennialism and American Culture*. Philadelphia: Temple University Press, 1987.

Dochuk, Darren. *From Bible Belt to Sunbelt: Plain Folk Religion, Grassroots Politics, and the Rise of Evangelical Conservatism*. New York: W.W. Norton, 2011.

English, Adam C. "Christian Reconstruction after Y2K: Gary North, the New Millennium, and Religious Liberty in America." In *New Religious Movements and Religious Liberty*, edited by Derek Davis and Barry Hankins. Waco, TX: Baylor University Press, 2003.

Even, Raymond A., and Francis B. Harrold. *The Creationist Movement in Modern America*. Boston: Twayne, 1991.

Goldberg, Michele. *Kingdom Coming*. New York: W.W. Norton, 2006.

Grant, George. *The Changing of the Guard: Biblical Principles for Political Action*. Vol. 8 of *Biblical Blueprint Series*. Gary North, ed. Tyler, TX: Dominion Press, 1987.

Grant, George. *In the Shadow of Plenty: The Biblical Blueprint for Welfare*. Vol. 4 of *Biblical Blueprint Series*. Gary North, ed. Tyler, TX: Dominion Press, 1986.

Grover, Alan N. *Ohio's Trojan Horse*. Greenville, SC: Bob Jones University Press, 1977.

Hague, Euan, Heidi Beirich, and Edward H. Sebesta. *Neo-Confederacy: A Critical Introduction*. Austin: University of Texas Press, 2008.

Hall, Verna M. *The Christian History of the American Revolution*. San Francisco: Foundation for Christian Education, 1975.

Hall, Verna M. *The Christian History of the Constitution of the United States*. San Francisco: Foundation for Christian Education, 1966.

Harding, Susan. *The Book of Jerry Falwell*. Princeton, NJ: Princeton University Press, 2000.

Harvey, Paul. *Redeeming the South: Religious Cultures and Racial Identities Among Southern Baptists 1865–1925*. Chapel Hill: University of North Carolina Press, 1997.

Hunter, James Davison. *Before the Shooting Begins: Searching for Democracy in America's Culture Wars*. New York: Free Press, 1994.

Hunter, James Davison. *The Culture Wars: The Struggle to Define America*. New York: Basic Books, 1991.

Ingersoll, Julie J. *Evangelical Christian Women: War Stories in the Gender Battles*. New York: New York University Press, 2003.

Ingersoll, Julie J. "Rank and File Evangelicals and the Activist Elite: Views of Pluralist Democracy." In *The Conservative Christian Movement and American Democracy*, edited by Steven Brint and Jean Schroedel, 179–208. New York: Russell Sage Foundation, 2009.

Ingersoll, Julie J. "Religion and Politics: The Impact of the Religious Right." In *Faith in America*, edited by Charles Lippy, 59–78. Santa Barbara, CA: Praeger Press, 2006.

Ingersoll, Julie J. "Religiously Motivated Violence and the Abortion Debate." In *Oxford Handbook of Religion and Violence*, edited by Mark Juergensmeyer, Margot S. Kitts and Michael Jerryson. New York: Oxford University Press, 2013.

Jordan, James B. *The Sociology of the Church: Essays in Reconstruction.* Tyler, TX: Geneva Ministries, 1986.

Joyce, Kathryn. *Quiverfull: Inside the Biblical Patriarchy Movement.* Boston: Beacon Press, 2009.

Juergensmeyer, Mark. *Terror in the Mind of God.* Berkeley: University of California Press, 2000.

Kik, Marcelus. *Revelation Twenty: An Exposition.* Philadelphia: Presbyterian and Reformed Publishing, 1955.

Kunzman, Robert. *Write These Laws on Your Children: Inside the World of Conservative Christian Homeschooling.* Boston: Beacon Press, 2010.

LaHaye, Tim. *The Battle for the Family.* Old Tappan, NJ: Fleming H. Revell, 1982.

LaHaye, Tim. *The Battle for the Mind.* Old Tappan, NJ: Fleming H. Revell, 1980.

LaHaye, Tim. *The Battle for the Public School.* Old Tappan, NJ: Fleming H. Revell, 1983.

LaHaye, Tim. *Faith of Our Founding Fathers.* Brentwood, TN: Wolgemuth and Hyatt, 1987.

Lakoff, George. *Moral Politics: How Liberals and Conservatives Think.* Chicago: University of Chicago Press, 1996.

Lakoff, George. *Whose Freedom? The Battle over America's Most Important Ideal.* New York: Farrar, Straus, and Giroux, 2006.

Lamis, Alexander P. *The Two-Party South.* Oxford: Oxford University Press, 1990.

Lienesch, Michael. *Redeeming America.* Chapel Hill: University of North Carolina Press, 1993.

Lincoln, Bruce. *Authority: Construction and Corrosion.* Chicago: University of Chicago Press, 1994.

Lincoln, Bruce. *Discourse and the Construction of Society.* New York: Oxford University Press, 1992.

Lincoln, Bruce. *Holy Terrors: Thinking About Religion after September 11.* Chicago: University of Chicago Press, 2002.

Lincoln, Bruce. *Myth, Cosmos and Society.* Cambridge, MA: Harvard University Press, 1986.

Livingstone, David N. *Darwin's Forgotten Defenders: The Encounter Between Evangelical Theology and Evolutionary Thought.* Grand Rapids, MI: William B. Eerdmans, 1987.

Loewen, James W., and Edward H. Sebesta. *The Confederate and Neo-Confederate Reader.* Jackson: University of Mississippi Press, 2010.

Luker, Kristen. *Abortion and the Politics of Motherhood.* Berkeley: University of California Press, 1984.

Marsden, George. *Fundamentalism and American Culture: The Shaping of Twentieth-Century Evangelicalism 1870–1925.* Oxford: Oxford University Press, 1980.

Marsden, George. "Preachers of Paradox." In *Understanding Fundamentalism and Evangelicalism*. Grand Rapids, MI: William B. Eerdmans, 1991.

Marsden, George. *Reforming Fundamentalism*. Grand Rapids, MI: William B. Eerdmans, 1987.

Mason, Carol. *Killing for Life*. Ithaca, NY: Cornell University Press, 2002.

McCutcheon, Russell. *Critics Not Caretakers: Redescribing the Public Study of Religion*. Albany: State University of New York Press, 2001.

McCutcheon, Russell. *The Discipline of Religion: Structure, Meaning and Rhetoric*. London and New York: Routledge, 2004.

McCutcheon, Russell. *The Insider/Outsider Problem in the Study of Religion*. London and New York: Cassell, 1999.

McCutcheon, Russell. *Manufacturing Religion: The Discourse on Sui Generis Religion and the Politics of Nostalgia*. Oxford: Oxford University Press, 1997.

McDannell, Colleen. *Material Christianity: Religion and Popular Culture in America*. New Haven, CT: Yale University Press, 1995.

McVicar, Michael. *Christian Reconstruction: R. J. Rushdoony and American Religious Conservatism*. Chapel Hill: University of North Carolina Press, 2015.

Moen, Matthew C. *The Christian Right and Congress*. Tuscaloosa: University of Alabama, 1989.

Moen, Matthew C. *The Transformation of the Christian Right*. Tuscaloosa: University of Alabama, 1992.

North, Gary, ed. *Biblical Blueprint Series*. 10 vols. Ft. Worth, TX: Dominion Press, 1986–1987, and Tyler, TX: Dominion Press, 1978.

North, Gary. *Conspiracy: A Biblical View*. Ft. Worth, TX: Dominion Press, 1986.

North, Gary. *Fighting Chance: Ten Feet to Survival*. Cave Junction: Oregon Institute of Science and Medicine, 1986.

North, Gary. *Government by Emergency*. Ft. Worth, TX: American Bureau of Economic Research, 1983.

North, Gary. *Healer of Nations: Biblical Principles for International Relations*. Vol. 9 of *Biblical Blueprint Series*. Tyler, TX: Dominion Press, 1987.

North, Gary. *Honest Money: Biblical Principles of Money and Banking*. Vol. 5 of *Biblical Blueprint Series*. Tyler, TX: Dominion Press, 1986.

North, Gary. *Inherit the Earth: Biblical Principles for Economics*. Vol. 7 of *Biblical Blueprint Series*. Tyler, TX: Dominion Press, 1987.

North, Gary. *Introduction to Christian Economics*. Vallecito, CA: Craig Press, 1973.

North, Gary. *The Judeo-Christian Tradition*. Tyler, TX: Institute for Christian Economics, 1990.

North, Gary. *The Last Train Out: The Essential Survival Manual for the 80s and Beyond*. Ft. Worth, TX: American Bureau of Economic Research, 1983.

North, Gary. *Liberating Planet Earth: An Introduction to Biblical Blueprints*. Vol. 1 of *Biblical Blueprint Series*. Tyler, TX: Dominion Press, 1987.

North, Gary. *Marx's Religion of Revolution: Regeneration through Chaos.* Tyler, TX: Institute for Christian Economics, 1986.

North, Gary. *Millennialism and Social Theory.* Tyler, TX: Institute for Christian Economics, 1990.

North, Gary. *Moses and Pharaoh: Power Religion Versus Dominion Religion.* Tyler, TX: Institute for Christian Economics, 1985.

North, Gary. *None Dare Call it Witchcraft.* New Rochelle, NY: Arlington House, 1976.

North, Gary. *The Pirate Economy.* Ft. Worth, TX: American Bureau of Economic Research, 1987.

North, Gary. *Political Polytheism: The Myth of Pluralism.* Tyler, TX: Institute for Christian Economics, 1989.

Numbers, Ronald. *The Creationists: The Evolution of Scientific Creationism.* New York: Alfred A. Knopf, 1992,

Phillips, Kevin. *American Theocracy: The Peril and Politics of Radical Religion, Oil and Borrowed Money in the 21st Century.* New York: Penguin Books, 2006.

Poole, W. Scott. *Never Surrender: Confederate Memory and Conservatism in the South Carolina Upcountry.* Athens: University of Georgia Press, 2004.

Ribuffo, Leo P. *The Old Christian Right.* Philadelphia: Temple University Press, 1983.

Rodda, Chris. *Liars for Jesus: The Religious Right's Alternate Version of American History.* New Jersey: Self-published, 2006.

Rosin, Hannah. "God and Country." *New Yorker,* June 2005.

Rosin, Hannah. *God's Harvard: A Christian College on a Mission to Save America.* New York: Harcourt, 2007.

Rushdoony, Rousas John. *The Biblical Philosophy of History.* Phillipsburg, NJ: Presbyterian and Reformed Publishing, 1979.

Rushdoony, Rousas John. *By What Standard?* Fairfax, VA: Thoburn Press, 1958. Repr. 1983.

Rushdoony, Rousas John. *The Foundations of Christian Scholarship.* Vallecito, CA: Ross House Books, 1979.

Rushdoony, Rousas John. *The Institutes of Biblical Law.* Philadelphia: Presbyterian and Reformed Publishing, 1973.

Rushdoony, Rousas John. *Intellectual Schizophrenia: Culture, Crisis and Education.* Phillipsburg, NJ: Presbyterian and Reformed Publishing, 1961.

Rushdoony, Rousas John. *Law and Liberty,* Fairfax, VA: Thoburn Press, 1977.

Rushdoony, Rousas John. *Law and Society.* Vol. 2 of *The Institutes of Biblical Law.* Vallecito, CA: Ross House Books, 1984.

Rushdoony, Rousas John. *The Messianic Character of American Education.* Nutley, NJ: Craig Press, 1963.

Rushdoony, Rousas John. *The Mythology of Science.* Nutley, NJ: Craig Press, 1967.

Rushdoony, Rousas John. *The Nature of the American System.* Nutley, NJ: Craig Press, 1965.

Rushdoony, Rousas John. *The Politics of Guilt and Pity.* Fairfax, VA: Thoburn Press, 1970. Repr. 1978.

Rushdoony, Rousas John. *The Philosophy of the Christian Curriculum.* Vallecito, CA: Ross House Books, 1981.

Rushdoony, Rousas John. *The Politics of Guilt and Pity.* Nutley, NJ: Craig Press, 1970.

Rushdoony, Rousas John. *Revolt Against Maturity.* Fairfax, VA: Thoburn Press, 1977.

Rushdoony, Rousas John. *Systematic Theology.* 2 vols. Vallecito, CA: Ross House Books, 2000.

Rushdoony, Rousas John. *This Independent Republic.* Fairfax, VA: Thoburn Press, 1978.

Rushdoony, Rousas John. *Thy Kingdom Come.* Philadelphia: Presbyterian and Reformed Publishing, 1971.

Schaeffer, Francis. *The God Who Is There.* Downers Grove, IL: Intervarsity Press, 1968.

Schaeffer, Francis. *How Should We Then Live.* Old Tappan, NJ: Fleming H. Revell, 1976.

Schaeffer, Frank. *Crazy for God: How I Grew Up as One of the Elect, Helped Found the Religious Right, and Lived to Take It All (Or Almost All) of It Back.* New York: Carroll and Graf, 2008.

Sharlet, Jeff. *The Family.* New York: HarperCollins, 2008.

Shupe, Anson. "Christian Reconstruction and the Angry Rhetoric of Neo-Postmillennialism." In *Millennium, Messiah's and Mayhem,* edited by Thomas Robbins and Susan J. Palmer, 195–206. New York: Routledge, 1997.

Slater, Rosalie. *Teaching and Learning America's Christian History.* San Francisco: Foundation for Christian Education, 1965.

Sommers, Christian Hoff. *Who Stole Feminism?* New York: Simon and Schuster, 1994.

Standeart, Michael. *Skipping Toward Armageddon: The Politics and Propaganda of the Left Behind Novels and the LaHaye Empire.* New York: Soft Skull Press, 2006.

Stephens, Randall J., and Karl W. Giberson, *Anointed: Evangelical Truth in a Secular Age.* Cambridge: Belknap Press, 2011.

Suton, Ray. *Second Chance: Biblical Principles of Divorce and Remarriage.* Vol. 10 of *Biblical Blueprint Series.* The Gary North, ed. Tyler, TX: Dominion Press, 1988.

Sutton, Ray. *Who Owns the Family: God or the State?* Vol. 3 of *Biblical Blueprint Series.* Gary North, ed. Tyler, TX: Dominion Press, 1986.

Thoburn, Robert. *The Children Trap: The Biblical Blueprint for Education.* Vol. 6 of *Biblical Blueprint Series.* Gary North, ed. Tyler, TX: Dominion Press, 1986.

Tower, Wells. "The Kids Are Far Right." *Harper's,* Nov. 2006, 41–51.

Walton, Rus. *Fundamentals for American Christians.* Nyack, NY: Parson, 1979.

Walton, Rus. *One Nation Under God.* Nashville, TN: Thomas Nelson, 1975; and Grand Rapids, MI: Thomas Nelson, 1986.

Wilcox, Clyde. *Onward Christian Soldiers? The Religious Right in American Politics.* Boulder, CO: Westview Press, 1996.

Williams, Daniel K. *God's Own Party: The Making of the Christian Right.* Oxford: Oxford University Press, 2010.

Witham, Larry A. *Where Darwin Meets the Bible: Creationists and Evolutionists in America.* Oxford: Oxford University Press, 2002.

Woodberry, Robert, and Christian Smith. "Fundamentalism and Conservative Protestants in America." *Annual Review of Sociology* 24 (1998): 25–56.

Index